Fictional Traces: Receptions of the Ancient Novel
Volume 2

ANCIENT NARRATIVE

Supplementum 14.2

Editorial Board
Gareth Schmeling, *University of Florida, Gainesville*
Stephen Harrison, *Corpus Christi College, Oxford*
Heinz Hofmann, *Universität Tübingen*
Massimo Fusillo, *Università degli Studi dell'Aquila*
Ruurd Nauta, *University of Groningen*
Stelios Panayotakis, *University of Crete*
Costas Panayotakis (review editor), *University of Glasgow*

Advisory Board
Jean Alvares, *Montclair State University*
Alain Billault, *Université Paris Sorbonne – Paris IV*
Ewen Bowie, *Corpus Christi College, Oxford*
Jan Bremmer, *University of Groningen*
Stavros Frangoulidis, *Aristotelian University of Thessaloniki*
Ronald Hock, *University of Southern California, Los Angeles*
Irene de Jong, *University of Amsterdam*
Bernhard Kytzler, *University of Natal, Durban*
Silvia Montiglio, *Johns Hopkins University*
John Morgan, *University of Wales, Swansea*
Rudi van der Paardt, *University of Leiden*
Michael Paschalis, *University of Crete*
Judith Perkins, *Saint Joseph College, West Hartford*
Tim Whitmarsh, *Corpus Christi College, Oxford*
Alfons Wouters, *University of Leuven*
Maaike Zimmerman, *University of Groningen*

Subscriptions and ordering
Barkhuis
Zuurstukken 37 9761 KP Eelde the Netherlands
Tel. +31 50 3080936 Fax +31 50 3080934
info@ancientnarrative.com www.ancientnarrative.com

Fictional Traces:
Receptions of the Ancient Novel
Volume 2

edited by

Marília P. Futre Pinheiro

Stephen J. Harrison

BARKHUIS PUBLISHING &
GRONINGEN UNIVERSITY LIBRARY
GRONINGEN 2011

Book design: Barkhuis

Cover Design: Nynke Tiekstra, Noordwolde

ISBN 978-90-77922-98-9

Image on cover: front cover of the fifth and sixth part of Palmeirim de Inglaterra, by Baltasar Gonçalves Lobato. – Lisbon: Nacional Library, [1990]. – 1 postcard, color. – Reproduction of the Lisbon edition: Jorge Rodrigues, 1602 (BNP Res. 796 A.). Location: Portuguese Nacional Library (BNP)

Copyright © 2011 the editor and authors

All rights reserved. No part of this publication or the information contained herein may be reproduced, stored in a retrieval system, or transmitted in any form or by any means, electronic, mechanical, by photocopying, recording or otherwise, without prior written permission from the authors.

Although all care is taken to ensure the integrity and quality of this publication and the information herein, no responsibility is assumed by the publishers nor the authors for any damage to property or persons as a result of operation or use of this publication and/or the information contained herein.

Table of contents

Editors' Introduction   IX

A THE RECEPTION OF THE ANCIENT NOVEL IN THE VISUAL TRADITION

HUGH MASON
Charikleia at the Mauritshuis   3

FAUSTINA C.W. DOUFIKAR-AERTS
Susanna and her Sisters. The Virtuous Lady Motif in Sacred Tradition
and its Representation in Art, Secular Writing and Popular Narrative   19

B ECHOES OF APULEIUS' *METAMORPHOSES* IN ART AND LITERATURE

BEATRICE BAKHOUCHE
Martianus Capella's *De nuptiis Philologiae et Mercurii*
or the Subversion of the Latin Novel   33

GERALD SANDY
Apuleius, Beroaldo and the Development
of the (Early) Modern Classical Commentary   47

FERRUCCIO BERTINI
The *Golden Ass* and its *Nachleben*
in the Middle Ages and in the Renaissance   61

MICHELE RAK
From word to image: notes on the
Renaissance reception of Apuleius's *Metamorphoses*   83

CHRISTIANE REITZ & LORENZ WINKLER-HORAČEK
Love on a wallpaper: Apuleius in the boudoir … 95

C THE RECEPTION OF PETRONIUS' *SATYRICON*: PERENNIAL PATTERNS

NIKOLAI ENDRES
Petronius in West Egg: The *Satyricon* and *The Great Gatsby* … 111

NIALL W. SLATER
'His Career as Trimalchio': Petronian Character
and Narrative in Fitzgerald's Great American Novel … 125

MASSIMO FUSILLO
Petronius and the Contemporary Novel:
Between New Picaresque and Queer Aesthetics … 135

D THE RECEPTION OF THE ANCIENT NOVEL IN DRAMA

JON SOLOMON
Callirhoe and Operatic Heroines derived from Ancient Novels … 147

SIMONE BETA
Le dieu Pan fait pan pan pan de son pied de chèvre:
Daphnis and Chloe on the stage at the end of the nineteenth century … 157

TIZIANA RAGNO
Widows on the operatic stage:
The 'Ephesian Matron' as a dramatic character
in twentieth-century German musical theatre (esp. 1928-1952) … 169

STEPHEN HARRISON
Apuleius On the Radio:
Louis MacNeice's BBC Dramatisations … 181

Abstracts	195
Contributors	203
Indices	207
Index locorum	208
General index	208

Editors' Introduction

This second volume of *Fictional Traces* (*Fictional Traces* II) contains fourteen articles dealing with the reception of the ancient novel in literature and art. These articles are revised versions of papers originally presented at the Fourth International Conference on the Ancient Novel (ICAN IV), which took place at the Fundação Calouste Gulbenkian, in Lisbon, on July 21-26, 2008. The papers are assembled in four groups according to a thematic arrangement. The first group contains two studies on the reception of the ancient novel in the visual tradition; the second includes essays that discuss the echoes of Apuleius' *Metamorphoses* in art and literature; the third category brings together papers involving the reception of Petronius' *Satyrica*; and finally the essays of the fourth section are unified by their focus on the reception of the ancient novel in the performative arts.

Hugh Mason's paper introduces the first series of two papers that illustrate the repercussions of the ancient novel in visual arts, in secular writing and in popular narrative. In "Charikleia at the Mauritshuis" Mason uses as an example of such influence a painting by Abraham Bloemaert in the Mauritshuis, the 17th century town house in Den Haag which is home to the (Dutch) Royal Collection of Paintings, that depicts Theagenes receiving the price at the Pythia from Charicleia. This painting, inspired by *Ethiopica* 4, 4, commemorated the wedding in 1625 of Amalia von Solms (1602-1675), and Frederik Hendrik of Orange (1584-1647), the third Stadhouder of the United Provinces of the Netherlands. It is a "history painting", a large-scale painting incorporating figures that, like episodes in history used as *exempla* in rhetoric, portray a narrative illustrating a human virtue of interest to the artist or his patron. In other words, it is the inverse of a literary *ecphrasis*, that is the verbal representation or literary description of a real or imaginary work of art (painting, sculpture, tapestry, architecture, bas-relief). As Mason stresses, the iconoclasm of the Reformation and the New Republic's need for its own imagery made secular history paintings especially popular in the Netherlands in the 16th century, just at the time when the ancient novels were becoming widely known. In this context, ancient novels provided artists with a fresh repertory of classical narratives for history paintings. The "mannerist" effects and other aspects of Heliodorus' *Aithiopika*, such as the tales of shipwrecks and pirates, the exotic environment and the high moral seriousness, made the novel very popular, and by far the best known and most admired of the ancient novels. So, the history illustrated by such painting suggests some parallels between Heliodorus' narrative of a marriage achieved after desperate adventures and the princely couple's own experience. Bloemaert's painting, which iconographically recalls his *Adoration of the Magi*, may also give some indication of how the Prince viewed his wife, and consequently present an outstanding example of ideas of companionship and even equality in marriage that are characteristic both of the ancient novels and of contemporary Dutch culture.

The second article of this series, "Susanna and her Sisters. The Virtuous Lady Motif in Sacred Tradition and its Representation in Art, Secular Writing and Popular Narrative", by Faustina C.W. Doufikar-Aerts, is focused on the development of the virtuous lady motif as represented in the biblical story of Susanna and the Elders. This ancient motif can be found in many works of literature, art and music. It also survived in novellas and narratives in several languages of the Middle East, and it became a favorite subject of iconography both in early Christianity and later in medieval illuminated Bibles and books of *exempla*. However, research and criticism have been concentrated on issues such as the story's origin and date of composition, as well as on its close connection with the Book of Daniel (13) in the Septuagint and Theodotion (*floruit* 2nd c. A.D.), and little attention has been paid to other evidence of "Susanna" in a non-biblical context. Doufikar-Aerts widens the scope of the analysis, uncovering other testimonies of the Biblical story, by reviewing and comparing other versions related to the traditions of the Samaritans, Shi'ite and Sunnite Muslims, Copts and Ethiopian Jews, and by establishing their relation to the Biblical source. Doufikar-Aerts' analysis leads to the conclusion that the Susanna story originated in the ancient world, and that it is probably much older than the version that became known through the Septuagint and Theodotion. She also argues that other branches (apparently more closely linked to Jewish historiography) could originate from a parallel line, and that, in the wake of this tradition, other versions were created. She also argues that it cannot be ruled out that the Biblical story of Susanna was an excerpt taken from a pre-existing legend or story which had a mythical character, and that from this legend only the Susanna part survived in the Bible for its function as an edifying parable. However, an investigation on the novelistic character of the episode of Susanna's trial plot reveals that "In spite of their diversity the Susanna stories agree on a crucial statement; a complete orchard of different trees has passed under review here, brought up as silent witnesses of Susanna's crime, but they all evidenced the same thing: how the name of a tree could make the difference between life and death."

The next category, "Echoes of Apuleius' *Metamorphosis* in Art and Literature", is comprised of five essays unified by their focus on Apuleius' novel and its *Nachleben* during the Late Antiquity, Middle Ages and the Renaissance. With Martianus Capella's *De nuptiis Philologiae et Mercurii* we are drawn away from the strict field of the ancient novel. In fact, the fictional setting is one among many other genres or sub-genres, such as *fabula*, epic poetry, drama, didactic prose, and religious poetry, that were remarkably explored by Martianus Capella's matchless literary competence. *De nuptiis Philologiae et Mercurii* is the story of a young mortal, Philology, whom the God Mercury decides to marry. A reader that would be eager to find the usual romantic events would be inevitably disappointed, insofar as the love story remains peripheral. The novel is but a generic component of a work which is regarded by the author himself as an "I don't know what." In a paper entitled "Martianus Capella's *De nuptiis Philologiae et Mercurii* or the Subversion of the Latin Novel", Beatrice Bakhouche dissects the novelistic texture and the highly cryptic construction of the work to illuminate the relationship that the *Wedding* maintains with its Latin models and, specifically, with Apuleius' *Golden Ass*. In this respect, three peculiarities stand out. First, "The plot of the *Wedding* could be compared with the story of Eros and Psyche in the *Golden Ass*, but with a kind of reversal, since the young Psyche is considered to be a goddess and, because of this, she cannot find a husband." Second, "Apuleius frames the story of the two young people within the revenge of Venus who sees her worship neglected due to the amazing beauty of Psyche, whereas the young couple in the *Wedding* meet no opposition." Third, by employing a great variety of topics and levels of language and style, *De Nuptiis*, as Apuleius' novel, stands for an "aesthetics of hybridization." Moreover, in many aspects, the *Wedding* incorporates the codes of the novelistic genre (e.g., the polyphony of authorial voice, several levels of narrative, the intertextual dimension). Nevertheless, Martianus' cunning games of mirrors in which his work refracts the numerical harmony of the universe and the author reflects his heroine (Philology), confirming himself worthy of the immortality acquired by knowledge and eloquence, confirms the pedagogic aim of Martianus Capella's work: a high level of knowledge (*sapientia*) is accessible to everyone, provided it is preceded by study and hard work.

In an essay entitled "Apuleius, Beroaldo and the Development of the (Early) Modern Classical Commentary", Gerald Sandy addresses the issue of the place of Filippo Beroaldo's commentary (1500) on Apuleius' *Golden Ass* in the historical development of early modern and modern classical commentaries and simultaneously attempts to isolate some of the features that contributed to its success in the sixteenth and seventeenth centuries. Filippo Beroaldo (1453-1505) was a popular professor of rhetoric at the University of Bologna and, as Sandy stresses, "One of his remarkable achievements was to produce publications that simultaneously met the demands of scholars (*docti*), the educated public (*studiosi*) and students (*scholastici*)". Sandy also adds that Beroaldo's success depended on his astute understanding of the needs of his students and readers. Details that at first glance might appear to be extraneous to his explanation of an issue usually have relevance to it. Moreover, he states exactly what the relevance is, instead of leaving it to the reader to infer it from a list of presumably germane but undifferentiated citations of ancient authorities. Since most of the students at the University of Bologna were pursuing legal studies, Beroaldo repeatedly elucidates Roman legal terms and practices, frequently advising his students and readers to be alert to Apuleius' nuanced manipulation of specialized vocabulary. At first glance, many words do not appear to be worthy of further consideration, because they do not seem to involve any obscure or recondite subject of study. However, "throughout his comments on the tale of Cupid and Psyche, which belongs to the world of fairy tales seemingly far removed from the concerns of Roman law, Beroaldo highlights the vocabulary and practices of the Roman law of marriage." Besides the explanations of Roman law, Sandy's analysis also focuses on three other features of Beroaldo's commentary which helped to ensure its success: explanations of the finer points of the Latin language, engagement with ancient sources and engagement with post-classical scholarship. Sandy notes that for Beroaldo, Apuleius was a stylistic and moral authority and, as a conclusion, he states that "Probably because he was used to teaching hundreds of students each day, Beroaldo was able to judge his readers' needs and, accordingly, to present the *Golden Ass* as a repository of Roman law, Latin style and Platonist-inspired moral paradigm."

Ferruccio Bertini, in turn ("The *Golden Ass* and its *Nachleben* in the Middle Ages and in the Renaissance"), examines the critical, conceptual and philological problems of the textual tradition of Apuleius' The *Golden Ass* and its *Nachleben* during the Middle Ages and the Renaissance, in the light of the different critical interpretations of the novel's argument. His inquiry begins with a lexicological analysis of the meaning of the term *curiositas* (the key concept of the novel) in Greek and Latin, and continues with the statement that the *Metamorphoses* may be considered a Dantesque *Divina Commedia ante litteram*, because in both there is a clear difference between simple curiosity and authentic knowledge. Bertini points out that in Plutarch too there exists a difference between *curiositas* (πολυπραγμοσύνη) and authentic knowledge, because in the term *curiositas* there is no eschatological perspective. He also states that the word comes very probably from a Menandrean slave, who in a fragment of a lost comedy represents the typical πολυπράγμων, declaring that "Nothing is sweeter than to know everything". After defining what we usually mean by the words πολυπραγμοσύνη and *curiositas* in Greek and Latin, Bertini explains how they become emblematic in the eleven books of Apuleius' novel. Bertini's main goal is to evaluate the different critical opinions on *The Golden Ass* and to present his own interpretation of the novel. For that, relying on ancient authors and texts (Artemidorus, Macrobius, Hieronymus, Iulius Capitolinus, Lactantius, Ausonius, Augustinus, Fulgentius, and the anonymous *Historia Apollonii regis Tyri*), he revisits the exegetical tradition of the *Golden Ass*, from the second century AD. to the seventeenth century as well as the main questions concerning the history of the transmission and interpretation of the text. For instance, he argues (in agreement with most modern scholars) that the *fabella* of Cupid and Psyche is not an insertion in the novel, but an integral part of it, supplying in advance an interpretative key to understand the meaning of the whole novel. However, Boccaccio occupies a predominant place in Bertini's overview: as is well known, stories of adulterous love in the *Decameron*, taken from the ninth book of the *Metamorphoses*, illustrate the debt of the Florentine writer towards Apuleius.

Michele's Rak's essay, "From word to image: notes on the Renaissance reception of Apuleius's *Metamorphoses*" represents an aspect of an ongoing project investigating love in European culture. In this context, Rak uses an interdisciplinary approach and focuses on the European artistic representation of Cupid and Psyche, trying to reconstruct the multifaceted representation of the story in frescoes, paintings, statues, sketches, panels, plays and literary works in early modern Italian culture. Referring specifically to literary and visual sources that contain different interpretations of Apuleius's tale, he demonstrates how each of the works analyzed reflects various ways in which love has been conceived in different cultural contexts and elucidates their role as significant pieces in the complex mosaic of European thought. In early modern Europe, the myth of Cupid and Psyche circulated through printed editions, translations and literary adaptations, poetic paraphrases and theatre adaptations. Towards the end of the fifteenth century many intellectuals began to read and interpret Apuleius's work. *The Golden Ass* or *Metamorphoses* was mainly read as a pagan and lascivious text whose meanings had to be decoded and manipulated. It was in early modern Ferrara, Rome and Modena, towards the end of the fifteenth century, that some of the printed editions of *Metamorphoses* started circulating, and that consequently "the iconic, allusive and spiritual journey of Psyche began." In early modern Europe, Cupid and Psyche became a fashionable subject for paintings, sketches and prints, games and cards, encouraging a philosophical analysis of Apuleius' tale. The strong visual impact of some passages of *The Golden Ass*, mostly the tale of Cupid and Psyche, has facilitated its reception among different cultures through the centuries. For instance, as Rak states, the fact that the human body had become a focal point of observation in Renaissance painting, visual arts, medicine, and scientific treatises facilitated the wide circulation of the Apuleian text in Renaissance Italy. Raphael's *Loggia di Amore e Psiche* (Villa Farnesina, Rome) is a model of this artistic tendency. Raphael and some of his pupils (Raffaellino del Colle, Giovan Francesco Penni, Giulio Romano, and Giovanni da Udine), decorators and makers of design sketches drew from several illustrated sources, especially printed editions of the *Metamorphoses* containing engraved images and representations of Apuleius' tale, which became a popular subject for interior decorations and privately owned objects.

The next and last essay in this series by Christiane Reitz and Lorenz Winkler-Horaček ("Love on a wallpaper: Apuleius in the boudoir") moves us again into the domain of artistic representation. The object of study is a set of grisaille wallpapers from the Empire period that draws on the story of Amor and Psyche. First printed in 1815 in Paris by Joseph Dufour after the designs of Merry-Joseph Blondel (1781-1853) and Louis Lafitte (1770-1828), the wallpaper was a great success and was sold until 1924 all over Europe. As Reitz and Winkler-Horaček stress, in antiquity, artifacts depicting Amor and Psyche, rather than focusing on the narrative aspect, concentrate on the allegorical force of the two concepts, the unity of "Soul" and "Love" as part of a religious perception. From the Middle Ages onwards, and specially in the Renaissance, the main interest lies in the narrative element. In their article, Reitz and Winkler-Horaček take a twofold approach. Firstly, they concentrate on the narrative technique of the images in comparison with that of the novel of Apuleius, and the extended prose version by Jean de La Fontaine (*Les Amours de Psyché et de Cupidon*, 1669). Secondly, looking at two episodes in particular, they show how the artists constructed the scenes by elaborately combining different sources. They point to the fact that the story, the heroine, who looks different in every panel according to her state of mind and fortune, the setting, the allusions to ancient sculpture, and the interior design form an artificial cosmos. In several scenes, "visual codes deriving from the ancient iconography of the goddess Venus are applied to Psyche", which means that Venus and Psyche overlap. Designed to appeal to highly educated customers, who are moreover drawn into the story by short subtitles, the wallpapers give insight into the vision of antiquity in 19th century Europe through the reconstruction of ancient narrative texts. During the more than hundred years of their successful marketing, the wallpapers reflect their buyer's antiquarian taste for details and decorations, which matches a general tendency for a nostalgic return to the mythical past.

The next set of papers deals with the reception of Petronius' *Satyrica*. Three of the most famous references in modern literature to Petronius are in the epigraph to T.S. Eliot's *The Waste Land*, in James Joyce's *Ulysses*, and in F. Scott Fitzgerald's *The Great Gatsby*. However, the *Satyrica* has received little attention in Fitzgerald studies, which is, according to Nikolai Endres ("Petronius in West Egg: The *Satyricon* and *The Great Gatsby*"), "all the more remarkable considering that Fitzgerald had originally entitled his novel *Trimalchio* or *Trimalchio in West Egg*". It is, therefore, symptomatic of a change of perspective in the study of Fitzgerald's work that two papers in this series are consecrated to the American writer's famous novel. Nikolai Endres' essay is centered on the analysis and discussion of the two narrators' characters (Petronius' Encolpius and Fitzgerald's Nick Carraway), and their desire for greatness. *The Great Gatsby*, like the *Satyrica*, portrays a quick-tempered yet surprisingly sentimental narrator who flounders but also threads his way through a world that rarely meets his expectations. As Endres stresses, not only Trimalchio and Gatsby (the incarnation of an indigenously American breed, the self-made man), but also Nick Carraway and Encolpius would like to lead a life of fairy tale and romance, only to be disappointed by pedestrian reality. And behind the narrators we find the hidden authors. Endres' discussion stresses the theatricality and inauthenticity of any form of human intercourse in Fitzgerald's novel, and the permanent discrepancy between the ideal and the trivial reality. Both Nick and Encolpius fail in their effort to turn banality into melodrama, that is, to promote the narrow scope of ordinary life to the level of grandeur through the appropriation of great literary models. They fail because they lack the critical awareness to see that no imitation can be anything but a caricature. Both

Petronius and Fitzgerald introduce into their stories characters that are their doubles in the sense that they aspire to giddy heights in their fiction to compensate for the self-confessed failure in their private lives. Nick is both Nick and Gatsby, both little and great, Encolpius is also both Encolpius and Trimalchio, both little and great too. As Endres stresses, "In the patchwork of incongruity, modes of life are denigrated and human values satirized. In both the *Satyricon* and *Gatsby*, the beginning is ashes, the end melodrama."

The second essay on Fitzgerald's "great American novel" offers us a different perspective. In an article entitled " 'His Career as Trimalchio': Petronian Character and Narrative in Fitzgerald's Great American Novel", Niall Slater re-examines the considerable rearrangements and the important rewriting undertaken by Fitzgerald when he revised the first version of his novel. Although it has long been known that Fitzgerald considered calling his greatest novel *Trimalchio in West Egg*, the full dimensions of Petronian influence on the original design for *The Great Gatsby* could not be clear until the text of his first version was published by James L. W. West in 2000. Slater begins by drawing attention to the unsolved question of how Fitzgerald knew Petronius, especially if we consider that the syllabuses of the two Latin courses he took at Princeton do not include Petronius, as well as the fact that Fitzgerald portrays himself as "a poor Latin scholar". So, Slater thinks that most probably he would have read Petronius in English. He also argues that, while the great majority of this earlier text remained in *The Great Gatsby* as finally published, there are substantial differences, particularly in the portrayal of Gatsby's assumption of the role of profligate host, which the Encolpius-like narrator Nick Carraway labels "his career as Trimalchio," and in the re-structuring of the narrative that reshapes our views of its characters. Such changes show a significant Petronian influence in Fitzgerald's novel and allow us "to see fuller dimensions of Petronian influence on the novel's original design". The narrative structure borrows from but significantly transforms the Petronian precedent. Where Encolpius provides an often satiric but static and detached viewpoint on the Trimalchian spectacle, Carraway's perspective over time allows for both significant change and growth in both his own and Gatsby's characters as well as a deepened appreciation of the protagonist's crafted Platonic self-image. At last, if Fitzgerald perceives himself as Gatsby and still more as Nick Carraway (if there is much of Fitzgerald in Gatsby and still more of him in Nick Carraway), we could say that the deviation from the Petronian chronotope at work in the original version of the novel (*Trimalchio*) portrays a deeper insight into Fitzgerald own double (or triple) personality.

Similarly historically oriented is Massimo's Fusillo's contribution on Petronius' contemporary reception. The *Satyricon* becomes in the twentieth century a model for experimental novels and for open and encyclopedic forms, especially with respect to the revival of the picaresque pattern. Its expressive polyphony is linked with a polyhedric and promiscuous view of sexuality, that also recalls crucial contemporary issues, such as camp and the performative idea of gender. In an article that bears the title "Petronius and the Contemporary Novel: Between New Picaresque and Queer Aesthetics", Fusillo starts by defining the main features of the picaresque, to finally conclude that the new picaresque contemporary novel can be as productive as the old one. A certain number of Petronius's innovative features look towards the modern novel and contemporary experimentation, such as: the absence of teleology (i.e., the labyrinthine and anarchic course of the narration as well as its paratactic and hectically episodic organization), its open form, theatricality ("his characters ... conceive their adventures in terms of sublime literary models, epic and tragic, and read their experience as a continuous performance", and realism. In turn, the new picaresque is an interesting example of how the 20th century novel can re-use and transform traditional narrative patterns. As stressed by Fusillo, "The paratactic and associative structure of the canonical antecedents is now aimed at expressing a shattered identity, a cosmic dissatisfaction, a profound nomadism." In order to show how, in different cultural contexts, the transcultural label of picaresque can be applied to the novel, Fusillo focuses on texts coming from different moments of the 20th century, Céline's *Voyage au bout de la nuit* and (principally) the third, expanded new version (1993) of Arbasino's *Fratelli d'Italia* (1963), which he considers according to the postmodern aesthetics of the "camp", an outstanding category in Anglo-Saxon culture, first defined by Susan Sontag in 1967, that "indicates a mixture of irony, theatricality, aestheticism, and juxtaposition of incongruous elements; a playful re-use of consumer culture; a refined contamination of kitsch with cultivated, high-brow elements." Petronian ambivalent resumption of consumer genres (mime, pantomime, sentimental novel) can be read through the lens of contemporary camp and as its embryonic archetype.

The last group of papers explores the theme of the reception of the ancient novel on stage. The first of these deals with the influence of the novels' heroines on opera. Relatively few operas have been inspired by ancient novels, but Jon Solomon's article ("Psyche, Callirhoë and Operatic Heroines Derived from Ancient Novels") presents some important examples. Two notable heroines, Apuleius' Psyche and Chariton's Callirrhoe, gained considerable popularity, the former particularly in late-Renaissance France, and the latter shortly after the publication of Jacques Philippe d'Orville's *editio princeps* in 1750. The operatic genre, as Solomon stresses, owes its existence largely to the dramatic format of ancient Greek tragedy. The new and innovative musical style, the *stile rappresentativo*, and what the creative humanists of the Florentine Camerata called *dramma per musica*, aimed at resembling, as much as practicable, ancient Greek musical theatre. Most baroque operas were based on ancient myth and history, although the narrative structure and subject matter (coincidental appearances, episodic narratives, and geographical exoticism) of many early operas as well as most operas of the eighteenth century are the same we find throughout the extant ancient novels. Nevertheless, as Solomon explains, opera was a relatively conservative artistic genre and audiences and critics tend to prefer what is familiar to them, that is, ancient myth and history. He also notes that adaptations from ancient narratives and myths often occur in clusters. One of them produced Francesco Cavalli's Venetian opera *Amore inamorato*, that was inspired by the Cupid and Psyche story. Soon after came Tomaso Breni's *Psiche* (1645) performed in Lucca, and Marco Scacchi's *Le nozze d' Amore e di Psiche*, with a libretto by Puccitelli, performed in Gdansk, Warsaw, and Cracow in 1646. Besides presenting us with a list of musical works inspired by a reinvigorated interest in the Cupid and Psyche story in the middle of the seventeenth century, Solomon also points to a adaptation of this portion of Apuleius' *Metamorphoses* in libretto form. Of great interest also is the Sacchini/Verazi *Calliroe* (1770), which was performed several times (in Padua, in Naples, again in Pisa, in Milan, and in Florence). Solomon also alludes to Auguste Mariette's plot outline for *Aida*, set by Giuseppe Verdi, and commissioned by Khedive Isma'il to celebrate the inauguration of his Cairo opera house in 1870. As for Longus' *Daphnis and Chloe*, it has not surprisingly found its most familiar home in ballet. Finally, Solomon refers as one of the most interesting and appropriate operatic versions of Petronius' *Satyrica*, Bruno Maderna's last work, *Satyricon* (1973), "a pastiche of traditional music and electronic tape intertwined with *commedia dell'arte* motifs and a variable sequence of sixteen scenes—matching effectively the episodic nature of the ancient novel."

In his contribution, the second of the series, entitled "Le dieu Pan fait pan pan pan de son pied de chèvre: Daphnis and Chloe on the stage at the end of the nineteenth century", Simone Beta analyses the theatrical adaptations of Longus' novel in the second half of the nineteenth century. His aim is to throw new light on the appeal of this Greek novel in theatre and music.

At the same time, he underlines which elements the composers (together with their librettists) took from the Greek original and how they organized this material in their works. His overview starts from the vaudeville by Clairville and Cordier, performed in 1849 and set to music by Jacques Offenbach in 1860. After this comic operatic version (which was restaged in 1866 with a few significant differences), Fernand Le Borne, a Belgian pupil of Massenet, composed the "drame pastoral" *Daphnis et Chloé*, performed in Brussels in 1885. At the end of the century, Paris hosted two other adaptations of Longus' novel: the "Pastorale en un acte" by Henri Busser (a good friend of Debussy) in 1897 and the "comédie lyrique en trois actes" by Charles Henri Maréchal in 1899. Through study of the librettos, Beta analyses the differences among these adaptations and the parody composed by Angelo Casirola and published in 1894. In this modern adaptation, the authors of the libretto (Lebrun, Gramet, and Larseneur), take one of the most famous moments of Daphnis and Chloe's discovery of sex, and turn it "into a funny and disrespectful farce." In this paper, Beta also briefly mentions the ballets inspired by Longus's novel, from the one planned by Claude Debussy in cooperation with the novelist Pierre Louÿs to the celebrated version composed by Maurice Ravel in 1912 for a production by the Russian choreographer Mikhail Fokine, first performed by the Ballets Russes, the celebrated dance company led by Sergej Diaghilev, in Paris, at the Théâtre de Châtelet, on 8 June 1912. As a conclusion, Beta stresses that "The everlasting success of one of the most celebrated compositions of Maurice Ravel, compared with the oblivion into which the five operatic versions dealt with in this paper have sunk, is clear evidence that, sometimes, music and gestures move the soul more effectively than music and words."

The latest phase of the *Nachleben* of the "Widow of Ephesus" story includes several operatic adaptations of the Petronian novella version. The aim of Tiziana Ragno in her paper, " Widows on the operatic stage: The 'Ephesian Matron' as a dramatic character in twentieth-century German musical theatre (esp. 1928-1952)", is to investigate some of these operatic transpositions produced (and concentrated) in Germany from the 1930s onwards, and to compare them to assess to what extent the Petronian narrative "hypotext" was adapted and re-invented. This specific form of "hypertextuality" (from *diegesis* to *mimesis*) probably finds good grounds in some dramatic features belonging already to the Petronian source (*e.g.* the triangular structure, the nurse as "go-between", the voyeuristic atmosphere and the repeated allusions to the widow's "performance"). Ragno also stresses that in the past some theorists (*e.g.* G. E. Lessing) illustrated the difficulties of transposing this story into dramatic form and postulated that the "actual" presence on stage of its characters could deprive them of any "symbolic" features. Then, the operatic adaptations can be considered as a sort of "field tests". In fact, in some cases the librettists reproduce just the "symbolic" perspective, making the characters universal (e.g. presenting the widow not as a female individual but as a paradigmatic "persona") or adding further meanings to the literal ones. Hence, in K. A. Hartmann's short opera *Die Witwe von Ephesus* (1930), the plot is treated in a satirical light, revealing the composer's social engagement and his socialist political views that prefigure his stand against Nazi dictatorship. Therefore, Hartmann "practises one of the most efficacious means of modernizing the ancient plot by using prophetic tones and hinting at contemporary times." In terms of intersemiotic translation, the librettist (Erich Bormann) produced a "travesty" that exploits and manipulates the original story as a "pre-text", submitting it to a process of overall "re-semantization". This operation, which consists in a "reduction" or "compression" of the subject, is achieved, for instance, with the "contraction" of the cast (e.g. the suppression of characters and the combination of different roles). Accordingly, W. Fortner's pantomime, *Die Witwe von Ephesus* (1952), points to a manner of musical-dramatic development of the ancient tale, being inspired by an analogous "stylization technique" but without Hartmann's strong adulteration of the source: here, the "effet de réel" is diminished by inserting a teller's voice. Finally, there are two other cases, again from Germany, of musical-theatrical transposition of the "Widow of Ephesus" theme. The first (E. d'Albert, *Die Witwe von Ephesus*, 1928) appears closely connected with the "Cena Trimalchionis", and in the second (R. Wagner-Régeny, *Die Witwe von Ephesus*, 1950), the ancient tale was once again rewritten in the light of antimilitarist beliefs.

Besides opera, ballet, and theatre, the radio can be also a medium for a dramatized transposition of the ancient novel in a contemporary context. Stephen Harrison in his essay "Apuleius On the Radio: Louis MacNeice's BBC Dramatisations" focuses on two unpublished radio plays by the Anglo-Irish poet, classical scholar and prolific author Louis MacNeice (1907-1963). These radio plays, of which the scripts are preserved in the BBC archives, are based on Apuleius' *Metamorphoses* or *Golden Ass* and the Cupid and Psyche story, and were both originally produced and broadcast in 1944. In this paper, Harrison's aim is to provide a first critical assessment of how the Apuleian text was rewritten by MacNeice, as well as to stress the significant differences of the Irish writer's scripts in comparison with its original. In the *The Golden Ass* adaptation, Harrison stresses "the relevance of the plot of

Apuleius' novel in a wartime context where Nazism and its followers, now at last being defeated, could be described as asinine," and he also observes that MacNeice's drastic abbreviation of Apuleius' plot puts into practice a form of "reduction" that is due to the various constraints and conventions of the radio play form and to the need for simple and effective construction. On the other hand, some strategies of selection and modification of the original text were also applied by MacNeice to Apuleius, such as the addition of characterising speeches and the use of a musical accompaniment. In the second piece, the version of the tale of Cupid and Psyche, the fairytale aspect of the story and its amusing features are emphasized. As Harrison stresses, the two pieces are complementary in that the *The Golden Ass* script passes over the extensive Cupid and Psyche episode very briefly, while the Cupid and Psyche script focuses on that episode. Both scripts are generally in prose, while using verse for some marked and solemn passages that are supported by a musical score. Harrison's contribution also looks at the way in which Apuleius' narratives are transposed and reshaped for a shorter form, without a strong adulteration of the source, but according to MacNeice's priorities and BBC-style educational, entertaining and even informative interests.

Marília P. Futre Pinheiro
Stephen J. Harrison

A

The Reception of the Ancient Novel

in the Visual Tradition

Charikleia at the Mauritshuis

HUGH J. MASON
University of Toronto

The subject of this paper is a painting on permanent display in the Mauritshuis, the 17th century town house in Den Haag that houses the (Dutch) Royal Collection of Paintings (Figure 1).[1] It was signed in 1626 by the artist Abraham Bloemaert, who lived from 1566 to 1651, and worked primarily in Utrecht. Although he was a Catholic and produced religious art for churches in the Spanish Netherlands, his faith did not prevent him from enjoying the patronage of the Calvinist Princes of Orange. Admired as a landscape artist, he also accepted commissions for religious paintings, but apparently did few portraits. He was reputed to prefer work based on the imagination (*uit dem Geest*) to that drawn from nature (*naar der Natuur*).[2]

The painting has been in the possession of the House of Orange since its commission. An inventory of the palace at Noordeinde, dated to 1632, lists a painting of "Theagenes and Chariclea by Bloemaert,"[3] in the private apartment of Amalia of Solms (1602-1675). She was the wife of Prince Frederik Hendrik of Orange (1584-1647), the third Stadhouder of the United Provinces of the Netherlands. (See figure 2 for the couple's place in the House of Orange and European princely families.)

The palace inventory suggests that the painting was the personal property of the Princess; dated a year after her marriage to Frederik Hendrik, it probably commemorated the wedding, and may have been a gift from her husband.[4]

---

[1] Mauritshuis, inv # 16. Van der Ploeg and Buvelot 2006, 24, ill.18; Van der Ploeg and Vermeeren 1997, 100-105, cat. 2.
[2] Biography by Martin Jan Bok in Rothlisberger 1993, 1.549-666; van Manders 1999, 98.
[3] Van der Ploeg and Vermeeren 1997, 107 and notes 11-12.
[4] Van der Ploeg and Buvelot 2006, 24; van der Ploeg and Vermeeren 1997, 101, 104.

Figure 1. Abraham Bloemaert, *Theagenes and Chariclea.* Canvas 157.2 x 157.7. Signed *A. Bloemaert fec./1626.* Mauritshuis, Den Haag, inventory 16.

The persons named in the inventory are the principal characters of the *Aithiopika* of Heliodorus, and the painting is identified in catalogues with a title like "Theagenes receiving the palm of honour from Chariclea."[5]

Book 3 recounts how the couple fell in love at first sight on the first day of the Pythian Festival. Book 4, chapter 4, reports events on the second day, in which Theagenes competed in the race-in-armour. This is the scene portrayed in our painting:

---

[5] Roethlisberger 1993, 1: 239, and II, figure 595.

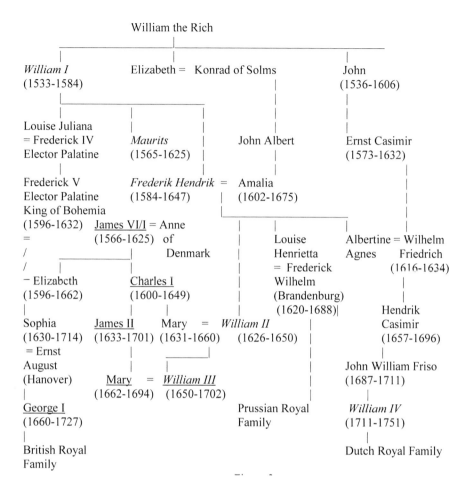

Figure 2. House of Orange. *Stadhouders* of the United Provinces *in Italics;* English Monarchs Underlined

"He turned aside and looked askance at Ormenos. He then lifted his shield on high, threw back his head and, fixing his gaze on Charikleia, he sped onward like a dart to its mark … He ran up to Charikleia, flung himself with intense energy into her bosom as though he were unable to check the impetus of his pace, and, as he received the palm … he kissed the girl's hand."

Many details in the painting, such as Charikleia's purple robe, laurel crown, and torch, derive from the first description of her appearance, in Book 3.

Bloemaert produced two other paintings illustrating the *Aithiopika*. The first, (Figure 3), signed in 1625, is now in Potsdam (having passed to the Brandenburgs through Amalia's daughter). It portrays the opening scene of the novel, and is usually entitled something like "Theagenes and Charikleia in the Midst of the Murdered Pirates."[6] The other, signed by Bloemaert in 1628, represented the first meeting of Theagenes and Charikleia, but was lost in the Second World War.[7]

Bloemaert's Charikleia painting is one of the earliest in the Royal Collection, as indicated by its inventory number (16).[8] Frederik Hendrik succeeded his (much) elder brother Maurits as Stadhouder in 1625, and married his cousin Amalia von Solms in the same year. Nothing in the Royal Collections can be traced to his father William the Silent or to his brother Maurits; both men were too busy with the war with Spain to collect art. Very few of the paintings listed in the 1632 Noordeinde inventory can be dated before 1625.[9]

Our painting is an example of what was termed at the time a "history," a large-scale painting incorporating figures, and illustrating a narrative. The theory behind such paintings was strongly influenced by classical and post-classical rhetoric, as explained by the contemporary critic Karel van Mander.[10] Chapter 5 of his essay *De Grondt* is entitled "Van de ordinanty en de Inventy der Historien;" the Latin rhetorical terms *ordinatio* and *inventio* are hardly changed at all to make them Dutch words. Like episodes in history used as *exempla* in rhetoric, a history painting typically portrayed a narrative that illustrated some human virtue, such as constancy.

The sources of the histories illustrated by such paintings corresponded closely to the *exempla* stressed in post-classical rhetoric: "biblical;" "historical," (from *secular* history from antiquity to the present); or "fabulous," based on classical mythology, and often derived from Ovid's *Metamorphoses*.

The ancient novels first became familiar to Western European patrons and artists early in the 16th century, just when we meet the first "history" paintings with *exempla* from secular history, seen in Venice in the works of

---

[6] Potsdam-Sansouci Inv. GK I 2531; Roethlisberger 1993, I. 278, cat. 424, II, figure 594; Van der Ploeg and Vermeeren 1997, cat. 3, 104-107.

[7] A black-and-white reproduction has survived; van der Ploeg and Vermeeren 1997, 104.

[8] Van der Ploeg and Vermeeren 1997, 100-107; Spicer and Orr 1997, 325; van der Ploeg and Buvelot 2006, 24.

[9] Van der Ploeg and Vermeeren 1998, 98, cat. 1; 142-145, cat.10a and 10b; Van der Ploeg and Buvelot 2006, 179.

[10] Van Mander 1973, 1.126, chapter 5.

Titian and Veronese. This is also the period of the Protestant Reformation, which in the Netherlands took a strongly iconoclastic turn in the 1560s, bringing to an end the role of the Catholic Church as a patron of artists. New patrons, such as the princely families, city and provincial governments of the United Provinces of the Netherlands, were greatly interested in history paintings, both "Biblical" (reflecting pietistic Calvinist religious tradition), and secular, highlighting the new State and its institutions.

In this context, ancient novels provided artists with a fresh repertory of classical narratives for history paintings. Their visual narrative form, incorporating *ekphraseis,* or descriptions-in-words, of visual phenomena, was especially appropriate for history paintings.

The Cupid and Psyche narrative in Apuleius' *Metamorphoses* was the first ancient fiction to be adapted by artists, early in the 16th century.[11] Bloemaert created a "Marriage of Cupid and Psyche" in the 1590s, now in Hampton Court,[12] but the theme was generally not very popular with Dutch painters.[13]

The other novels were less frequently the subject of history paintings; but Heliodorus' *Aithiopika* was very popular as a topic for history paintings in the late 16th and early 17th centuries. The text is particularly rich in visual terminology in the first few chapters, when Heliodorus describes how a group of bandits come across Charikleia leaning over a wounded Theagenes. Bloemaert's other Heliodorus painting, now in Potsdam (figure 3), portrays the incident, and captures the dramatic force of the scene by employing what are known as "mannerist" effects, such as exaggerated foreshortening, something he had also attempted in an earlier (1591) *Death of the Niobids*.[14] As in Heliodorus' narrative, the focus begins with the dead figures and then narrows to the young couple.

Bloemaert's paintings are not the only representations of the *Aithiopika* from the first half of the 17th century.[15] Between 1605 and 1609, Ambroise Dubois painted a series for the Royal Château at Fontainebleau,[16] and in 1635 Gerrit van Honthorst produced four ceiling panels for Kronborg, the

---

[11] Spicer and Orr 1998, 3.
[12] Hampton Court Inv. 949; White 1982, cat. 1, 5-6; Roethlisberger 1993, cat. 11.
[13] An *Amor and Psyche* by Gerrit van Honthorst, from 1625, has not survived. Judson and Ekkart 1999, 106, cat. 109.
[14] Roethlisberger 1995, 278, cat 424; Niobids, cat.14; Seelig 1997, 203 and 351, abb. 1; Judson and Ekkart 1999, 128-129 and note 3.
[15] Stechow 1953; Hägg 1983, fig 21-22, 62; Sandy 1982, 120-124.
[16] Béguin 1960, 124; Lévêque 1984: 32, 42, 43, 49.

Danish Palace at Elsinore.[17] Eleven paintings in Kassel, purchased by the Landgrave in 1749, were apparently taken from a Danish palace in 1658-60.

Figure 3. Theagenes and Charikleia among the pirates. Potsdam-Sanssouci, Inv. GK I 2531

They are ascribed to Karl van Mander III, official portraitist at the Danish court.[18] There are also single paintings by Nicholas Knüpfer in Stockholm,[19] and Hans Horions in Glasgow.

The paintings at Fontainebleau do not appear to be related stylistically to the subsequent versions;[20] but Bloemaert, van Honthorst, Knüpfer and Horions were all in contact in Utrecht, and it is generally assumed that Bloe-

---

[17] Beckett 1916: Council of Europe 1988, 83-84, catalogue 229-232; Judson and Ekkart 1999, 128-131, cat. 138-141, plates 62-65; Leth 1969, 20.
[18] Andrup 1932; Council of Europe 1988, 17, 76, 103-104, cat 319-320; van Mander 1973, 1991.
[19] Stechow 1953, 151 and plate 18b.
[20] Stechow 1953, 150.

maert influenced the later painters.[21] Except for Dubois, who was a French speaker from the Southern Netherlands, all the artists had ties to the United Provinces; van Honthorst was a student and close associate of Bloemaert,[22] Knüpfer came to Utrecht from Leipzig, and became an assistant in Bloemaert's workshop,[23] as did Horions. The Honthorst ceilings, the Kassel series and Knüpfer's Stockholm painting are all associated with the rule in Denmark of King Christian IV (1588-1648), whose art collection was almost entirely by artists from the Netherlands.[24] His artistic ties to the United Provinces reflected his diplomatic situation. Like the House of Orange, he was closely tied to the Stuarts in England (his sister had married James I); Danish contingents served in the armies of the United Provinces in their long conflict with Spain; and Dutch commercial interest in the Baltic resulted in support for a regime in Denmark that imposed low tolls on ships passing through the Straits.

Why were the *Aithiopika* of Heliodorus so attractive as a theme to Dutch artists? They were of course by far the best known and most admired of the Ancient Novels, following the first printed edition from 1534, and several successful translations, including Jacques Amyot's French version from 1547 and the Latin translation by Warschewicki that accompanied the second major edition in 1551.[25]

The Dutch of the period were particularly fond of tales of shipwrecks and pirates, all of which are amply illustrated in Heliodorus.[26] The unprecedented widening of their horizons through exploration and commercial expansion in the 17th century, meant that they responded well to Heliodorus' approach to the "other," exotic, Egyptian/Ethiopian world. There is also a singularly Dutch event in the *Aithiopika*; in Book 9, 4-5, Heliodorus reports how during the siege of Syene, the besiegers opened the banks of the Nile, leaving the city like an island surrounded by water. The incident has been used to date the novel, because of similarities to an account by Julian of Constantius' siege of Nisibis in 350 CE. But "Opening the Dikes" was a core element of the Dutch national mythos, most famously in the siege of Leiden in 1574, and more recently in Utrecht in 1624.

---

[21] Judson and Ekkart 1999, 130, cat. 140.
[22] Spicer and Orr 1997, 382-383; Judson and Ekkart 1999, 1, 25, 46.
[23] Spicer and Orr 1997, 383-4.
[24] Council of Europe 1998, 17, 73, 85; Judson and Ekkart 1999, 20, and cat. 138-146, 161-169.
[25] Sandy 1982, 102-103; Maillon 1935, xlviii; Colonna 1938, LI.
[26] Schama 1987, 28-32.

The high moral seriousness of Heliodorus' work also would sit well with the tone of Dutch Calvinism; Heliodorus' view of the mysterious workings of Fate matched the typical mood of the Netherlands in the 17th century, and the commonly expressed fear that an Act of God might turn to ruin all the unprecedented wealth and prosperity of the Golden Age. There was much more emphasis in the 17th-century Netherlands than elsewhere on companionship and even equality in marriage, along with praise for women's courage and resolution.[27] All of which recalls David Konstan's 1994 discussion of the "Sexual Symmetry" portrayed in the Greek Novels in contrast to the conquest-and-dominance themes present in other classical literature about love.

Heliodorus had less influence on Dutch literature than on French and English; the first novel in Dutch, Johan van Heemskerck's *Batavische Arkadia,* was published in 1637, *after* our painting. There does not appear to have been a Dutch translation of Heliodorus at the time our painting was composed;[28] but those who could afford to commission large-scale paintings, would certainly be able to read Amyot's French or Warschewicki's Latin versions.[29] There was scholarly interest in Heliodorus in the Netherlands, in the works of the Amsterdam humanist Vossius (Gerhard Johann Voss) (1577-1649)[30] and of Joseph Justus Scaliger, who was at Leiden from 1593 to 1609.[31]

So Bloemaert's 1626 painting does correspond to a context of great interest in Heliodorus in the Netherlands around 1600; but it was also a personal commission by the *Stadhouder* of the United Provinces, and deserves to be analysed in terms of his court culture and politics.

Frederik Hendrik was the youngest child of William the Silent, Prince of Orange. William had been the Deputy, or *stadhouder,* in the Netherlands, of the Holy Roman Emperor. When the States General, the representative body of the Provinces, formally abjured their Spanish overlord in 1579, they appointed William to the same position. The Netherlands thus began their independent existence with an *elected* head of state, and much Dutch politics would centre on the conflict between a monarchist and centralizing "Orange" party, close to the Stadhouder, and a republican and federalist "States" party.

---

[27] Schama 1987, 398-430.
[28] Hägg 1983, 193.
[29] Frijhoff and Spies 2004, 239, 243-246 and Schama 1987, 618-619 (Appendix I).
[30] Colonna 1938, XXVI.
[31] Sandy 1982, 99; Maillon 1935, LXVI.

William the Silent was assassinated early in the War of Independence, and Maurits, his older son, was not married and had no legitimate children. It was only with the succession of Frederik Hendrik that dynastic issues became important. As Maurits was dying from a chronic liver condition in 1625, he was able to secure from the States General the succession of his brother Frederik Hendrik as Stadhouder and Captain General. While these negotiations were proceeding, the dying Maurits also pressured his brother to marry; his wedding to his cousin Amalia von Solms took place on 4 April 1625, just days before Maurits' death.

It was Frederik Hendrik and his wife who began to make dynastic claims for the House of Orange, asserting that their son should succeed his father by hereditary right. Associated with their plans for a hereditary monarchy was the establishment of a court in The Hague that could be compared to those of France, Spain and England. The art that they collected was just as significant to their dynastic claims as their palaces and court protocol.

In establishing their courts, and in their artistic patronage, Frederik Hendrik and Amalia drew heavily on their family connections. Frederik Hendrik's mother, who belonged to a leading Huguenot family, arranged for her son to have as his godfather Henri IV of France (at that point Protestant King of Navarre). Even after Henri's conversion and succession to the throne of France, he supported his godchild Frederik Hendrik and invited him to serve for a year (1598) as a page at his court at Fontainebleau.

Amalia's father was High Steward at the court of the Palatine Elector in Heidelberg. When Elizabeth Stuart, the sister of Charles I, married the Elector's son, Frederick V, in 1613, Amalia became her lady-in-waiting. Frederick was declared King of Bohemia and Holy Roman Emperor in 1619, but was driven out of Bohemia by Catholic forces the following year. Amalia accompanied Elizabeth from Heidelberg to Prague to The Hague, where they maintained a court in exile from 1621, with the financial support of both her brother Charles and of the Estates General of the Netherlands.

It was at the exiled Bohemian court in The Hague that Amalia and Frederik Hendrik became acquainted. Much of what they attempted artistically after 1625 was influenced by the tastes and interests of the exiled King and Queen of Bohemia, and through them to the Stuarts in Britain.

They soon became distinguished patrons of Golden Age Art. At the urging of Frederik Hendrik's secretary, Constantijn Huygens (1596-1687), they acquired some stunning Rembrandts, and a wide range of typically Dutch work – landscapes, still lives, and genre pieces – much of it still on display in the Mauritshuis.

Some of the art they commissioned was conventional court stuff – formal portraits, state occasions and the like, especially in the "Orange Room" (*Oraniensaal*) which Amalia had constructed in her palace of Huis ten Bosch after Frederik Hendrik's death.[32] But the paintings that they acquired early in their rule are much more personal. Many reflect a taste for the pastoral,[33] such as a painting by Gerrit von Honthorst, illustrating *Granida and Daifilo*, a pastoral play in Dutch by Pieter Cornelisz Hooft, published in 1615.[34] The Stadhouder and his wife shared the taste for pastoral with the Bohemian court;[35] soon after they settled in The Hague, in 1622, Frederik called himself in a letter to Elizabeth, "Poor Celadon," alluding to a character in another pastoral romance, *Astrée* by Honoré d'Urfée (1567-1625).[36] Since van Honthorst was already working for the Bohemian court at the time of the wedding of Frederik Hendrik and Amalia, it has been suggested that his painting of *Granida* was a *wedding* gift to the Stadhouder and his wife from the Bohemian Royal Family.[37] We know that another pastoral painting, a *Shepherd and Shepherdess* by Paulus Moreelse, was given to Amalia as a wedding present, by the States of Utrecht in November 1626.[38] When Frederik Hendrik and Amalia had a new palace constructed at Honselaarsdijk in 1635, they commissioned a series of paintings from several artists that illustrated the *Pastor Fido* of Giovanni Battista Guarini, first performed in 1596, staged in Amsterdam as early as 1609,[39] and translated into Dutch by Constantijn Huygens in 1623.[40] Abraham Bloemaert contributed an *Amaryllis and Myrtillo* to the Honselaarsdijk series.[41]

Since Bloemaert's illustrations of Heliodorus belong to the same period and courtly environment as van Honthorst's *Granida* and show many similar techniques, critics of the Bloemaert paintings sometimes treat the *Aithiopika* as a work "with similar Arcadian implications" as French and Dutch pastor-

---

[32] Utrecht Centraal Museum 5571; Judson and Ekkart 1999. cat. 189, 159-161, plates XIV and 101; Van der Ploeg and Vermeeren 1997, cat. 14, 52-55, 156-159.
[33] Kettering 1983, Spicer and Orr 1997, 355.
[34] Spicer and Orr 1997, cat. 57, 307-309
[35] Kettering 1983, 10-12. See also Sutton 1984, cat. 7, plate 42, 140-141; Roethlisberger 1993, cat. 449.
[36] Spicer and Orr 1997, cat. 27, 210-213.
[37] De Meyere 1998, 96.
[38] Van der Ploeg and Vermeeren, cat. 18-19, 175-181, cat. 26, 204-207; Spicer and Orr 1997, cat. 53, 293-296, 323-325.
[39] Van der Ploeg and Vermeeren 1997, 58 and cat. 29, 216-225; Spicer and Orr 1997, cat. 59, 313-315; Kettering 1983, 112, 119, figures 157-163
[40] Spicer and Orr 1997, 314 and 430, note 2.
[41] Spicer and Orr 1997, cat. 59, 313; Roethlisberger 1993, cat. 513.

al.⁴² They ignore its darker tone; no 17th century pastoral opens with a scene of death and destruction like Heliodorus' novel (and our Figure 2). The dates are also not so firm that we can state with certainty whether Bloemaert's Heliodorus paintings come before or after the Stadhouder's commissioning of pastorals. Bloemaert's first full-size pastoral genre piece is dated to 1627,⁴³ in the middle of the Heliodorus group, so it may be that the Heliodorus paintings led to the creation of pastoral history paintings rather than the other way round.

One feature of contemporary court culture, especially among the Stuarts in London, was the *"portrait historié,"* in which patrons were portrayed as gods or goddesses, nymphs and shepherds, or even as characters in specific romances.⁴⁴ Jan Mijtens (1614-1670) portrayed a married couple as Granida and Daiphilo.⁴⁵ Van Honthorst did many *portraits historiés* including Frederick of Bohemia as a Roman Emperor,⁴⁶ Amalia von Solms as both Diana and Flora,⁴⁷ and Frederick and Elizabeth of Bohemia as Celadon and Astraea.⁴⁸

Is then our painting also a *portrait historié*, with Amalia serving as the model for Charikleia? With regret, we must decide that it probably was not. Figure 4 shows Amalia just before her wedding; she was a brunette, and Charikleia a blonde. There does not appear to me to be a close resemblance.⁴⁹

Paulus Moreelse and Gerrit van Honthorst did produce *portraits historiés* in Utrecht, but there is no sign that Bloemaert ever did. In fact, the taste for them may have begun with van Honthorst's representing Charles I and Henrietta as Apollo and Diana, in 1628, *after* our painting.⁵⁰

Nevertheless, the case should be made that Theagenes and Charikleia were intended in some way to represent the Prince and Princess.

There is every indication that the Princely couple chose Heliodorus for the painting, rather than accept a completed painting from Bloemaert. For

---

[42] G. Seelig in Spicer and Orr 1997, 315, and 430, notes 9-11; Seelig 1997, 193-212.
[43] Christopher Brown in Sutton 1984, 140-141, cat. 7, plate 42. Roethlisberger 1993, cat. 449.
[44] Kettering 1983, 70-82; Judson and Ekkart 1999, 45.
[45] Frijhoff and Spies 2004, 438; cf Kettering 1983, figures 55-56, 142-156
[46] Spicer and Orr 1997, cat. 27, 210-213; Judson and Ekkart 199, cat
[47] M. Tietoff-Splithoff in Keblusek and Zijlsmans 1997, 171 , fig, 159; 197. fig. 174; Judson and Ekkart 1999, 235, cat.297, 247, cat. 310, pl. 197.
[48] White 1982, xxv-vi and figure 4; 58, cat. 77, plate 66; Kettering 1983, 67; Spicer and Orr 1997, cat. 27, 210, and 418, n. 4. Judson and Ekkart 199, 161, cat. 192, pl, 102.
[49] Keblusek and Zijlsmans 1997, 185, fig. 172.
[50] Judson and Ekkart 1999, 107-108, pl. 45, 45a.

both the Potsdam and the Mauritshuis paintings, there are earlier *modellos*, and Bloemaert appears to have changed both paintings to satisfy his patron.

Figure 4: Anonymous, *Portratit of Amalia of Solms*, 1625. Panel, 77 x 66.5. Olsztyn (Poland), Olsztyn Museum.

How did Frederik Hendrik and Amalia became interested in Heliodorus? It is unlikely that the Fontainebleau paintings were in existence when Frederik Hendrik was a page at Henri's court in 1598, although at age 14, he might have been aware of French interest in the novelist. It is possible that he did see them during a shorter visit to Fontainebleau in 1609.[51] Frederik Hendrik was trained in Greek and Latin and was a student at Leiden after 1594. His studies there focused on mathematics and military history; he is known to have read both Polybius, and Caesar. He was indeed in Leiden at the same time as Scaliger; but Scaliger refused to give public lectures, and it is unlikely that Frederik Hendrik learned about Heliodorus from him. The Prince *might* have had enough Greek to read Heliodorus in the original; but he was completely fluent in French, using it as much as, or more than, Dutch, as we can tell from his correspondence with Constantijn Huygens, so that it is more likely that he read Heliodorus in Amyot's translation.

I suggest that it was Frederik Hendrik's secretary and confidant, Constantijn Huygens, who introduced the Prince and his wife to Heliodorus. Huygens was a poet, a musician, a scholar, an accomplished Latinist. He was widely read in Classical and contemporary literature and also an unabashed romantic. His love poetry to his wife, Suzanna van Baerle (1599-1637), whom he called "Sterre" (Star) is one of the best examples of the theme of married love as companionship. We also know that he possessed a copy of the *Aithiopika* (Huygens 1903), and that it was he who brought Rembrandt to the attention of the Prince. I have not (yet) discovered anything in his voluminous correspondence that mentions Heliodorus or Bloemaert, but I'm still looking.

I mentioned before that the Bloemaert paintings were intended to commemorate the marriage of Frederik Hendrik and Amalia. This point is reinforced by van Honthorst's ceilings at Kronborg, which were clearly influenced by Bloemaert's paintings. The Kronborg ceilings were accompanied by little scenes in which Cupids carry little plaques with the monograms of the Danish Royal family and of the bride of the Crown Prince, Magdalena Sibylla of Saxony.[52] The couple was married in 1634, and the Cupids, along with the illustrations of the Aithiopika, were installed in the palace of Kronborg in 1635. The paintings and Cupids were all commissioned to celebrate the wedding. Heliodorus, it is asserted by critics of the Kronberg ceilings, was selected as "a romance about a happy love affair which ends in the preparation for a wedding feast."[53] Christian IV and/or van Honthorst certainly drew on Bloemaert's paintings of the *Aithiopika* to celebrate the Danish royal marriage; it is reasonable to conclude that they did so because

---

[51] Van der Ploeg and Vermeeren 1997, 18, 104.
[52] Judson and Ekkart 1999, 130-131, cat. 142-145, pl. 66-69.
[53] Charlotte Christensen in Council of Europe 1988, 83-84.

Bloemaert, Huygens and/or Frederik Hendrik had chosen the *Aithiopika* to celebrate the Dutch princely wedding.

All the paintings from the Netherlands and Denmark suggest strongly that the *Aithiopika* was adopted as a model for Weddings in Princely Courts. This may be true of the series at Fontainebleau, but I feel much less certain of my understanding of the dynastic and marital politics of Henri of Navarre than I am of the Dutch and Danish courts.

The marriage of the Danish Crown Prince was entirely conventional, an arranged affair between two young members of what has been rightly described as the "Calvinist International." But the Royal Marriage of Theagenes and Charikleia was achieved despite overwhelming odds, and the *Aithiopika* is so much more than "a romance about a happy love affair which ends in the preparation for a wedding feast." What, besides their royal and noble descent, seemed to Frederik and Amalia to reflect their own situation?

There was something very unusual about the wedding of Frederik Hendrik and Amalia. Carried out in the shadow of the death of Maurits, it was celebrated with none of the pomp and ceremony of a great wedding. From prompting by Maurits to proposal by Frederik Hendrik, to acceptance by Amalia and the actual ceremony, the whole affair was very rushed. They had known each other for some time, possibly since she arrived at The Hague with the Winter Queen. Although she was his cousin, Amalia did not appear to be the kind of dynastic match that an ambitious monarchist might make. With the Bohemian court existing essentially on the generosity of Charles I and the States General, she brought, as the English ambassador said, "nothing but herself to the wedding." But they were not an acknowledged couple, and Frederik Hendrik was known to have sexual partners. We are told that before their engagement was announced, Frederik Hendrik was deeply embarrassed by gossip at the Bohemian court about them.[54] He denied that there was any relationship, even though it was acknowledged and approved, apparently, by his brother, and noted by his devoted secretary Constantijn Huygens. It is now impossible to recover what the circumstances of their relationship were before their marriage; but it is clear that there was something in the adventures of Theagenes and Charikleia that led the couple to associate their courtship with the novel.

I would suggest that they did indeed fall in love at first sight, or something like it, when they met in The Hague, at the "Bohemian" court; one could see how Charikleia's odd position in Delphi might be seen as a model to the awkward Bohemian court-in-exile. What I also would argue is that

---

[54] Tiethoff-Spliethoff, 1997, 164-165.

Amalia, like Charikleia, insisted on postponing intimacy until marriage. The embarrassment, irritation and secrecy about the relationship that we find in the contemporary accounts probably can be explained because the court gossip assumed they were having an affair when in fact they weren't. From their later lives together, it is indeed clear that Amalia was, like Charikleia, a strong and equal partner in the relationship; and there is no mention of Frederik Hendrik having a mistress after his marriage.

Studies of later reception may, perhaps even should, prompt reconsideration of the original context of the work under consideration. The 17th-century artistic representation of *Aithiopika* frames it as a narrative of *royal* courtship and adventure. When we recall the role of Royal Narratives in the beginning of the Ancient Novel (in the *Cyropaedia),* and its special position in the relatively late *King Apollonius of Tyre,* should we look for a "Royal" context in the Severan or Constantinian world into which to fit Heliodorus?

References

Andrup, O. 1932, "Noter verdrørende Karel van Manders Biographi I-II," *Kunstmuseets Aarskrift* 30-31, 141-182.
Beckett, F. 1916. "Pigen fra Aethiopien," *Kunstmuseets Aarskrift* 2, 25-37.
Béguin, S. 1960. *L' École de Fontainebleau.* Paris, Gonthier-Shers.
Blok, P.I. 1907. *History of the People of the Netherlands. Part 4.* Translated by O.A. Bierstadt. New York and London: G.P. Putnam's.
Colonna, A. ed. 1938. *Heliodori Aethiopica.* Rome: Regia Officina Polygraphica.
Council of Europe. 1988. *Christian IV and Europe. The 19th Exhibition of the Council of Europe, Denmark 1988.*
De Meyere. J.A.L. 1998. *"Granida en Daifilo" 1625 van Gerard van Honthorst: onderzuik en restauratie.* Utrecht: Centraal Museum.
Frijhoff, W. and M. Spies. 2004. *Dutch Culture in a European Perspective, Volume 1. 1650: Hard-Won Unity.* Basingstoke and New York: Palgrave Macmillan.
Groeneweg, I. 1997. "Court and City: Dress in the Age of Frederik Hendrik and Amalia." In Keblusek and Zijlmans 1997, 200-218.
Hägg, T. 1983. *The Novel in Antiquity.* Oxford: Blackwell.
Hardie, P. 1998. "A reading of Heliodorus, *Aithiopika,* 3.4.2 –5.2." In R. Hunter (ed.), 19-39.
Hunter, R. ed. 1998. *Studies in Heliodorus.* Cambridge Philological Society, supplementary volume 21. Cambridge: Cambridge Philological Society.
Huygens, C. 1903. *Catalogus der Bibliotheek van Constantyn Huygens.* 's Gravenhage: Stockum & Zoon.
 Online at http//www.xs4all.nl/~adcs/Huygens/varia/catal-voorrede.html.
Judson J. R. and R.E.O. Ekkart. 1999. *Gerrit van Honthorst, 1592-1656.* Dornspijk: Davaco
Keblusek, M. and J. Zijlmans, editors. 1997. *Princely Display. The Court of Frederick Henry of Orange and Amalia van Solms.* The Hague: Historical Museum.

Kettering, A.M. 1983. *The Dutch Arcadia. Pastoral Art and its Audience in the Golden Age.* Totowa, NJ: Allanheid, Osmun and Montclair NJ: Abner, Schram.

Lévêque, J.-J. 1984. *L'École de Fontainebleau.* Neuchâtel: Ides et Calendes.

Maillon, J. translator. 1935. Héliodore, *Les Éthiopiques.* 3 vols. Paris: Les Belles Lettres.

Prak, M. 2005. *The Dutch Republic in the Seventeenth Century.* Translated by D.Webb. Cambridge: Cambridge University Press.

Roethlisberger, M. 1993. *Abraham Bloemaert and his Sons: Paintings and Prints.* 2 vols. Doornspijk: Davaco.

Sandy, G.N. 1982. *Heliodorus.* Boston: Twayne.

Schama, S. 1987. *The Embarrassment of Riches. An Interpretation of Dutch Culture in the Golden Age.* New York: Knopf.

Seelig, G. 1997. *Abraham Bloemaert (1566-1651). Studien zur Utrechter Malerei um 1620.* Berlin: Mann.

Spicer, J. and L.F. Orr. 1997. *Masters of Light: Dutch Painters in Utrecht during the Golden Age.* New Haven and London: Yale University Press.

Stechow, W. 1953. "Heliodorus' Aethiopica in Art." *Journal of the Warburg and Courtauld Institutes* 16, 144-152.

Sutton, P. 1984. *Masters of Seventeenth-Century Dutch Genre Painting.* Philadelphia: Philadelphia Museum of Art.

Tiethoff-Spliethoff, M. 1997. "Role-Play and Representation. Portrait Painting at the court of Frederik Hendrik and Amalia." In Keblusek and Zijlmans, editors, 161-200.

Van der Ploeg, P. and Q. Buvelot. 2006. *Royal Picture Gallery Mauritshuis. A Princely Collection.* The Hague: Royal Picture House Gallery.

Van der Ploeg, P. and C. Vermeeren. 1997. *Princely Patrons. The Collection of Frederick Henry of Orange and Amalia of Solms in The Hague.* The Hague: Mauritshuis.

Van Mander, K. 1936. *Dutch and Flemish Painters.* Translated by C.van de Wall. New York: McFarlane, Warde, McFarlane.

— 1943. *Het Schilder-Boek. Het leven der doorluchtige Nederlandsche en Hoogduische schilders.* Amsterdam: Wereldbibliotheek.

— 1973. *Den Grondt der edel vry schilder-const.* Edited by Hessel Miedema. Utrecht: Haentjens Dekker & Gumbert.

— 1999. *The Lives of the Illustrious Netherlandish and German Painters.* Edited by H. Miedema. Volume 6. Doornspijk: Davaco.

White, C. 1982. *The Dutch Paintings in the Collection of Her Majesty the Queen.* Cambridge: Cambridge University Press.

Susanna and her Sisters

The Virtuous Lady Motif in Sacred Tradition and its Representation in Art, Secular Writing and Popular Narrative

FAUSTINA C.W. DOUFIKAR-AERTS
Universität Mainz - VU Amsterdam - Leiden University

More than six decades have passed since the prolific Flemish author Marnix Gijsen published *Het Boek van Joachim van Babylon*.[1] In this novel he placed the Biblical story of Susanna and the Elders in a new perspective by creating a framework of an unsuccessful marriage between Joachim and his wife Susanna. Although she was the perfect wife, unequalled in beauty – the Helen of her time – she remained mentally unapproachable for her husband and he felt that she treated him with mere patronizing kindness. The book caused a great deal of controversy, not in the least because of some agnostic thoughts raised by Joachim in the story.[2] Gijsen's literary creation depended on readerly knowledge of the story of Susanna and the Elders, which had been a favorite subject of iconography since early Christianity and later in medieval illuminated Bibles and books of exempla.[3] Moreover, the Susanna motif had been elaborated in Flanders earlier in the *Rijmbijbel*, the Middle Dutch version of the Bible composed in rhyme by Jacob van Maerlant in 1271.[4]

---

[1] *Het boek van Joachim van Babylon* (The Book of Joachim of Babylon), Den Haag 1947, written by Johannes Alphonsius Albertus Goris (1899-1984), who used the pseudonym Marnix Gijsen.

[2] Within a decade two books were written in reply to Gijsen's novel: *Het Antwoord van Suzanna aan Joachim van Babylon* (The Answer of Suzanna to Joachim of Babylon) by Esther de Raad (pseudonym for Mellie Uyldert) and *Een vrouw met name Suzanna* (A Woman Called Suzanna) by Yvonne de Man.

[3] Frescoes representing Susanna and the Elders can be found in the third century Roman Catacomb of Priscilla and on several sarcophagi from this period. See Smith 1993. Also see below, note 34.

[4] Jacob van Maerlant's 'Rijmbijbel' (composed in 1271) edited by M. Gysseling 1983. Verses 16932-16984.

The Susanna story became known in two different versions: primarily, it was part of the Book of Daniel (13) in the Septuagint.[5] The other version is the more detailed adaptation attributed to Theodotion (*floruit* 2nd c. A.D.). The origin and date of composition of the Susanna story have been under discussion from the time of Julius the African in the third century A.D. Some details in it, specifically a Greek play on words, point to a composition in Greek. Other particulars seem to bear witness of a Hebrew or Aramaic origin.[6] A recent study proposes dating the story to the early first century B.C. – the period of Queen Salomé Alexandra – on the grounds of textual and internal evidence, such as the themes of witnesses and gender relations.[7]

In the past century research and criticism, predominantly in the fields of theology, literature and gender studies, has concentrated on the origins and relationship of the Susanna story in the Septuagint and Theodotion.[8] So far, little attention has been paid to other versions of 'Susanna', according to the traditions of the Samaritans, Shi'ite and Sunnite Muslims, the Copts and Ethiopian Jews, as handed down in Arabic and Ge'ez (classical Ethiopic). In this piece I will focus on these particular traditions and on the question of how the motif inspired authors to create edifying tales and short narratives.

In the celebrated collection of the *Arabian Nights* we find 'The tale of the pious Israelite woman'; she was falsely accused of adultery by two sheikhs, who sought her love and both of whom she had turned down. She narrowly escaped from execution by the intervention of a twelve-year-old boy, the future prophet Dāniyāl, who questioned the two sheikhs separately on their testimony. They testified differently about the spot and the tree under which they allegedly witnessed 'Susanna' committing the crime, and, eventually, were struck by a bolt of lightning. The account in the *Arabian Nights* gives a very condensed version, but the details are explicit enough to consider the Israelite woman, whose name is not mentioned, to be no other than Susan-

---

[5] The Story of Susanna and the Elders belongs to the apocryphal part of the Book of Daniel; it does not occur in the Hebrew version of the Bible, but to the Greek translation of the Old Testament, the Septuagint, it is a canonical text.
[6] See Zimmermann 1957-1958, p.238. Also see Koenen 1998.
[7] Clanton 2003, 121-140.
[8] Engel 1985, *Die Susanna-Erzählung*; Zimmermann 1957-58; J.W. van Henten 1989, 'Het verhaal over Susanna als een pre-rabbijnse midrasj bij Daniel 1:1-2'; Ilan 1999, ' "And Who Knows Whether You Have not Come to Dominion for a Time Like This?" (Esther 4;14): Esther, Judith und Susanna as Propaganda for Shelamzion's Queenship'; Carroll 1983, 'Myth, Methodology, and Transformation in the Old Testament: The Stories of Esther, Judith, and Susanna'. Bal 1993, 'The Elders and Susanna'.

na.⁹ In fact, the details have much in common with another Arabic narrative, related by Dāwud al-Antaqī (David of Antioch) in his compilation of 'love-stories'.¹⁰ This account is clearly based on the biblical tradition, which is confirmed by Al-Antaqī who explains that 'the story of Sūsan' was famous among the people'. Moreover, it had been translated 'from the Book of Daniel in the Torah'. The author may have believed his source on this point, but an analysis of the text shows that it obviously derives from the Theodotion version. The translation in full of al-Antaqī's *Qissat Sūsan* may serve here as a basis for reviewing and comparing the variants of the story:

> The famous story of Sūsan, about which there has been a lively debate among the people. The author, may God be pleased with him, who knew many different languages and spoke many tongues, rendered this story about her from the word of God Almighty in the Torah. He stated that the story that follows is a translation from the Book of Dāniyāl, may peace be upon him.
>
> When it was the third year of the reign of Yuwākīm the King of Judah, the King of Bābil, Bukhtnasar (Nebuchadnezzar), arrived at Urshalīm (Jerusalem), that is, in Arabic, Bayt al-Maqdis (the Holy House). And the Lord handed it over to him. Then, he brought what was in the temple to Shinghār (Shinar), and this is a place known as the Holy House.¹¹ When they had agreed upon the legitimacy of [the application of] the Mosaic laws, he appointed two elders as judges, who were renowned among the Israelites for their devoutness and abstinence. They sat in judgment upon the people, having been lodged near the house of Yuwākīm. The latter had a wife named Sūsan. She excelled in beauty and loveliness, and she was a treat and a blessing to the eye, while both their¹² parents were honorable

---

⁹ *The Alif Laila or Book of the Thousand Nights and One Night,* in the edition by W.H. McNaghten 1839, pp. 406-407: 'The Story of the Devout Israelite Woman' (حكاية المرأة العابدة في بني إسرائيل).

¹⁰ Dāwud al-Antaqī († 1599), *Tazyīn al-Aswāq fī Akhbār al-'Ushshāq* (The Embellishment of the Markets on the Stories of Lovers) ed. Dār Hammad wa Mahyū, Beirut 1982, 2 vols., 1, pp. 280-281. The Susanna-story is to be found in the chapter entitled: *Qissat Sūsan* (The Story of Susanna). A similar but more elaborate recension can be found in an 18ᵗʰ-century (?) ms. in the Coptic Museum in Cairo, Biblica, 39, no. 9, ff. 183-187. See below, note 25.

¹¹ This introduction refers to Dan. 1:1-2 the canonical part of the Book of Daniel.

¹² It is not clear whether this refers to her parents and to her husband's parents as well – perhaps meaning that they were a respectable couple – or that is was a mistake for *her* parents.

people among the Israelites. She used to go into her garden for a walk every day. The two judges had watched her there, and they fell in love with her, to the point that she distracted them from the administration of justice. Each of them kept it a secret from the other until one day at noon of a very warm day, they said to one another: 'It is extremely hot, let us go for a rest'. They left, both hiding their intention to come back, hoping to win the lady over. When they met each other again, each of them questioned the other about his return. Then, they both revealed that love for her [Yuwākim's wife] had possessed them and they agreed upon [having] her.

She entered the garden with her maidens, for she wanted to bathe, while they kept themselves hidden. When she sent the maidens for oils and salves the two men appeared and closed the gates, saying to her: 'If you do not fulfill our demand we will announce that we found you with a youth and that you therefore sent the maidens away. You know our position among the Israelites!' Sūsan answered: 'By God, I would never provoke the Lord' and she screamed. But the judges also began to shout and one of them left to open the gate. The servants came near and they [the judges] told them their story. They [the servants] were highly amazed because they had not observed any misbehavior on her part. Then, Yuwākīm arrived and they notified him about the matter and that they had not been able to seize the young man. People gathered around and the two sheikhs moved toward Sūsan to unveil her and they spoke: 'We testify on her that she entered the garden with two maidens whom she sent away after which she locked the gates. Then there came a young man from behind a tree who made love to her. When we witnessed the sin, we yelled but the man escaped.'

Sūsan wept and lifted her eyes up to heaven saying: 'Oh God Eternal, Who knows all hidden things, You know that they lie about me.' But they took her to be executed. Then Dāniyāl, peace be upon him, who was a thirteen-year-old boy, came forward crying out to them: 'Stop it, she is not guilty of the things she has been accused of'. Then, he ordered them to separate the two and he asked one of them: 'From under which tree appeared the young man?' and he answered: 'From under the terebinth', and he said: 'You are a liar, and an angel of God bears witness against you of your deceit'. Then he dismissed him and sent for the other and questioned him: 'From under which tree came the youth?' and he said: 'From under the oil-tree', and he said: 'You lied', and he raised them, and thus they were exposed. Then, a blaze came down, which burnt them, and God spared innocent blood. And the reputation of Dāniyāl, peace be upon him, became great.

The last remark, as well as several other details, such as the bathing, can only be found in Theodotion. The *Arabian Nights*' version also follows this tradition, but it apparently preserved, in spite of its abbreviated form, a significant feature which is not transmitted in the *Qissat Sūsan* by al-Antaqī: in the *Arabian Nights* it is told that the sheikhs – obviously the substitute for the Elders – put their hands on the convicted woman's head, saying: 'Praised be the Lord, who sent His punishment upon you!' This corresponds to an essential element in the description of the trial, the laying on of hands. In the biblical context, this act is be understood as a judicial ritual only to be performed by the High Priest, Rabbis and Elders.[13]

Another point worth attention in these two Arabic versions is the names of the trees that play a role in the false testimonies. In the *Arabian Nights*' version, these are the pear-tree and the apple-tree, whereas in al-Antaqī's account these trees are the terebinth and the oil-tree.[14] The Susanna stories in the Septuagint and Theodotion match each other in giving the mastic tree and the evergreen oak. In Greek the names of these trees, *schínos* and *prínos*, give rise to a play on words which refers to the punishment of the Elders.[15] This detail no longer occurs in the Arabic versions, apparently because the play on words would lose its relevance in translation. Therefore the transmitters may have permitted themselves to choose a pair of trees more familiar to their audiences. Besides, in al-Antaqī, Daniel's reaction to the false testimony by the first witness saying 'an angel of God bears witness against you of your deceit' – which at first seems to be a loose end – is likely to actually refer to the Greek text, which says 'You have lied against your own head, for the angel of God has received the sentence from God and will immediately cleave you in two'.[16] With regard to Daniel's age, mentioned exclusively in al-Antaqī and the *Arabian Nights*, thirteen and twelve years old respectively,

---

[13] As noticed by Smith, *opus cit.,* 6 with regard to Daniel 13:34.
[14] The ms. in the Coptic Museum (see below) has the terebinth and the almond tree.
[15] The word σχῖνος refers to: σχίσει: he cleaves. Daniel 13:55: the angel of God (..) will cleave you in two; πρῖνος refers to: πρίσαι: he cuts. Daniel 13:59: the angel of God (..) will cut you in two.
[16] Daniel 13:55.

this aspect is reminiscent of the Syriac 'Book of the Child Daniel', which may have influenced these Arabic versions.[17]

A third, and highly interesting representation of the Susanna story can be found in a ninth-century (?) folk-tale, entitled *Hadīth al-Jumjuma ma'a al-Malik* ('The Story of the Skull and the King'). Fabrizio Pennacchietti has edited the text for the first time from a *codex unicus* under the title *Susanna nel deserto*, with a commentary and Italian translation.[18] In this delightful booklet we find a variant of the Susanna story, which differs in many respects from those mentioned earlier. It is a short story, in which the Susanna motif has been integrated in a frame story. The scene of action is situated at the court of an ancient great king of the Israelites in an undefined distant past. The narrative time covers three generations; that of the Israelite king, of his daughter, princess Rabbāb, and his grand-daughter Sawsana, the actual heroine of the story. She was born by a virgin birth from her mother, princess Rabbāb. The king's daughter had miraculously conceived by eating fruit from a mysterious tree. This tree grew on the top of a skull buried in her father's garden. Long ago, this skull of enormous proportions had been discovered by the king in a cave during a hunt, and brought home. There it was given to the gardener to be buried in the palace garden. When the heroine, Sawsana, had learned about her amazing origin, she decided to devote her life to the Lord. Two hermits, living in a monk's cell next to hers, invited her to come and recite the Psalms, but when they tried to harass her she cunningly escaped and locked herself in her tower. The two hermits, named Hiram and Huraym,[19] then returned to her father's city to accuse her of adultery. The king was obliged to sentence his grand-daughter to death, but at the very last moment he observed a group of children playing a game of the trial of Sawsana. Then, he learned that the judge always has to question the witnesses, separately. When he applied this method to Hiram and Huraym they were exposed as impostors and sentenced to death. They were stoned and

---

[17] In the Heraclean, the Syriac New Testament, according to the revision by Thomas of Herkal (7th c.). Also see Gaster 1925-1928, 'The Story of the Daughter of Amram: the Samaritan Parallel to the Apocryphal Story of Susanna', 208.

[18] Pennacchietti 1998, *Susanna nel deserto. Riflessi di un racconto biblico nella cultura arabo-islamica*, testo, traduzione, commentari, Torino 1998. I thank Pennacchietti for kindly providing me with his book, which inspired me to start on this investigation. An English translation appeared in Pennacchietti 2006, *Three Mirrors For Two Biblical Ladies. Susanna and the Queen of Sheba in the Eyes of Jews, Christians, and Muslims*, 28-39.

[19] The names, Hiram and Huraym, consist of the radicals occurring in the Arabic verb *harima* (= to become old or senile), which possibly points to the old aged *sheikhs*, or Elders.

burnt to ashes, just as they had wished to happen to Sawsana. All the events took place in absence of Sawsana, who was still in devotion in her monk's cell.

As far as the Susanna part of the story is concerned, the details, such as the fact that the assault is carried out by hermits in a deserted area, away form the city, and the nature of their punishment, point to a strong relation of the *Hadīth al-Jumjuma ma'a al-Malik* with the story in the 14th-century Samaritan Chronicle of Abu 'l-Fath, written in Arabic.[20] This version of the story derives in its turn from the Samaritan Book of Joshua, also in Arabic, the original Hebrew version of which is dated by Gaster to 69-117 A.D.. The parallels between the *Hadīth al-Jumjuma* and Abū 'l-Fath's *Chronicle* have been listed by Pennachietti, who already noticed the striking similarity of these two versions.[21] The correspondence is mainly related to the circumstances of the events. In both stories the slanderous accusations are made by hermits living in seclusion, who first bid Susanna – in Abū 'l-Fath she is nameless and referred to as 'the daughter of the High Priest 'Amram' – to recite the Scriptures in their presence. The girl parries the harassment by the ascetics by flattering them. She invites them to her home but then hastily barricades the door. The following accusation, trial and, finally, the condemnation of the hermits take place in the city, in her complete absence and without her knowledge. And just as in the *Ḥadīth al-Jumjuma* it is a children's game – not Daniel's intervention – that changes the outcome.

Pennachietti also pointed to motifs common in Abū 'l-Fath and the 'Acts of Sūsenā', the Falasha variant of the Susanna-story. This text is found in a Homily written in Ge'ez, the liturgical language also in use by the Jewish communities of Ethiopia.[22] Although there are a few differences in the details of the story – Susanna is a widow, the slanderers are three in number, and her savior is the angel Michael – the purport is still the same. The fact that she explicitly devotes herself to the Lord would be an argument to arrange the Ge'ez Homily in the same category with the tradition of Abū 'l-Fath and the *Hadīth al-Jumjuma*.

In these five representatives of the Susanna story we can roughly discern two types, which cross over the boundaries of religion. Firstly, the Samaritan version which is expressed, apart from Abū 'l-Faṭh's (hi)story, in the Ethiopian-Jewish Homily and the Muslim tale of the King and the Skull. In none

---

[20] *Abulfathi Annales Samaritani*, edited by Eduard Vilmar 1865, 108-113.
[21] Pennachietti 1998, 87-88.
[22] The text has been edited and translated by Wurmband 1963, 'A Falasha Variant of the Story of Susanna', 30-34.

of these Daniel actually plays a role, neither does the bath-scene. Next to this we find the Theodotion-related versions in the *Arabian Nights* and the compilation of 'love-stories' by al-Antaqī. The version as transmitted by al-Antaqī must have had some vogue, because it can also be found in Coptic collections of Biblica. An 18th-century Cairo manuscript in the Coptic museum contains a story about Sūsanah, the wife of Yuwāqīm, the daughter of Salqīwā (Hilkiah), an elaborate account and even more in line with this tradition. It particularly dwells on the rituals taking place during the trial. It is said that 'the two transgressors of the Nāmūs (law) ordered that she be unveiled to pass judgment and so that they could feast their eyes on her beauty. All the people gathered there cried when they saw her being exposed to be brought up for trial. And the two sheikhs, the judges, were among the people and they laid their hands on Sūsanah's head'. Here we see that the laying on of hands – a feature of the *Arabian Nights* that is missing in al-Antaqī – and the unveiling – a feature of al-Antaqī which, in its turn, is missing in the *Nights* – occur together in the Coptic manuscript, which is clearly linked to Theodotion.

This text also throws light on the angel, referred to by Daniel, when he accused one of the Elders of deceit; although the Greek play on words connecting the trees' names to a punishment loses its meaning when translated into another language, the phrases have been preserved in the Arabo-Coptic text. The episode runs as follows:

> Dāniyāl spoke to him [the judge]: 'Oh sower of Canaan,[23] not of Judah, beauty has led you astray and lust has turned your heart away. This is how you behaved against the daughters of Israel, for they mourn because they are subjected to you. But Judah[24] did not endure your crime. Now then, tell me under which tree did you discern the two meeting each other?' He said: 'It was under the almond tree.' And Dāniyāl said to him: 'You lied, and your deceit has decided upon your head. Behold, an angel of the Lord has brought a spear to be planted firmly in your heart in order to eliminate you.'[25]

This text demonstrates that al-Antaqī almost certainly shortened a similar text. This explains the occurrence of some cryptic phrases and the fact that some of the components differ from the ones appearing in the *Nights*.

---

[23] In Theodotion (56): seed of Canaan.
[24] One Judean?
[25] Ms. in the Coptic Museum in Cairo, Biblica section I, ser. No. 39, no. 9, p. 186v.-187r.

Yet, we can define a third category in the Susanna tradition, the existence of which is not really surprising, although it remained practically unnoticed as part of the Susanna tradition.[26] In the collection of Qisas al-Anbiyā' (Lives of the Prophets) by the Shi'ite compiler 'Abd Allāh ibn Muhammad Radī al-Husaynī[27] a chapter is devoted to the story of the young Daniel. Husaynī derived the tale from *Al-Kāfī fī 'Ilm ad-Dīn* ('The adequate book on theology') by Muhammad ibn Ya'qūb ibn Ishāq al-Kulīnī († 939), whose report is said to go back – via a reliable chain of transmission – to as-Sādiq, the 6th Shi'ite Imām (702-765). Characteristic of this Susanna-story is that her name is not mentioned, as in the *Arabian Nights* and Abū 'l-Fath. On the other hand, more than average attention is paid to Daniel, who is said to have been an orphan, raised by an old Israelite woman.

The story is different in the sense that the husband of the virtuous Israelite lady commits his wife to the care of the judges of his own. He asks them to vouch for her welfare while he is on a mission for the king. However, as soon as he has gone they start to make the lady improper proposals and when she refuses they threaten her, saying: 'By God, when you decline we will surely testify to your adultery, before the king!' And so it happened. The king has to sentence her to death. However, while waiting for the execution for three days, the king asks his minister for advice. The latter accidentally observes a group of playing children. One of them, named Dāniyāl, takes a seat on an improvised throne pretending to be the king. He appoints the others to play the role of the lady and the two judges. Then, he separates them and questions them one after the other to testify about where, when, and with whom the lady's crime took place. When Dāniyāl, in his role of the king, finds out that their answers contradict, he judges that they have given false testimonies and that they ought to be punished. The minister, who has been watching the whole game from a distance, straightaway hastens to inform the king about this event. The king decides to interrogate the witnesses once more, separately. They fail to agree in their testimony, precisely as had happened during the children's play. Then, the king who was relieved at the outcome orders the treacherous judges to be put to death.

The Shi'ite tradition transmitted by Husaynī has all the essential clues of the tale, without giving identical details. This is probably due to the fact that it is part of a collection of Lives of the Prophets, sacred stories that highlight

---

[26] The work is not mentioned by Pennachietti.
[27] Guesses about the dating of Husaynī vary from the 10th c. (Ahlwardt) up to the 19th c. (Aichele). A few parts of his work were published in Walther Aichele's article 'Biblische Legenden der Schī'iten aus dem Prophetenbuch des Hoseinī' in 1915.

the deeds and marvels of pre-Islamic messengers and holy men. The compilation also consists of episodes about David, Jesaya, Jona and Jesus. The main concern of Husaynī's Susanna-story is the glorification of the Prophet Daniel; the trials and tribulations of the virtuous lady are secondary and subordinate to the portrayal of the young Dāniyāl. On the basis of its components the story should be classified as a half-way composition. It agrees with the *Arabian Nights* and al-Anṭaqī in focusing on the young Daniel, in describing the lady as an Israelite woman, and in attributing the harassment and false accusations to two judges, not hermits. The lady is, also similarly, troubled in her own house. On the other hand it corresponds with the *Hadīth al-Jumjuma* and Abū 'l-Fath in the fact that the king/grandfather and the high-priest/father, respectively, who are obliged to sentence their kin to death, are relieved and helped out by the three-days' respite before the execution.[28] As in Husaynī it is the observance of a children's game that causes the resumption of the trial and its dramatic change of outcome. For that matter, this motif is not exclusive to the Susanna tradition. It also occurs in the Jewish David and Salomon cycle, which has its Islamic counterpart in the collection of Lives of the Prophets by Abū Rifāʿa ʿUmāra ibn Wathīma. Here, a falsely accused woman escapes execution when a mock trial played by young Sulaymān (Solomon) and his friends brings Dāwud (King David) around. He re-opens the trial and questions the witnesses separately, which leads to the exposure of the false testimonies.[29] Although the tale of the David/Solomon cycle is quite different in detail from the Susanna story, it may point to the fact that the motif could be traced back to the common pattern of the Clever Child.[30]

In the above, seven 'Susannas' have been under consideration. They represent three categories, the varieties of which may be explained as follows. The Susanna story originated in the ancient world; it is probably much older than the version that became known through the Septuagint and Theodotion. The characteristics of these other branches – which are apparently more closely linked to Jewish historiography – could originate from a parallel line that resulted, in an early stage, in the Samaritan version of Abū 'l-Fath. In the wake of this tradition a tale, the *Hadīth al-Jumjuma*, was created, composed of the core of the story with the addition of other plots and legends that recall elements in Greek mythology. The virgin pregnancy of the heroine's mother, caused by the fruit of a mysterious tree, recalls the

---

[28] In the Homily it is the king/father who has his daughter thrown in a deep pit.
[29] The text has been edited by R. G. Khoury in *Codices Arabici Antiqui*, 'Les Légendes prophétiques dans l'Islam', 123-126.
[30] See Gaster, *op.cit.*, 209.

birth of Adonis[31] and of the Phrygian shepherd Atys, whose mother, Nana, had conceived by putting a ripe pomegranate in her bosom.[32] It cannot be ruled out that the Biblical story of Susanna was an excerpt taken from a pre-existing legend or story which is still mirrored in the *Hadīth al-Jumjuma* and which had a mythical character. From this legend only the Susanna part survived in the Bible for its function as an edifying parable. The Susanna tradition as given by Theodotion came to form part of early Christian discourse on morals, marital chastity, celibacy and virginity.[33] It gave rise to expressions of religious and secular figurative painting and sculpture. The aspect of iconography could not systematically be examined within this synopsis, but it must be noticed that the Susanna motif has been in vogue from antiquity up to the present in a multiplicity of artistic representations. A future study of this pictorial tradition would be a worthwhile project.[34] In these seven representations of 'Susanna' the focus was not predominantly on her chastity, but on diverse elements – on the wickedness of false testimonies, the importance of impartial justice, the necessity of hearing witnesses separately and the glorification of Daniel.

In spite of their diversity the Susanna stories agree on a crucial statement; a complete orchard of different trees has passed under review here, brought up as silent witnesses of Susanna's crime, but they all evidenced the same thing: how the name of a tree could make the difference between life and death.

---

[31] According to one of the versions in Greek mythology Adonis' mother, Myrrha, had been turned into a myrrh tree. She gave birth to her son when a boar used its tusks to tear the tree's bark off.

[32] A ripe almond is also mentioned as a variant.

[33] See Smith 1993.

[34] For the early Christian period this has been done by Smith 1993. The first representations of the Susanna story can be found on the frescoes of the Priscilla Catacomb in Rome (ca. 200-250 AD). See above, note 3. Exceedingly interesting in its turn are the five scenes engraved in crystal, produced for the Frankish Lothar II of Lotharingia (AD 855-69) which is preserved in the British Museum. From the 15th cent. edifying and artistic images of Susanna and the Elders enjoyed great popularity. This is, for instance, attested in the pen-drawn miniatures in the *Historiebijbel* (Historybible), ms. 78 D 38 in the KB in The Hague, dated ca. 1430; engravings by Georg Pencz (ca. 1532), Hans Collaert (ca. 1590) and Jacob Matham (1599); the oil paintings by Tintoretto's (1560-62); Annibale and Ludovico Carracci (1590-91and 1616, resp.); Peter Paul Rubens (1607); Rembrandt Harmenszoon van Rijn (1647). In more recent times we find a Susanna-miniature in an early 19th-century handwritten Coptic bible (Lehnert and Landrock 2000, p. 25). Even today the motif inspires painters like Daniel Malikov and Schigolev Oleg and many others. For an overview of the artistic tradition of Susanna images see: www.3r-kontext.de/susanna.html.

Bibliography

Aichele, W. 1915. 'Biblische Legenden der Schī'iten aus dem Prophetenbuch des Ḥoseinī', *Mitteilungen des Seminars für Orientalische Sprachen* 18, 27-57.

Antaqī, Dawūd al-, 1982. *Tazyīn al-Aswāq fī Akhbār al-Ushshāq* (The Embellishment of the Markets on the Stories of Lovers). Edition. 2 vols., I, Beirut: Dār Hammad wa Mahyū.

Bal, M. 1993. 'The Elders and Susanna', *Biblical Interpretation. A Journal of Contemporary Approaches* 1/1, 1-19.

Carroll, M.P. 1983. 'Myth, Methodology, and Transformation in the Old Testament: The Stories of Esther, Judith, and Susanna', *Studies in Religion* 12/3, 301-312.

Clanton, D.W. 2003. '(Re)dating the Story of Susanna: A Proposal', *Journal for the Study of Judaism* 34/2, 121-140.

Engel, H. 1985. 'Die Susanna-Erzählung', in: *Orbis biblicus et orientalis* 61, Freiburg.

Gaster M. 1925-1928, 'The Story of the Daughter of Amram: the Samaritan Parallel to the Apocryphal Story of Susanna', *Studies and Texts in Folklore, Magic, Medieval Romance, Hebrew Apocrypha and Samaritan Archeology*, 3 vols., I, London, 199-210.

Gijsen, M., *Het boek van Joachim van Babylon*, Den Haag 1947.

Gysseling, M. 1983. 'Jacob van Maerlant's Rijmbijbel', in: *Corpus van Middelnederlandse teksten*, II, 3, edition, Leiden.

Henten, J.W. van 1989. 'Het verhaal over Susanna als een pre-rabbijnse midrasj bij Daniel 1:1-2', *Nederlands Theologisch Tijdschrijft* 43, 278-293.

Ilan, T. 1999. ' "And Who Knows Whether You Have not Come to Dominion for a Time Like This?" (Esther 4:14): Esther, Judith und Susanna as Propaganda for Shelamzion's Queenship', *Integrating Women into Second Temple History*, Tübingen.

Khoury, R. G. 1978. 'Les Légendes prophétiques dans l'Islam d'après le manuscrit d'Abū Rifā'a 'Umāra b. Wathīma b. Mūsa b. al-Furāt al-Fārisī al-Fasawī. *Kitāb Bad' al-Ḫalq wa Qisas al-Anbiyā'*', in : Codices Arabici Antiqui III, Wiesbaden.

Koenen, K. 1998. 'Von der todesmutigen Susanna zum begabten Daniel: Zur Überlieferungsgeschichte der Susanna-Erzählung', *Theologische Zeitschrift* 54, 1-13.

Lehnert and Landrock (publ.), *Illustrations from Coptic Manuscripts*, Cairo 2000.

Man, Y. de 1956. *Een vrouw met name Suzanna*, Amsterdam.

McNaghten, W.H. 1839. *The Alif Laila or Book of the Thousand Nights and One Night*, vol. 2. Edition, Calcutta.

Pennacchietti, F.A. 1998, *Susanna nel deserto. Riflessi di un racconto biblico nella cultura arabo-islamica, testo, traduzione, commentari*, Torino: Silvio Zamorani editore.

Pennachietti, F.A. 2006, *Three Mirrors For Two Biblical Ladies. Susanna and the Queen of Sheba in the Eyes of Jews, Christians, and Muslims*, New Jersey: Gorgias press.

Raad, E. de 1950, *Het Antwoord van Suzanna aan Joachim van Babylon*, The Hague.

Smith, K.A. 1993. 'Inventing Marital Chastity: the Iconography of Susanna and the Elders in Early Christian Art', *The Oxford Art Journal* 16/1, 3-24.

Vilmar, E. 1865. *Abulfathi Annales Samaritani, quos ad fidem codicem manu scriptorum E Bodlejani Parisini ed. et prolegomenis instruxit Eduardus Vilmar*, (Kitāb al-Tarīkh, Abū 'l-Fath as-Sāmirī). Edition. Gotha.

Wurmband, M. 1963, 'A Falasha Variant of the Story of Susanna', *Biblica* 44, 29-45.

Zimmermann, F. 1957-1958. 'The Story of Susanna and its Original Language', *The Jewish Quarterly Review* 48, 236-241.

B

Echoes of Apuleius' *Metamorphoses* in Art and Literature

Martianus Capella's *De nuptiis Philologiae et Mercurii* or the Subversion of the Latin Novel

BEATRICE BAKHOUCHE
Université Paul Valéry Montpellier III

The *Wedding of Philology and Mercury* by Martianus Capella is a difficult and confusing work. This fifth century African author writes for his son a long text blending prose and poetry in the manner of Varro's Menippean satires, relating in nine books the wedding ceremony between Philology and the God Mercury. The first two books set the stage (Mercury decides to take a wife; his brother Phoebus recommends Philology to him, and his choice is approved by Jupiter and Juno, then by the Council of the gods) and narrate the initial action: the apotheosis of Philology by magical means. The work from Book 3 then largely consists of a parade of seven girls offered by Mercury to his betrothed, each of them displaying a scholastic discipline. The first three treat the literary subjects, grammar, dialectic and rhetoric, which will be designated the *trivium* in the Middle Ages, and the last four the 'mathematical' sciences, geometry, arithmetic, astronomy and music, the future medieval *quadrivium*. This work is never included amongst the Latin novels – usually restricted to the *Satyrica* of Petronius and the *Golden Ass* of Apuleius – and this generic marginality can also be found in the French editions of the different books where the fictional setting is never taken into account.

The novelistic texture of the work should be investigated in order to allow us to illuminate the relationship that the *Wedding* maintains with its Latin models and, specifically, with Apuleius' *Golden Ass*. Can we speak of an 'anti-novel', and, in that case, what is the meaning of a narrative if it is considered as allegorical? Finally, what is the meaning of the omnipresence of the author in his work, which keeps distance through novelistic illusion? These are the questions that the present study will try to answer.

The novelistic frame and its borders

In the texture of the *Wedding*, a careful reader can easily find common novelistic structures. For instance when Philology and Mercury first meet, the latter is going out of the *palaestra* while the former is picking flowers, as Philology recalls:

> *ipsi sociandum esse Cyllenio, quem licet miro semper optarit ardore, tamen uix eum post unctionem palaestricam recurrentem, cum flores ipsa decerperet praelectis quibusdam herbusculis, conspicata* (§100).

When Mercury, following the advice of his brother Apollo, decides to marry this girl, he does not meet any opposition from his parents – Jupiter and Juno – who approve the wedding jointly with the senate of the gods (Book 1). Therefore, what is usually the climax of a love story – the wedding – is announced here from the very beginning.

After the second book when the young girl joins her divine betrothed, the seven further books are marked by the different moments of the ceremony, by Mercury's gift and the wedding contract:

> *Tunc exsurgens uirginis mater poscit de Ioue superisque cunctis uti, sub conspectu omnium, quicquid sponsalium nomine praeparauerat Maiugena traderetur ac demum dos a uirgine non deesset, tuncque tabulas ac Pappiam Poppaeamque legem sinerent recitari* (§ 217).

Except in Book 2 (and parentheses where the author Martianus Capella speaks), the whole story takes place in heaven, so that we can speak of unity of place. The unity of time seems concentrated in a single night: when Philology appears, at the beginning of Book 2, the night is already well advanced (*adulta iam nocte* § 99). At the beginning of the climactic Book 9, Venus becomes impatient with all the displays of knowledge by the *virgines dotales* which postpones the union itself:

> *Iam facibus lassos spectans marcentibus ignes*
> *instaurare iubet tunc hymenea Venus :*
> *'quis modus' inquit 'erit? quonam sollertia fine*
> *impedient thalamos ludere gymnasia?...* (§ 888).

And, when the last girl finishes speaking, everybody gets up to celebrate the union:

> *tunc… Ioue assurgente diuisque praeambulis coemesin modulata in thalamum quoque uirginis magna cunctorum uoluptate peruenit* (§ 996).

The story told by Martianus Capella could constitute the outcome of a beautiful love story except that the story is hardly about love between two young people: the choice of Philology by Mercury is negative, in a sense, and, at least, not personal. As we know, the name of the young girl is suggested to the young god by his brother, after some abortive attempts at marriage. Apollo describes him to his parents as burning with love (§ 36):

> *'Nam illum iam pridem' ait 'Philologiae sentio amore torreri eiusque studio comparatas habere complures in famulitio Disciplinas, ipsum linguae insignis ornatibus fandi nimiam uenustatem, quo placeret uirgini, consecutum, deinde barbito aurataque chely ac doctis fidibus personare…'.*

Besides, the young betrotheds never speak to each other and, during the ceremony, Mercury is the subject of lascivious glances from Venus who is sharply reprehended by Juno (§ 727).

The sequence of the plot clearly has coherence. But is it a novelistic plot? It is certainly not the plot of an adventure novel because there is no blocking character. The plot of the *Wedding* could be compared with the story of Eros and Psyche in the *Golden Ass*, but with a kind of reversal, since the young Psyche is considered to be a goddess and, because of this, she cannot find a husband. On the other hand, Apuleius frames the story of the two young people within the revenge of Venus who sees her worship neglected due to the amazing beauty of Psyche, whereas the young couple in the *Wedding* meet no opposition.

As *satura*, the *Wedding* could belong to the novelistic form which, in Antiquity, is characterized by the mixture of tones and types. Martianus' character Satura too stands for an aesthetics of hybridization:

> *Haec quippe loquax docta doctis aggerans*
> *fandis tacenda farcinat, immiscuit*
> *Musas deosque, disciplinas cyclicas*
> *garrire agresti cruda finxit plasmate…* (§ 998)

The new and technical *materies* recalled at the very beginning of the book must be bedecked with the finery of literary invention, if the author does not want put the readership to sleep. The topos of *mel miscere* is a statement of the poetics of *lepos*. And the very type of Satura, through culinary metaphor (*farcinat*), defines itself here as what it is: a 'pot-pourri'.

Indeed, as in the novels of Petronius or Apuleius, the mixture of kinds is at work here: marking the superiority of fiction in literature, the Latin novel borrows from all the existent literary types. The grandiose adjoins the comic: for instance, after the speech of Arithmetic produced a sacred silence (§ 803, *sacrum paululum fuit reuerendumque silentium*), an untimely snore from Silenus, who has fallen asleep under the influence of wine, makes the divine audience laugh. And Satura sharply criticizes Martianus for daring to introduce such a vulgar scene into the dramatic texture (§ 807)! It seems as though the comic scene around Silenus, eminently picturesque and 'living', is the work of Martianus, but that the scenario escapes from the author who is really unaware which girl will come in. *Satura* knows more about this than Martianus. The animation of tone and the dynamics of the tale mimic life itself, while the author speaks to a non-being, Satura. But, as we know, the small detail which 'authenticates' is the supreme means of referential illusion.

A retractatio of the Apuleian model?

The novel in Antiquity is characterized by a strong intertextual dimension. In the *Wedding,* the passages which can be qualified as fiction introduce numerous echoes of previous literature and especially, as can be easily seen from the list of *auctores* in Willis' edition, of the writings of Apuleius.

Similarities between the two authors

The *Golden Ass* introduces autobiographical features, in as much as the hero, Lucius, looks like his creator: both demonstrate a great curiosity, and a great interest in magic and mystery religions (cf. III, 15 and *Apol.* 55). They also both plead in Rome (XI, 28 and 30). In the *Wedding,* the self-representation of the author permits the elucidation of some data. Some of these confirm what we know about Apuleius: first, both are Africans and lawyers. On the other hand, magical practices and mystery cults, which Philology devotes herself to in Book II, lead us to think that such plausible discussions imply that these matters were not completely unknown to our author.

Structure of the fabula

Martianus Capella calls his *satura* a *fabula*, adding to the 'pot-pourri' element the character of a fiction or drama. From the very beginning, Apuleius uses the same term to qualify the story he is going to tell:

> *At ego tibi sermone isto Milesio uarias fabulas conseram auresque tuas beniuolas lepido sussurro permulceam – modo si papyrum Aegyptiam argutia Nilotici calami inscriptam non spreueris incipere –...* (I, 1).

Is this coincidental? Philology, informed of her forthcoming marriage with a god, already misses the stories told by human beings, and that she will not hear any more from the gods. Her words recall the prefatory sentence of the *Golden Ass*:

> *Nam certe mythos, poeticae etiam diuersitatis delicias Milesias historiasque mortalium, postquam supera conscenderit, se penitus amissuram non cassa opinatione formidat* (II, 100).

If Wolf (1997: 50) could point out the problematic features of the Milesian tale in Apuleius, it is even more difficult in the case of the young and pure Philology. Indeed, the Milesian tale is a type of short and licentious story supposed to amuse, and the best examples of Milesian *fabulae* in Latin literature are the stories of the young boy from Pergamum and of the *matrona* from Ephesus in the *Satyrica*. In the *Golden Ass* by Apuleius, on the other hand, a lot of tales are intended to amuse, but typically Milesian bawdy narratives are not so numerous. In the *Wedding*, we find no trace of them. The same reference to a literary genre that is not represented in reality refers probably more to intertextual codification than to a literary reality or a psychological likelihood.

Besides, among the other principles which govern the novel's structure, the one of fitting and of the delegation of speech, which leads to the making of a plot with different stories fitted together, characterizes Apuleius' work as well as Capella's one. If the novel is a tale containing tales, it is borne out from the first pages of the *Wedding*; the author plays three different roles: in the invocation to Hymenaeus, he takes the position of a priest, as pointed out by his son. In his debate with his son to justify his initial request, he introduces this request as a *captatio* of Hymenaeus so that 'the wedding is proclaimed'. Everything takes place as though the wedding which is going to be the subject of work was a reality, as though the fiction – one more time – had become true, and even as though the intervention of Martianus could favour this realization. Martianus establishes himself, in his answer to his son, as a listener-transmitter of Satura's tale:

> ... 'Ne tu' inquam 'desipis admodumque perspicui operis egersimon <non> noscens creperum sapis, nec liquet Hymenaeo praelibante disposita nuptias resultare. Si uero concepta cuius scaturriginis uena profluxerint properus scrutator inquiris, fabellam tibi, quam Satura comminiscens hiemali peruigilio marcescentes mecum lucernas edocuit, ni prolixitas perculerit, explicabo…' (I, 2).

The polyphony of authorial voice, in the *Wedding*, could correspond, in a sense, to the code of the novelistic genre.

Another novelistic principle is the resumption of a same topic treated in different ways. Specularity and circularity are also inscribed in the *Wedding* as if it mimed the contents of books, *disciplinae cyclicae* (IX, 998). The plays of echoes are structural, thematic and lexical. If we stick only to the 'authorial intermezzos' which constitute the bones of the work, they are clearly shot through with the resumption of the same topics. So, the rare term of *egersimon* (I, 2) is repeated at the beginning of book IX (§ 911). In a more general manner, the pairing of laughter and education is fundamental to the work: mockery, ubiquitous in the chosen passages, is inseparable from laughter, which comes in the middle of the intermezzo of Silenus in book VIII (cf. § 809 : *denuo me risus inuasit*). Camena, in book III, is already introduced *iocante rictu* (222). Also, Satura is characterized as *iocularis* or *iocabunda* (VI, 576). And, in this passage, laughter is linked to intelligence: *ride, si sapis, o puella, ride*, in a quotation from Martial (II, 41,1). Similarly, the announcement, in III, 220, of serious books on the arts distinguish them from the general banter.

Transformation and curiositas

The topic of transformation, very fashionable in Rome (cf. Ovid) is important in the novel: Apuleius tells of Thrasyleon dressed up as a bear (IV, 14-21) or of Tlepolemos pretending to be a robber (VII, 5-12). However there are misleading appearances which work only as an element of the novel. More profoundly, what is at the very heart of the *Golden Ass* is definitely Lucius' transformation into an ass (and all the adventures which result from it) before the hero regains his human appearance. Yet, by returning him to human form, Isis does not bring Lucius back to his previous social and moral status, but makes him a new human being.

If *curiositas* is the source of Lucius's misfortunes, it is also the origin of Philology's outstanding destiny; 'curiosity' is a form of attention to reality. It is the wish to know everything in any domain: trying to approach the divine, Lucius uses magical practices, and, as the priest of Isis said, 'he met the poor reward of his impious curiosity' (XI, 15). On the contrary, Philology spends the whole night studying, so that she ends up discovering the secrets of nature, better than the gods themselves:

Est igitur prisci generis doctissima uirgo,
conscia Parrhasio cui fulgent sidera coetu,
cui nec Tartareos claustra occultare recessus
nec Iouis arbitrium rutilantia fulmina possunt ;
fluctigena spectans qualis sub gurgite Nereus,
quaeque tuos norit fratrum per regna recursus,
peruigil immodico penetrans arcana labore,
quae possit docta totum praeuertere cura
quod superis praescire datum. Quin crebrius in nos
ius habet illa, deos urgens in iussa coactos ;
et quod nulla queat superum temptare potestas,
inuito scit posse Ioue... (I, 22).

Philology appears as an anti-Lucius, in so far as Apuleius' novel ends as the *Wedding* begins. Lucius is seen as a priest dressed in linen (XI, 23, 4), like Philology in Book 2 (*ex illa herbarum felicium lana*); this priestly dress is noted elsewhere by Apuleius in the *Golden Ass* (XI, 23 and 27) and especially explained in *Apology* 56, 2:

> *Quippe lana, segnissimi corporis excrementum, pecori detracta, iam inde Orphei et Pythagorae scitis profanus uestitus est ; sed enim mundissima lini seges, inter optumas fruges terra exorta, non modo indutui et amictui sanctissimis Aegyptiorum sacerdotibus, sed opertui quoque rebus sacris usurpatur.*

From this perspective, the transformation of Philology could be read as a new version of the *Golden Ass*: the positive version of entry into knowledge which allows its possessor to gain access to the status of the gods. In this regard, the work of Capella can be read as a novel about initiation. But Philology has nothing more to learn, she contents herself, when she goes up to heaven, confirmed in her knowledge.

Games of mirrors in the Wedding

This study can be concerned with the picaresque novel, because *Wedding* can be read as a novel of training. The paradox however is that this training does not concern the heroine whose divine and astral apotheosis merely sanctions the high level of knowledge already reached. In a complex and in cipher production, it is now necessary to study the different games of mirrors in which the novel refracts the universe and the author his heroine.

A totalizing work, or from the novel to the cosmos

The tale of the wedding of Philology and Mercury offers a 'totalizing' stage design: if we stick only to the 'authorial intermezzos', that is the passages where the author puts himself on stage, they offer a broad palette of metrical and literary kinds:

> I, 1: prayer to Hymenaeus in elegiac couplets, followed by a mini-scene of 'historical' comedy,
> II, 219: afterword of *fabula* in iambic *senarii*, the metre of the *diverbium* in the theatre,
> III, 221: mini-dialogue between Camena and the author in iambic catalectic dimeters,
> VI, 567-574: hymn to Pallas in dactylic hexameters, followed by a scene of comedy in prose,

VIII, 804-805: prose and iambic catalectic dimeters for a scene close to a parody of the satire,
IX 997-1000: general afterword in iambic *senarii* in imitation of dramatic poetry.

These passages not only exemplify the matchless literary competence of our author. Mastering all types, all styles, all rhythms, Martianus surely displayed a remarkable capacity in the literary domain. But, if we go farther, everything seems as if Martianus wanted to embrace all literary types – epic poem, theatre, prose, religious poem, religious hymn – in a single totalizing of literary creation. The work is therefore conceived as a whole.

Moreover the personification of Satura makes his work a living being. To this – Platonic – presentation of writings as living beings is linked the picture of the author as a father. This is how Martianus appears, invoked by his son by an exasperated *mi pater*. This biological father (is he really father?) is genuinely the father of a speech which represents the world. Besides, the harmonic construction of the macrocosm, such as found in the *Timaeus*, apparently matches the building of the book-microcosm which seems to be submitted to numerical harmonies. The numerical relationship at the base of harmony is noted from the beginning of the work (I, 11-12) and, if we mark out the numbers 2 (the number of the *fabula*'s books), 3 (the number of books about literary disciplines), and 4 (the number of books about arithmetical sciences), we get the three fundamental numbers from which the demiurge builds the world's soul in the *Timaeus*. There are also these same numbers which allow the establishment of the harmonic relationship, as the musical chords of the fourth (4/3), fifth (3/2) and octave (2/1) which will be found in Book 2 when Philology moves through the interplanetary spaces.

The mimesis is therefore accomplished: by making the book the picture of the universe, by introducing a synthesis of the complete model of the world, its author Martianus, its 'father', plays the role of a true demiurge!

Martianus as a double of Philology

In general, the picaresque novel narrates in the first person the adventures of the hero-storyteller. Can it therefore concern our author whose Satura points out the absence of *sapientia*, the foolishness? If it did, it would be necessary for us to note any intellectual, philosophical or religious progress of this storyteller who appears readily in his own fiction from the beginning to the end of the *Wedding*. But this is not the case. Martianus is however not only the author whose function is questioned; he is not only the extra-diegetic actor who discusses his production, he is also present within this production, as the spectator of a play which seems to be played without him.

A matchless director, Martianus is presented, paradoxically, at the same time as a *deus ex machina* and as an innocent actor within a play which seems to be larger than him. But this simplicity is apparent, as well as his devalued role.

When Martianus announces twice the arrival of a *uirgo* as if he were present at the scene (cf. VI, 580 *prospicio*; VIII, 810 *ecce*), not only does he join the members of the divine council who attend the parade, but he also confirms himself as possessor of the immortality acquired by the knowledge – just like Philology!

If our author devalues his own scientific knowledge, he really enjoys revealing his workmanship in rhetoric, evincing himself therefore an orator emeritus. But, when, in Book 2, each Muse celebrates, in an aretalogical mode, the remarkable merits of the young Philology, Clio praises her superiority in the field of rhetoric, which opens up for her the Milky Way where the human heroes of adventure worthiest of divine honours are welcomed, as we have already read in the Cicero's *Somnium Scipionis* or in Manilius' *Astronomica* (I, 703-808). It is the union of wisdom and eloquence, as in Cicero, that allows one to rise above his condition and to merit astral immortality.

Therefore, even if he cannot sit among the sages who are worthy of the same astral apotheosis as Philology's in the *Wedding*, he can be part of the cohort of remarkable men (V, 429 *ingens illustrium uirorum… agmen*) like Cicero and Demosthenes who accompany Rhetorica. His superiority in rhetoric will earn Martianus a seat in heaven, as announced by the divine council in I, 94:

> *Sed postquam Iuppiter finem loquendi fecit, omnis deorum senatus in suffragium concitatur, acclamantque cuncti fieri protinus oportere, adiciuntque sententiae Iouali, ut deinceps mortales, quos uitae insignis elatio et maximum culmen meritorum ingentium in appetitum caelitem propositumque sidereae cupiditatis extulerit, in deorum numerum cooptentur.*

On the other hand, it is the voice of Martianus that we hear from the beginning of the *Wedding*, of a Martianus who starts singing a hymn to Hymenaeus, like a priest, as his son sharply reproaches him:

'*quid istud, mi pater, quod nondum uulgata materie cantare deproperas et ritu nictantis antistis, priusquam fores aditumque reseraris, humnologeis?*... (§ 2).

We can see in this initial presentation a partial anticipation of Philology who, in Book 2, is dressed in pure linen and takes on the appearance of a wise Indian:

(Phronesis) uestem peplumque lactis instar fulgidum dedit, quod uel ex illa herbarum felicium lana, qua indusiari perhibent Indicae prudentiae uates accolasque montis umbrati, et, quantum usus eius telluris apportat, ex candentis byssi netibus uidebatur (§ 114).

Also, the author refracts the picture of a Philology whose knowledge he tries to equal – across his literary as well as scientific capacities. It is a question for him of displaying the same encyclopaedic knowledge, because this very knowledge will open the doors of heaven for him, in an astral apotheosis similar to Philology's one in Book 2, when she discovers, in the Milky Way, a whole race of remarkable men (§§ 206-213). The motif of late-night work is applied to the author at the end of Book 2, as well as to his heroine for whom *vigilare* is a constant feature.

From the author to the reader

The fit of structures allows the highlighting of several levels of enunciation: through the novel of Philology, we read the one of Martianus, the hero whose adventures are narrated in the first person. At this second level, the novel of Martianus emerges therefore as 'homodiegetic': the function of storyteller is taken on by a storyteller who is inserted into the tale and who is 'narrating' and 'narrated' at the same time.

And by managing the different subjects of the *enkyklios paideia* (grammar, dialectic, rhetoric, geometry, arithmetic, astronomy and music) in order to make seven books be 'recited' by seven different girls, Martianus gives an example of a high level of knowledge accessible to everyone, given hard work. Therefore, the hero of this novel of training will be the author who confirms himself as an example to be imitated by his reader - especially by the first of them, his own son. The pedagogic aim of Martianus Capella's work is in the production of his son as the first addressee as much as in the production of the unknown reader as a more generic addressee.

The liberal arts have a meaning only if they allow us to account for the world, to make the universe understandable. They teach the way which leads to philosophy, in the ancient world, then to theology in the Middle Ages. It is not about 'general culture', as Nuchelmans (1957) thinks, but about a way which leads to a superior knowledge, philosophy or God. Philology has a role, in the *Wedding*, which is surely not the same as that of the *virgines dotales* : she does not show the direction to be followed, but she illustrates the result to be gained when this direction is followed. She represents the scholar, the philosopher, the true beauty which goes hand in hand with genuine *sapientia*. She is shown for what she is and not for what she does. She has the right to ascend to heaven thanks to her knowledge. We attend the deification of a learned person, a deification merited by his knowledge. From this perspective, Philology represents the ideal to be reached by every 'learning' person and Martianus is her mediator on earth.

And if the philosophy hereafter 'consists in the only wish to know godhead better by a habitual contemplation and a simple devotion' as seen in the *Asclepius*, neither the theurgy nor the mysterious or magical practices recalled in Book 2 allow this favoured access to the divine. But study and hard work accomplish it, as exemplified by Philology's apotheosis, accompanied in her ascent by a young person called *labor*. In a minor mode, it is also what Martianus wants to teach.

In conclusion, it should be pointed out that the structure of the *Wedding of Philology and Mercury* is indebted, in a certain sense, to the framework of a novel like the *Golden Ass*. However, the tension between the heroine, in a sense abstract and disembodied, and the author, who shows himself, at the first level, as an inscribing tool, is not really suitable for a novelistic type of writing.

From the very beginning, there are comings and goings from reality to fiction, from the myth to the truth. The multiplicity of appearances leads to the uniqueness of the fiction-making and of the reality. In this eminently thought-out and constructed work, the animation and the animation of the tale mimic life, paradoxically.

The *Wedding* is much more than an encyclopaedia; it is a genuine Neoplatonist declaration of faith that plays a secret game. It is up to the reader to decipher this dense, complex, deliberately veiled work. It is only at this price that he will acquire a knowledge able to give its possessor the astral apotheosis which awaits all great men, all great intellectuals.

Bibliography

Bakhouche, B. 2008. 'Le je auctorial dans les Noces de Philologie et Mercure de Martianus Capella'. *Actes du colloque Fait littéraire et auctorialité*, ENS Lyon 24-25 novembre 2006, e-review Interférence (http://ars-scribendi.ens-lsh.fr/).

Grebe, S., 2003. 'Scientific and Narrative Arguments in Martianus Capella', *Latin vulgaire latin tardif* 6, 139-155.

Lemoine, F., 1972. *Martianus Capella A Literary Re-evaluation*, Munich.

Lenaz, L., 1975. *Martiani Capella De nuptiis Philologiae et Mercurii liber secundus*, Padua.

Nuchelmans, G., 1957. 'Philologia et son mariage avec Mercure jusqu'à la fin du XIIe siècle', *Latomus* 16, 84-107.

Stahl, W.H., Johnson, R. & Burge, E.L., 1971. *Martianus Capella and the Seven Liberal Arts*, 2 vol., New York-London.

Wolf, E., 1997. *Le roman grec et latin*, Paris.

Zaffagno, E., 1996. 'La 'persona' di Marziano Capella nel *De nuptiis*', *Giornale italiano di filologia* 48, 223-251.

Apuleius, Beroaldo and the Development of the (Early) Modern Classical Commentary

GERALD SANDY
University of British Columbia

The Apuleian corpus was one of the first classical Latin works to appear in print (Rome, 1469). Apuleius' *Golden Ass* also enjoys the distinction of being the subject of one of the earliest humanist commentaries on a classical Latin author, that of Filippo Beroaldo (1453-1505), the popular professor of rhetoric at the University of Bologna whose lectures drew hundreds of students each morning. Here I will try to give an impression of Beroaldo's commentary on the *Golden Ass* by highlighting a few general characteristics and then focusing on his scholarship, that is, his command of the sources and his engagement with the scholarship of the past and that of the *recentiores*. I hope to demonstrate that Beroaldo's commentary underlies and anticipates many modern interpretations of Apuleius' novel.[1]

Contemporary biographies stress Beroaldo's erudition and prodigious memory, citing Pico della Mirandola's characterization of him as a talking library:

> ...vivam quandam bonarum omnium artium et rerum loquentem Bibliothecam videri, quod nihil usquam tam vel abstrusum vel difficile, nihil tam vetustate reconditum, quod non ille recens promptum facile expeditum, ac velut apud se domi natum haberet. Erat enim veterum rerum om-

---

[1] I have discussed some of these issues more fully in Sandy 2007. I have expanded abbreviations and ligatures, used modern punctuation and adopted modern orthographical forms such as initial capitals for proper names and at the beginnings of sentences. I have, however, retained most humanist spelling such as *pene* for *paene* and *foelix* for *felix*. I have also added breathings and accents to Greek words. I use the abbreviations of the *Oxford Latin Dictionary* for Latin authors and their works and those of *L'année philologique* for journals.

nium nec Latinarum modo, sed et Graecarum quoque et externarum immensa quadam incredibilique memoria.[2]

His colleague at the University of Bologna, Codro Urceo (1446-1511), said of Beroaldo that he had almost single-handedly established the rules for writing commentaries, *legem...commentandi non servasse modo...sed prope constituisse*.[3] In his commentary on Propertius (1487) Beroaldo states that the commentator is infused with the same divinely inspired creative spirit as the creative artist is and defines the role of the commentator thus:

Interpres involucra explicat, obscura illustrat, arcana revelat et quod ille [viz. poeta] strictim et quasi transeunter attingit, hic [viz. interpres] copiose et diligenter enodat.
(The commentator unwraps what is wrapped, casts light on what is dark, reveals what is hidden and extensively and diligently untangles what the creative writer [left tangled because] he touched only superficially and in passing on the subject.)[4]

Filippo Beroaldo's commentary on Apuleius' *Golden Ass* (1500) is a large work of 286 folios preceded by some fifteen unnumbered folios that contain a '*Tabula uocabulorum in libris de asino aureo*' and an epistolary dedication. In his inaugural lecture on the *Golden Ass* Beroaldo provides a summary of his publications and readership as at 1500, the year in which the commentary was published. He states there that his publications are approved by the *docti* but actually used by, and intended for, the educated public (*studiosis*) and students:

Extant ingenii nostri, extant eruditionis, quantulacumque est, in omni scriptionis genere monumenta: orationes, poemata, epistolae, annotationes, commentarii, quae omnia, nisi mihi bibliopolae blandiantur, ex-

---

[2] Pins [1505], fol. sign. L iiii-iiii^{vo}, Bianchini (1548) and Meuschen (1735-1738), vol. 1, p. 125.
[3] Bianchini 1548, fol. sign. γ 1vo.
[4] See also Beroaldo's commentary on Suetonius (1493), *Elaboravi...ut nodosa enodarem, implicita explicarem, obscura clararem, sinuosa corrigerem, maculosa emacularem* (quoted from Casella 1975, 647). And cf. St. Jerome, *In Ionam*, praef. (*PL* 25, 1118), ...*commentatoris officium sit, ut quae obscura sunt breviter aperiat dilucidetque* and *In Zachariam* (*PL* 25, 1463), *Commentarios scribimus, quorum officium est, praeterire manifesta, obscura disserere*.

petuntur a studiosis, probantur a doctis, terentur manibus scholasticorum tam provincialium quam Italicorum.[5]

As he puts it in the same inaugural lecture:

> In this commentary (viz. the commentary on the *Golden Ass*) as in several others my intention …has been to the best of my ability to aid those who study (*studiosos*) the Latin language and Latin style as well as followers of humanistic studies (*humanioris disciplinae assectatores*).

Beroaldo's goal of catering simultaneously to the educated public and students appears to have been a good strategy to judge by the publisher's decision to print 1200 copies of the commentary at a time when less than half that number appears to have been the norm for Aldine editions of classical authors. Let's consider some of the elements that contributed to that success. I begin with Beroaldo's comment on *Golden Ass* 8. 2. 2 (…*erilis puella in boni Tlepolemi manum venerat*), fol. 166vo:

> 'In manum venerat.' Id est, denupserat T<l>epolemo eiusque uxor facta erat. Quod autem ait in manum convenerat usus est verbo nuptiali ex ritu scilicet consuetudineque priscorum; et ut id quod dicitur planius fiat scito duobus modis uxorem haberi solitam: usu et coemptione. Nam confarreatio, de qua suo loco dicetur, solis pontificibus conveniebat. Quae in manum per coemptionem convenerant eae matres familias vocabantur; quae autem usu nequaquam. Coemptio certis solemnitatibus peragebatur, et sese in coemendo inuicem interrogabant, uir ita, an mulier sibi materfamilias esse uellet. Illa respondebat uelle. Item mulier interrogabat an

---

[5] The fourth (unnumbered) 'page' of the speech headed '*Oratio Habita in Enarratione Lucii Apulei: Ad Commentarios Apuleianos*' = the last speech collected in Beroaldo 1500a. Cf. Beroaldo 1500, fol.1, *Existimavi me facturum operae pretium consulturumque pro virili parte studiosis Apuleianae eruditionis*…; and 1vo, *Solet haec* [*enarratio compendaria*] *quoque studiosis esse non iniucunda cognitio*, as well as *Declamatio An Orator Sit Philosopho et Medico Anteponendus* (Paris, 1501), (unnumbered) folio 3, …*ut uno volumine prosim medicinae et iuris civilis scientiae studiosis*; *Annotationes in Commentarios Servii in Virgilium* (Bologna, 1482), (unnumbered) folio 1vo: …*quod negotium dum Virgilianam poesim publico auditorio profiterer suscipere non recusavi ut auditoribus id a me efflagitantibus gratificaret. Quibus ista excipientibus dictavi…ut pro virili parte iuvarem Latinae linguae studiosos et potissimum Virgiliani poematis amatores*; and the first folio of the dedicatory epistle heading Beroaldo's commentary on Propertius (1487), *Nos talia intra duos sesquimenses elucubravimus ut tironibus placere possint nec veteranis displicere*.

uir sibi paterfamilias esse uellet, ille respondebat uelle. Itaque mulier uiri conueniebat in manum, et uocabantur hae nuptiae per coemptionem, et erat mulier materfamilias uiro, loco filiae. Auctor Ulpianus et post Ulpianum Boethius in Commentariis [Ciceronis] Topicorum (3. 4, ed. Girard and Sean). Qui (viz. Boethius) alio quoque loco tradit quaedam bona mulieris post eius mortem adipiscatur quae in viri manum convenerit. Efficitur enim per in manus conuentionem, ut quaecumque sunt mulieris, uiri fiant dotis nomine. Hanc solemnitatem numptiarum signavit Aulus Gellius (18. 6. 7) cum ait matremfamilias appellatam esse eam solam quae in mariti manum mancipiumque venisset; hoc idem denotat Servius Maronianus interpres scribens in xi commentario (on *Aeneid* 11. 581) matrem familias dici quae in matrimonio convenit per coemptionem per quondam iuris solemnitatem. Triviales magistri et minuti grammatistae quorum deus est Servius legentes haec Serviana annotamenta hallucinant atque cecutiunt; apud quos commentator commentatore, interpres eget interprete...Haec eo curiosius enarratiusque explicavi propterea quod non parum multi lectores per incuriam eruditionem in Apuleianis verbis delitescentem haud facile perspiciunt neque ultra primorem cutem descendunt, minime elaborantes sanguinem ac medullam verborum ipsius eruere atque penitus introspicere. Nos vero, qui posterorum negocium pro virili parte agere contendimus, pensiculate et diligenter perpendimus quae non sunt omnibus obvia, quae in secretariis doctrinarum recondita delitescunt; et ut in commentariis pristinis nostris dedimus operam ne paenitendi commentatores videremur, ita in his curabimus ne opera et impensa dispereat.

They illustrate at least four features of Beroaldo's commentary that helped to ensure its success: (1) explanations of Roman law, (2) explanations of the finer points of the Latin language, (3) engagement with ancient sources and (4) engagement with post-classical scholarship.

Explanations of Roman law

Most students enrolled in courses at the University of Bologna at the end of the fifteenth century were there to study Roman law. They were fortunate that the professor of rhetoric, the chair that Beroaldo held from 1478 until his death in 1505, had committed to memory the *libros...iuris consultorum*, according to his pupil and biographer Jean de Pins. For their benefit Beroaldo repeatedly cites the Roman *Digest* and the jurists, as he does in the comment quoted above and in the following comment:

> Non parum multa sunt quae cum legas primori cute nihil prae se ferant obscuritatis et disciplinae reconditae. Sed si introspexens curiosius, deprendas arcanam eruditionem semotamque, ut hic Apuleii locus est, quo non simpliciter sed scienter et ex legalis doctrinae verbis dictum est Psychen convenisse in manum mariti. Namque uxoris species duae sunt. Una matrum familias, altera usu mater familias esse non poterat nisi quae convenisset in manum… Itaque mulier viri conveniebat in manum et vocabantur hae nuptiae per coemptionem et erat mulier materfamilias. Quam solemnitatem Ulpianus et Boetius exponunt… Invenio apud auctores quod nubentes veteri lege Romana asses tris ad maritum venientes solebant ferre; atque unum quem in manu tenerent tamquam ementi marito, alium quem in pede haberent in foco larium familiarium ponere, tertium in sacciperiuo in compitio vicinali solere resonare. Enim legere mali 'in sacciperio' apud Nonium Marcellum quam uti legitur in vulgatissimis codicibus 'in sacciperone.' Nam sacciperium crumena maior est et minoris marsupii receptaculum. Plautus in Rudente (575) 'meum marsupium…in sacciperio.'[6]

After explaining in detail exactly what is meant by *coemptio coniugalis*, that is, the fictitious sale of a Roman bride, Beroaldo concludes:

> I have explained these matters in detail because most readers carelessly overlook the erudition lurking in Apuleius' words…I am determined to the best of my ability to attend to the interests of future readers and diligently to explain matters that are not obvious to everyone and that lurk hidden in the secret recesses of learning. Just as I endeavoured in my previous commentaries not to be seen as a blameworthy commentator, just so in this commentary I shall take care that my work and expenditure are not wasted.

Similarly, he comments on the phrase '*ligno ... vendito*' at *Golden Ass* 7. 20. 4 that Ulpian defines pieces of wood that have been sold with the word '*lignum*' in the singular, that is, 'fuel':

---

[6] Beroaldo 1500, fol. 134 on Apul. *Met.* 6. 24.

> As Ulpian writes, 'the term 'fuel' is general.' And we properly denote as 'fuel' whatever is prepared for making a fire...or for heating a bath or, I should say, '*hypothaustras*.' This word is used throughout Book 3 of *De Legatis* [*et Fideicommissis*] [i. e., Book 32 of the *Digest*], where Accursius offers a really remarkable interpretation. He explains '*hypothaustras*' as places where sick people stay, which the most zealous users of Latin call a '*valitudinarium*.' But it is not surprising that in the instance of this false word he has given a very false interpretation, since he suddenly hallucinates like a blind man [even] when faced with uncorrupted readings. I think that the word should be emended to '*hypocaustum*' or '*hypocausim*' or '*hypocaustarium*...' And so the sense of the juriconsult [Ulpian] will be that the phrase '*legata ligna*' denotes what is obtained for heating baths and steam-rooms and vapour-rooms...Such rooms are very common among those who live on the other side of the Alps (*transmontanos*), which they call '*stuffas*.' For at times barbarian words must be used to illustrate more clearly a rather erudite matter.[7]

He goes on in his comment to include the *modus operandi* of burglars, humanist prohibitions on the use of certain supposedly non-classical words and the desirability of discursiveness in commentaries, concluding:

> I frequently and willingly turn aside [from the topic under discussion] to comment on extraordinary matters of this sort because I know that they are in need of clarification and are more welcome to the educated public (*studiosis*) than ordinary comments are...I have followed the method [that I used in my commentary on (Cicero's)] *Tusculan Disputations* (1496) in order periodically to insert small flowers of learning and undo knotty passages in other writers in a desultory and discursive manner. Unless my friends are flattering me, readers will take great pleasure from this approach and like those who are fatigued gain relief from the [unremittingly] focused commentary.

True to his intention to explain only the *historicum sensum, et rerum reconditarum verborumque interpretationem* Beroaldo throughout his comments on the tale of Cupid and Psyche, which belongs to the world of fairy tales seemingly far removed from the concerns of Roman law, highlights the vocabulary and practices of the Roman law of marriage. The lemma (*Sic rite*

---

[7] Beroaldo 1500, fol. 159 on Apul. *Met.* 7.20.

Psyche convenit in manum Cupidinis) is replete with legal technicalities and the comment no less so. The comment is introduced thus:

> Many words do not appear to be worthy of further consideration. At first glance they do not seem to involve any obscure or recondite subject of study. If you probe more carefully, however, you will detect arcane and remote erudition, as in this passage of Apuleius, where the phrase '*Psychen convenisse in manum mariti*' is derived ingeniously and knowledgeably from the vocabulary of the legal discipline.[8]

Scholarship

Beroaldo anticipated by 500 years the most recent study of the legal terms in Apuleius as they apply to marriage and fugitive slaves.[9] He treated contemporary humanists with respect, practising Martial's rule, *parcere personis, dicere de vitiis*. I have found only two disagreements in his published works with contemporary humanists. In his comment on '*spatha*' (sword) at *Metamorphoses* 9. 40 Beroaldo remarks that the diminutive form '*spathalion*' is derived from '*spatha*,' "which Hermolaus Barbarus claims is derived from the name of the nymph Spatale. I, however, derive it from the Greek word '*spathao*,' which means 'to live extravagantly' (*delicate ago*), as in Aristophanes' *Clouds* (55)." The other criticism of a contemporary humanist occurs in the epistolary dedication of his commentary on Propertius (1487), where he characterizes Domizio Calderini's commentary of 1475 on the same author as so concise that he seems to be writing for his own benefit alone.[10]

He is equally respectful of ancient authorities. In what appears to be his first published work of critical scholarship, he undertakes to correct the geographical errors in Servius' commentary on Virgil not because he is prone by

---

[8] Beroaldo 1500, fol. 134 on Apul. *Met.* 6. 24.
[9] Osgood 2006.
[10] *Nec solos lectione esse dignos censeo antiquos commentatores. Verum etiam nostrorum temporum ingenia non despicio...Vigent hodie clarique sunt in studiis litterarum complusculi qui interpretando, commentando, explanando veterum poemata non mediocrem laudem consequuti sunt...Extant Domitii enarrationes luculenter quidem scriptae sed adeo concise ut sibi soli et musis sicuti dici solet cecinisse videatur. Nos talia intra duos sesquimenses elucubravimus ut tironibus placere possint nec veteranis displicere* (the recto of the first [unnumbered] folio of the epistolary dedication).

nature to find fault or to show off his own accomplishments but because the errors impede the progress of students:

> Cum errores commentatoris non minus obsint legentibus quam prosint bonae interpretationes institui summatim breviterque annotare loca quam plurima quae apud Servium magis obelisco quam asterisco dignissima esse existimavi. Quod negotium dum Virgilianam poesim publico auditorio profiterer suscipere non recusavi ut auditoribus id a me efflagitantibus gratificaret. Quibus ista excipientibus dictavi non eruditionis ostendendae gratia sed ut pro virili parte iuvarem Latinae linguae studiosos et potissimum Virgiliani poematis amatores.[11]

Like other humanists, Beroaldo reserves his harshest criticisms for the so-called scholastics. Accursius, the thirteenth-century jurist of the University of Bologna who compiled the glosses of the previous generations of glossators to the *Corpus Iuris*, is repeatedly ridiculed for his ignorance of Latin and Greek, e. g.:

> Ligno vendito. Lignis venditis singularis numeus pro plurali ligni appellatio. Ut scribit Ulpianus, nomen generale est, et proprie 'lignum' dicimus…Haec verba passim leguntur libro de legatiis tertio (De Legatis [et Fideicommissis] [i. e., Book 32 of the Digest]), ubi Accursius tamquam aliquid praeclarum interpretaretur. Hypothaustras exposuit loca esse ubi stant egroti, quod Latinitatis servantissimi valitudinarium appellant. Sed nil mirum si in dictione mendosa mendosissimum dedit interpretamentum, cum in sinceris cecutiens subinde hallucinatur. Ego emendandum censeo hypocaustum.[12]

The final example of Beroaldo's scholarship centres on his decision 'to evaluate carefully the opinions of eminent writers on the subject of eggs.' (folios 213-214, *Golden Ass* 9.33.5, lemma: *quotidianis partubus*). It pits Albertus Magnus, the *doctor universalis*, against classical authorities, taking as its starting point Albertus Magnus' alleged misunderstanding of Aristotle. 'Albertus Magnus, the ape of Aristotle (*Aristotelis simia*), hallucinates not so much when he ponders Aristotles' words as when he draws conclusions from them.' Beroaldo notes that the elder Pliny (*Nat.* 10. 74. 146) took all the

---

[11] From the verso of the first (unnumbered) folio after the dedicatory epistle that heads Beroaldo's *Annotationes…in Commentarios Servii Virgiliani Commentatoris* (1482).
[12] Beroaldo, fol. 159 on Apul. *Met.* 7.20.

information about the egg-laying proficiency of Hadrianic (i. e., Adriatic) hens from Aristotle (*GA* 749b 29-30 and *HA* 558b 17). He adds:

Albertus Magnus believed that Hadrianic hens took their name from the emperor Hadrian, who ruled Rome long after the time of Aristotle and after that of Pliny, when [in fact] they take their name from the Italian town of (H)adria. The famous and otherwise great philosopher suddenly errs in such matters because while fixing his gaze skyward he fails to see what lies at his feet.

Beroaldo then summarises Columella (*De Re Rustica* 8. 5. 11), the elder Pliny (*Natural History* 10. 74. 145) and Horace (*Satires* 2. 4. 14), all of whom are in agreement that oval eggs produce male offspring, round eggs female offspring. He adds:

> Please wait for the rest. Albertus Magnus, who is to be admired on subjects of natural history, writes this in Book 6 of *De Animalibus*. 'Aristotle says that oval eggs produce male offspring, round eggs female offspring. This is completely false. The mistake resulted from a corrupt text and not from the words of the philosopher. Because of [this corrupt text of Aristotle] Avicenna writes that male offspring and cocks are produced from short, round eggs; hens from long, pointed eggs; and that this accords with my experience with eggs.' From his words I have concluded that the codices of Aristotle at the time of Albertus himself were consistent with the opinions of Columella and Pliny on the subject of eggs producing female and male offspring and that Aristotle did write thus, as did Pliny, who was an excellent interpreter of Aristotle…To conclude this appendix (*parerga*), Aristotle perceived and wrote that female offspring are hatched from round eggs, male offspring from pointed eggs. Columella, Pliny and Horace, taking their lead from Aristotle, perceived and wrote the same thing…Let the natural scientists and philosophers debate, balance and examine these issues of philosophy and natural science. It is enough for me to confirm historical facts (*historica*).

In this instance Albertus Magnus is correct. It is instructive, however, to consider how Beroaldo was led to his incorrect conclusion, which reflects the prevailing mediaeval tradition. He has allowed the authority of classical writers to outweigh that of the scholastic *doctor universalis*.

Finer points of the Latin language

For Beroaldo, Apuleius was a stylistic and moral authority. Beroaldo quotes St. Augustine's assessment of his compatriot Apuleius as *magna…praeditus eloquentia* and offers his own assessment: *elegans, eruditus, emunctus*.[13] He adds, 'Therefore, reader, I entreat, advise and urge you to make this writer your constant companion as though he were a manual, or handbook.'[14] As he often does, Beroaldo adds a personal note, 'Moreover, there are not a few interspersed words [in the *Golden Ass*] in which I delight more than I use, many of which I shall take delight in using in the future.' Also as he often does, Beroaldo relates the subject to his teaching and its value for his students:

> Frequent reading of Apuleius is especially suitable for perfecting [one's proficiency in the Latin] language and the branch of eloquence that is called '*sermo<ci>natrix*.'

He rarely misses an opportunity to comment on stylistic matters, all the while adhering to his goal of explaining the *Golden Ass*, as in this comment (fol. 122) on the phrase '*inter Orci cancros*' at *Golden Ass* 6. 8. 7:

> Writers in antiquity used this word (viz. *cancros*) for '*claustra*' and '*septa*'; the diminutive form (viz. *cancelli*) is now used for the lattices that protect the windows of shrines and small churches… The word '*cancellare*' is very frequently used in idiomatic speech and by the uneducated. It does not, however, deviate from good Latin usage…The jurisconsult [Ulpian, *Digest* 28. 4. 2, writes], '*Cancellaverat quis testamentum…*' It is from this use of the word in a legal context that that the word '*cancellarii*' is now used. This usage is, to be sure, vulgar but nonetheless good Latin. Their function (viz. that of *cancellarii*) in writing is to delete and cross out what has been written…The sense in Apuleius is that Psyche is caught within *claustra* and *cancellarios* and that escape is no longer possible.

Finally, a few words should be said about Beroaldo's influence on interpretations of the *Golden Ass*. In the part of Beroaldo's preface that is headed

---

[13] Beroaldo 1500, fol. 1vo.

[14] *Ibid., Quamobrem te, lector, oro, moneo, hortor ut familiaris tibi fiat hic scriptor sitque tuum quasi manuale et enchiridion.*

'*Scriptoris Intentio atque Consilium*' Beroaldo affirms ('*ego...confirmo*') Apuleius' 'Intention and Purpose':

> (Apuleius') intention was to represent by means of the guise of transformation the nature and character of human beings so that we would be cautioned that we become asses instead of human beings when we behave brutishly and with asinine stupidity as a consequence of having been immersed in beastly sensual pleasures and when no spark of reason or virtue shines forth in us. The transformation back into a human being from an ass signifies that reason recovers its senses after it has trampled sensual pleasures and cast off the pleasures of the flesh and that the inner person, which is the real person, has returned with the guidance of virtue and religion from its filthy prison to its sparkling habitation.[15]

And in his epistolary *sphragis* headed '*Finis Commentariorum*' Beroaldo interprets the *Golden Ass* as the mirror of the human condition:

> Perusal of Apuleius' *Golden Ass* is like looking at a mirror-image of the human condition, and one views expressed in this guise our character and the image of our daily lives, the goal and greatest blessing of which are religion and the cultivation of divine majesty joined to erudition.[16]

To rephrase the well known statement of the grammarian Terentianus Maurus, *Pro captu commentatoris habent sua fata libelli*. Apuleius' *Golden Ass* became widely known in western Europe through the medium of Beroaldo's commentary.[17] He did not, however, 'almost single-handedly establish the rules for writing commentaries.' As Beroaldo himself recognised, he was

---

[15] *Verum sub hoc transmutationis involucro, naturam mortalium et mores humanos quasi transeunter designare voluisse, ut admoneremur ex hominibus asinos fieri, quando voluptatibus belluinis immersi asinali stoliditate brutescimus, nec ulla rationis virtutisque scintilla in nobis elucescit.... Rursus ex asino in hominem reformatio significat calcatis voluptatibus, exutisque corporalibus deliciis rationem resipiscere, et hominem interiorem, qui verus est homo ex ergastulo illo cenoso, ad lucidum habitaculum, virtute et religione ducibus remigrasse* Beroaldo 1500, fol. 2vo).

[16] Lectio *Asini Apuleiani nimirum speculum est rerum humanarum istoque involucro efficti nostri mores espressaque imago vitae quotidianae conspicitur, cuius finis et summa beatitas est religio cultusque divinae maiestatis una cum eruditione copulata connexaque* (Beroaldo 1500, fol. 280vo).

[17] Both Carver (2007) and Gaisser (2008) have recently discussed in detail Beroaldo's contribution to the reception of Apuleius' *Golden Ass* during the Renaissance.

working within a well established mediaeval tradition.[18] Beroaldo was not even the first humanist of his generation to produce a commentary on a classical Latin author, as Beroaldo himself acknowledges.[19] To what, then, can we attribute the success of Beroaldo's commentary on the *Golden Ass*? One of his remarkable achievements was to produce publications that simultaneously met the demands of scholars (*docti*), the educated public (*studiosi*) and students (*scholastici*), so much so that the younger Henri Éstienne pays tribute to Beroaldo (and Calderini) as the teacher of his generation.[20] Probably because he was used to teaching hundreds of students each day, Beroaldo was able to judge his readers' needs and, accordingly, to present the *Golden Ass* as a repository of Roman law, Latin style and Platonist-inspired moral paradigm. As the teacher of his age Beroaldo had a wealth of erudition and insight to offer to his hundreds of students each day in 1500, and we today would be well advised to take some of his lessons to heart.

Bibliography

Beroaldo F. 1500, *Commentarii a Philippo Beroaldo Conditi in Asinum Aureum Lucii Apuleii*, Bologna, Benedictus Hectoris.
— 1500a, *Orationes Multifariae a Philippo Beroaldo Editae Recognitaeque cum Appendicula Aliarum quoque Oratiuncularum*, Bologna: Benedictus Hectoris.
Bianchini, B. 1548, 'Philippi Beroaldi Vita per Bartolomaeum Blanchinum Bononiensem ad Camillum Palaeottum,' in (ed.) Filippo Beroaldo, *Caii Suetonii Tranquilli Duodecim Caesares, cum Philippi Beroaldi Bononiensis, Marcilique, item Commentariis Bapt. Aegnatii Aliorum Doctorum Virorum Annotationibus*, Lugduni: I. Frellonius, fol.sign. β8-γ1^{vo}. (A reissue of the edition of 1510.)

---

[18] Beroaldo 1500, fol. 2vo, *In exponendis auctoribus id quoque spectari querique solet: quae fuerit scribentis intentio atque consilium.*

[19] From the epistolary dedication of Beroaldo's commentary on Propertius (1487):
Nec solos lectione esse dignos censeo antiquos commentatores. Verum etiam nostrorum temporum ingenia non despicio...Vigent hodie clarique sunt in studiis litterarum complusculi qui interpretando, commentando, explanando veterum poemata non mediocrem laudem consequuti sunt...Extant Domitii enarrationes luculenter quidem scriptae sed adeo concise ut sibi soli et musis sicuti dici solet cecinisse videatur. Nos talia intra duos sesquimenses elucubravimus ut tironibus placere possint nec veteranis displicere.

[20] *Age enim, tu, quicumque Beroaldi aut Domitii scripta non unius assis prae iis quae hodie eduntur aestimanda putas, quid sine Beroaldo ac Domitio aliisque huiusmodi magistris scribi ab eorum posteris potuisse arbitraris? Quod si doctiores suis magistris, ut saepe fit, evaserunt discipuli, an magistri propterea e doctorum albo eradendi erunt?* (Quoted from C. Dionisotti (1968, 156), who quotes from Henri Éstienne's preface to the reissue (1567) of the *Liber de Rebus per Epistolam Quaesitis* attributed to the Calabrian humanist Aulo Giano Parr(h)asio.

Carver R. 2007, *The Protean Ass: The 'Metamorphoses' of Apuleius from Antiquity to the Renaissance*, Oxford, Oxford University Press.

Casella M. 1975, 'Il metodo dei commentatori umanistici essemplato sul Beroaldo,' *SMed* 16, 627-701.

Ciapponi L. (ed.) 1995, *Filippo Beroaldo the Elder, Annotationes centum: Critical Edition with Commentary*, Medieval and Renaissance Texts and Studies, No. 131, Binghamton, Medieval and Renaissance Texts and Studies.

Dionisotti C. 1968, 'Calderini, Poliziano e altri,' *Italia medioevale e umanistica* 11, 151-185.

Gaisser, J. 2008, *The Fortunes of Apuleius and the 'Golden Ass'*, Princeton, Princeton University Press.

Krautter K. 1971, *Philologische Methode und humanistische Existenz*, Munich, Fink.

Meuschen J. 1735-1738, *Vitae Summorum Dignitate et Eruditione Virorum, ex Rarissimis Monumentis Literato Orbi Restitutae*, Coburg: Steinmerkius. 3 volumes.

Osgood, J. 2006, '*Nuptiae Iure Civili Congruae*: Apuleius's Story of Cupid and Psyche and the Roman Law of Marriage,' *TAPA* 136, 415-441.

Osler D. 1989, 'Filippo Beroaldo e l'umanesimo giuridico,' in (eds.) L. Avellini, A. De Benedictis and A. Cristiani, *Sapere e/è potere. Discipline, Dispute e Professioni nell'Università Medievale e Moderna: Il caso bolognese a confronto*, Atti del 4° Convegno, Bologna, 13-15 aprile 1989, Bologna, Istituto per la storia di Bologna, 1990 (*recte* 1991), I, 233-241.

Pins J. de. 1505, *Divae Catherinae Senensis simul et Viri Philippi Beroaldi Bononiensis Vita*. Bologna: Benedictus Hectoreus.

Sandy G. 2007, '*LEX COMMENTANDI*: Philippe Béroalde et le commentaire humaniste', *BiblH&R* 69, 399-423.

The *Golden Ass* and its *Nachleben* in the Middle Ages and in the Renaissance

FERRUCCIO BERTINI
University of Genoa

At the beginning of the *Metaphysics* Aristotle says : πάντες ἄνθρωποι τοῦ εἰδέναι ὀρέγονται φύσει[1] 'All men tend naturally to knowledge', that is to what in Latin is defined as *cupiditas sciendi*. This longing for knowledge is usually symbolized by Odysseus or Ulysses, who, from his Homeric origins, assumed the emblematic role of spokesman of this fundamental human ambition. At some moments, however, this longing for knowledge can turn from a virtue into a vice; that happens when man, who has been created in God's image and likeness, seeks after a knowledge which determinedly denies any reference to his divine origin and is motivated only by haughtiness, vanity and ambition, and not by love for truth. So, whereas the Homeric Ulysses completes his numerous adventures and comes back home to the affection of his family, his Dantean counterpart instead becomes a mere symbol of aiming to know, ready to face any sort of danger just to placate his thirst for knowledge.

In Homer Odysseus does not himself long for knowledge, but is compelled to acquire it, whereas in Dante he confesses (*Inf.* 24, 94-99):

... né dolcezza di figlio, né la pièta
del vecchio padre, né 'l debito amore
lo qual dovea Penelopé far lieta,
vincer poter dentro da me l'ardore
ch'i' ebbi a divenir del mondo esperto
e delli vizi umani e del valore.

---

[1] Arist. *met.* 1. 980a.

So, while the Homeric Odysseus longs to come back to his Ithaca, his Dantean version is even concerned to convince his companions to venture their last undertaking (*Inf.* 26, 112-120):

'O frati', dissi, 'che per cento milia
perigli siete giunti all'Occidente,
a questa tanto picciola vigilia
de' nostri sensi ch'è del rimanente,
non vogliate negar l'esperienza,
di retro al sol, del mondo sanza gente.
Considerate la vostra semenza:
fatti non foste a viver come bruti,
ma per seguir virtute e canoscenza'.

In this case the need to 'go beyond' is considered typical of human nature, but his adventure will end up tragically, because he shows ὕβρις. The tragic end of Ulysses contrasts symmetrically with the ascent of Dante, and the two characters invert each other. Like all the damned, Ulysses is bound to the memory of the past and calls his own flight 'crazy', perhaps in the meaning of 'reckless'. Dante admires Ulysses and identifies with him, but takes care to distinguish his own Christian *virtus* from the 'crazy' pagan *virtus* of Ulysses, which leads him only to *canoscenza* and not to true *cognitio*. That is a proof of the basic difference which exists between the imperative for casual exploration and that for true knowledge, which are both fundamental for the *curiositas*.[2]

In Greek literature there is a treatise especially dedicated to define the word *curiositas*, that is Plutarch's Περὶ πολυπραγμοσύνης; there the term is explained as follows: 'Curiosity, that is the longing to know other people's troubles, is a mental disease, free from neither envy nor malice'.[3] Plutarch too distinguishes between *curiositas* (πολυπραγμοσύνη) and true knowledge,

---

[2] Cfr. Walde – Hofmann 1938, 314, *s.v. cura*, where the authors say that since antiquity the adjective *cūriōsus* means 'wißbegierig' and 'besorgt', that's 'eager to learn' and 'worried', what is confirmed in Ernout – † Meillet 1959⁴, 159, where you read: '*cūra* ne pouvait former que **cūrōsus*, (comme *fāma, fāmosus*): «qui prend soin, qui s'inquiete de» et, avec une nuance péjorative, «curieux (de), indiscret»; à l'époque impériale, *cūriōsus* désigne un «espion» (cfr. en argot français le «curieux» = juge d'instruction); *cūriōsitas*'.

[3] Plut. *de curios.* 515D: Οἷον εὐθὺς ἡ πολυπραγμοσύνη φιλομαθειά τίς ἐστιν ἀλλοτρίων κακῶν, οὔτε φθόνου δοκοῦσα καθαρεύειν νόσος οὔτε κακοθείας.

because in *curiositas* there is no eschatological perspective. The term derives, in all probability, from a Menandrian slave who, in a fragment of a lost comedy,[4] is represented as the typical πολυπράγμων, who claims οὐδὲν γλυκύτερόν ἐστιν ἢ πάντ' εἰδέναι, that is 'There is nothing sweeter that to know everything', but Πολυπράγμων is also the title of a comedy by Diphilus which Franco Ferrari[5] well translates in Italian as 'L'impiccione' ('The nosy parker').

Now that we have clarified the usual meaning of πολυπραγμοσύνη in Greek and *curiositas* in Latin, we can discuss the novel in which it becomes emblematic, that is Apuleius' *Metamorphoses* in eleven books, which may be regarded as a *Divine Comedy ante litteram*. In both works there is a clear difference between *curiositas* (in the sense of exploration) and knowledge (in the true scientific sense), symbolized in one case by Lucius' adventures in the first ten books and then by *true* knowledge acquired from the freely given aid of Isis in the eleventh, and in the other case by Ulysses' 'mad flight' in *Inferno* XXVI and a progressive *approach* to the true *canoscenza* in Dante, which will later be achieved by the aid of divine Grace. What immediately differentiates the young protagonist of the Apuleian novel is *curiosity*, and, in particular, passion for magic. A native of Patras, he comes to Thessaly (the traditional land of witches) to attend to some unspecified business affairs. Here he is a guest in the house of the rich usurer Milo, whose wife Pamphile is an expert in the magic arts (*vulgo* a witch). Lucius, possessed by his incurable *curiositas*, induces the young servant Photis (whose favour he has won) to allow him to watch Pamphile's transformation into an owl by using an ointment. Lucius then convinces Photis to consent to experiment with the ointment on him, but the servant picks the wrong pot and the poor Lucius becomes an ass.[6] Hence in *De civitate Dei*[7] Augustine gives the Apuleian *Metamorphoses* the name of *Asinus aureus*, that is 'The Golden

---

[4] Kock 1888, fr. 850, quotes from Cramer, *Anecd. Paris.*, 4, 418, ὡς φησι Μένανδρος φιλῷ, and then from Cic. *ad Att.* 4, 11, οὐδὲν γλυκύτερόν ἐστιν.

[5] Cfr. Ferrari 2001, 836-837, with notes p. 1064.

[6] See Norden 1986, 507, where he notes that Apuleius was unlucky to tell a story about an ass, since an ordinary Italian humanist had said that Apuleius' style was like the braying of an ass. I cannot identify this Italian, but the same joke is used by both a German and a Spanish humanist: Melancthon (*Eloquentiae encomium* 1523, 29): *quis Apuleium et eius simias feret? Sed recte Apuleius, qui cum asinum repraesentaret, rudere quam loqui mallet*; Vives (*De tradendis disciplinis* 1531, III, 482): *Apuleius in asino plane rudit, in aliis sonat hominem, nisi quod Florida sunt ridicula, sed excusat ea inscriptio*.

[7] 17, 18.

Ass', underlining that Lucius, although transformed into an ass, remains human in his soul. Moreover it is noticeable that in a work whose title is *Metamorphoses* 'there are only two metamorphoses: that of Lucius who changes himself into an ass and then the opposite, i.e. the ass which becomes again Lucius'. So Grilli,[8] who then goes on to inform us[9] that Richard Reitzenstein was the first to understand that the *fabella* of Cupid and Psyche is no mere insertion in the novel, but rather an integral part of it.[10] This is the usual explication, but the true explanation was that proposed by René Martin in a paper published about forty years ago.[11] It has been diligently quoted in all following bibliographies, but no-one has taken it into due account, considering his argumentations and conclusions. But in my opinion it contains the clear proof of the true meaning of the title: Apuleius entitled his novel *Asinus aureus*[12] for a good reason.

In the Plutarchan work *On Isis and Osiris* (362F) one finds a very instructive passage about the ass' role in the mythology and rites of Egyptian religion. 'Osiris and Isis thus changed from good daemons into gods. The weakened and shattered power of Typhon, which still gasps and struggles, is appeased and mollified by them partly by sacrifices, while at other times again they humiliate and insult it in certain festivals, jeering at men of ruddy complexion and throwing an ass down a precipice, as the people of Coptos do, because Typhon had a ruddy complexion (πυρρόν) and was asinine in form. The people of Busiris and Lycopolis do not use trumpets at all, because they make a noise like an ass; and they believe the ass to be in general not a pure, but a daemonic beast because of its likeness to Typhon, and when they make round cakes in the festivals of the months of Payni and Phaophi, as an insult they stamp on them an image of a tied ass. In the sacrifice to Helios, they instruct those who venerate the god neither to wear golden objects on the body nor to give food to an ass'.[13]

---

[8] Grilli 2000, 121.
[9] *Ibidem*, 124.
[10] Reitzenstein 1912.
[11] Martin 1970. Cfr. Fedeli 1988², 370, who remarks: 'Diversa è anche la funzione del caso: è vero che al suo dominio sembrano sottostare personaggi ed eventi; in realtà non è così, e limitati risultano il suo potere e la sua sfera d'azione. Non è il caso, infatti, bensì la *curiositas* a suscitare il fatale interesse di Lucio per le pratiche magiche'.
[12] Cfr. Augustin. *de civ. Dei* 18, 18: *libri quos Asini aurei titulo Apuleius inscripsit*.
[13] Tr. Gwyn Griffths 1970, 165.

Plutarch also gives us this piece of information (364B): 'The wiser of the priests not only call the Nile Osiris and the sea Typhon, but apply the name Osiris simply to the general principle and power of moisture, regarding it as the cause of generation and the essence of seed, while the name Typhon is applied to the whole dry and fiery and generally scorching element which is hostile to moisture; believing, for this reason, that he was of red and sallow complexion, they do not gladly encounter or willingly associate with men of this appearance'.[14] If to all this we add that in the writings of Platonic philosophers the ass was often introduced to symbolize the body and its sensuality and besides that in the Isiac mysteries, Typhon, the monstrous evil spirit identified with the Egyptian Seth, was represented by an ass-head, we can do nothing else than think that Martin was right.

But two years later, Gerald Sandy noticed that 'other critics have traced the function of *curiositas* in the *Metamorphoses*, but have failed to demonstrate that this motif is in any way accounted for in the surprising conclusion of Apuleius' version of the *Eselmensch*'.[15] Later on Sandy produces a very acute reason; through the comparison between Lucius and Psyche, who both deliberately ignore 'frequent warnings not to view firsthand the workings of the supernatural'[16] and by stressing words pronounced by Lucius himself at the beginning of the novel (*velim scire cuncta vel certe plurima*, *Met.* 1,2), he highlights how Lucius is comparable with Faust, but has a previous model in Odysseus: *nam et ipse gratas gratias asino meo memini, quod me suo celatum tegmine variisque fortunis exercitatum, etsi minus prudentem, multiscium reddidit* (*Met.* 9, 13). In this sentence, indeed, the words *etsi minus prudentem* and *multiscium* are especially emphasised, and underline at the same time all the distance and all the similarity existing between Lucius and Odysseus.

In book eleven Lucius will compensate for the frivolity and lust of previous books, so that he becomes (like Ulysses before him) *prudens Lucius*. His character, of course, is not changed, since *nec minus in dies mihi magis magisque accipiendorum sacrorum cupido gliscebat* (*Met.* 11, 21, 2), which shows the great hurry to be initiated into the Isiac mysteries which seizes Lucius; but, just as previously (*Met.* 3, 20), Photis had warned him against longing to approach magic rites too hastily, so it is now Isis' priest who tries to restrain his impulsiveness. As a matter of fact 'none of Isis' followers is foolish enough to seek initiation without the goddess's approval and thus

---

[14] Tr. Gwyn Griffiths 1970, 169.
[15] Sandy 1972, 179.
[16] *Ibid.*, 180.

risk self-destruction'.[17] At this moment Lucius understands at last that, in order to enter into the *arcana secreta*, he has to learn to be patient: *nec impatientia corrumpebatur obsequium meum, sed intentus mihi quiete et probabili taciturnitate sedulum quot dies obibam culturae sacrorum ministerium* (*Met.* 11, 22, 1). Sandy's contribution highlights how, in order to arrive at the conscious and quiet expectation of the last book, it was necessary to have the series of previous ten books which Ben Edwin Perry[18] had awkwardly defined as being full of futile frivolity. The eleventh book 'integrates the motifs of Lucius' *curiositas* and his desire to *scire vel cuncta vel certe plurima*. Among other things, he has learned to find satisfaction not in gratifying his curiosity but in fulfilling his spiritual need through devotion to Isis'.[19]

With good reason J. L. Penwill[20] can assert that, while Psyche 'has learnt nothing from her experiences [...], Lucius [...] *does* learn from his experience and correctly refuses to 'lift the lid' on matters which are required to be kept secret', stating this to the reader: *quaeras forsitan satis anxie, studiose lector, quid deinde dictum, quid factum; dicerem, si dicere licet, cognosceres, si liceret audire. Sed parem noxam contraherent et aures et linguas illae temerariae curiositatis* (*Met.* 11, 23, 5). The result is that by the end of the novel, Apuleius, who till then exalted *curiositas*, at last realizes its true nature and does not hesitate to define it deliberately as *temeraria*.[21] According to Grilli, a similar conjunction (*sacrilega curiositas*, *Met.* 5, 6, 6) is employed by Apuleius to explain why Psyche was pushed to reveal the sleeping Cupid, whereas the same adjective *temeraria* is employed again of Psyche, when, at the end of her sad story, she wants to try a portion of *divina formositas* hidden in the *ciborium* that Proserpina entrusted her with, forbidding her from opening it;[22] thus 'Psyche is the soul, the Roman soul pure and innocent, fit to attain the sublimity of Platonic love, in which immortality, free from the body, can be rediscovered'.[23] In a paper written some twenty years after his first, Penwill asserts: '*Bella fabella* says the ass at what he and its narrator see as the happy ending of the tale – but as Ovid, Persius and Apuleius are well aware, ass's ears, while they may be long and capable of

---

[17] *Ibid.*,182.
[18] Perry 1967, 244-245.
[19] Sandy 1972, 183.
[20] Penwill 1975.
[21] *Ibid.*, 58.
[22] Grilli 2000, 125.
[23] *Ibid.*, 128.

accurately picking up distant sounds,[24] are not the best organs for comprehending aesthetic, religious or philosophic truth'.[25]

Walsh reaffirms: 'The ass, the most stupid of domestic animals, is assigned to Typhon, the malevolent demon whom it resembles in stupidity and lust. Hence Lucius' transformation into a donkey, and his eventual resumption of human shape, pregnantly signify a relapse into bestial living and re-emergence into authentic humanity. It seems beyond doubt that, when Apuleius transformed the *climax* of the ass-story [...] into an apologia for the Isiac religion, he was inspired by Plutarch's *De Iside*. It is true that Plutarch's treatment is the more philosophical, whereas Apuleius emphasizes salient details of ritual and religious practice; but these variations are attributable to the differing purposes of philosopher and novelist. The moral of the *Metamorphoses* is that Lucius' avid curiosity to explore the realm of magic, attained by way of a sexual encounter with Photis, was punished because it was a perverted path to universal knowledge'.[26] It will be precisely Photis who informs the poor ass that to regain human shape in appearance, it will be sufficient that he eats some roses. That seems easy to say, but in reality, due to a series of misadventures that happen one after the other without a break during the whole development of the first ten books of the novel, poor Lucius can never come near to the flower he desires.

At a certain moment, while he is prisoner of some bandits in a cave, he listens to the story of Cupid and Psyche told by an old woman to console the young girl Charite in her care, kidnapped from bandits and imprisoned with him. The very long story goes from the end of the fourth book (4, 28) till nearly the end of the sixth (6. 24) and supplies in advance an interpretative key to understanding the meaning of whole novel. Psyche is the last of the three daughters of a king and she is the most beautiful, so to stir up Venus' envy. The goddess sends her son Cupid, who receives the charge to inflame the girl with his arrows in a dishonorable passion. But Cupid falls in love with her and abducts her to his palace, where she is served and honoured like a queen by Cupid's invisible servants. She, however, has to respect a condition – never to try to see the face of the man who abducted her, otherwise the enchantment will break. Poor Psyche, prisoner of solitude, obtains at least permission to see her two sisters, who, envious of her, insinuate that her

---

[24] See *met*. 9,13,3-5 with the remarks thereon of Laird 1990, 149-150; cf. also Penwill, 1975, 68-69.
[25] Penwill, 1998, 175; on this subject James 1987, 122 writes: 'The ass is proverbially insensitive to the finer thinks in life'.
[26] Walsh 1995, XXXII.

mysterious lover doesn't want to be seen because he is a monster. Psyche, like Lucius, doesn't resist *curiositas* and approaches her unknown lover with a dagger, with the intention to kill him, but from the lamp that she holds in her hand to reveal the sleeping god, a drop of hot oil falls, which wakes him up with a start. And Cupid flees away from Psyche who, breaking the pact, also breaks the enchantment: at this moment, in despair because, approaching the god covertly, she pricked herself with an arrow from the *pharetra* and fell hopelessly in love with him, the young girl wanders madly searching for her lost love. But she has to deal with Venus, who day after day more jealous of her beauty, imposes on her the completion of four very difficult tasks, the last of which consists of reaching the realm of the dead and receiving from Persephone a small pot that must be brought to Venus without opening it. But curiosity is again stronger than any fear and, after having opened the forbidden little pot, Psyche collapses in a lethal sleep. One time again, however, Cupid hastens freely to her aid, saves her and obtains from the king of the gods her immortality. From their union will be born a daughter, who will be called *Voluptas*.

This fable goes back over the whole of the novel's events which precede it: the erotic adventure, hence the curiosity punished through a sequence of misadventures and sufferings, which ends by free divine intervention, in the case of Lucius of the goddess Isis who, after appearing to Lucius in a dream, gives him the opportunity to eat from a rose garland during the celebration of her festival. Penwill remarks that this *fabella*, being in the centre of the first ten books of the novel, can be divided into three parts: 'The first of these is dominated by the motif of black magic, its practitioners and victims, and culminates in Lucius' transformation into an ass, itself a consequence of a curiosity against which he is repeatedly warned but which he continually seeks to gratify. The third (the post-'Cupid and Psyche' section) represents the world dominated by *Fortuna*, in which we find stories ranging from *Decameron* – style comedies of sexual intrigue […] 'Cupid and Psyche' is centrally placed as an explanatory myth. Psyche of course is the Greek word for soul and Cupido or Amor (he is given both names in the story) the Latin for sexual desire […]; the narration of the marriage rite with which it concludes employs a legal term, *convenit in manum*,[27] which signifies that the wife comes into the power and possession of her husband, and Jupiter pronounces that this marriage is to last for ever (*istae vobis erunt perpetuae nuptiae*)[28] […] The story is thus the narrative of a fall, a fall from which Isis alone can

---

[27] 6, 24, 4.
[28] 6, 23, 5.

redeem [...] Lucius' refusal to participate in what would reduce him to the level of the condemned woman with whom he is to copulate and to share her fate leads to his escape from the *voluptas*-dominated world depicted in Books 1-10, the world of black magic, blind fortune, and the flawed Olympians'.[29]

In a world like this, 'the birth of sexual pleasure may well be a matter for celebration'. From the Isiac point of view, however, pursuit of *voluptas*, identified as the offspring of Cupid and Psyche, threatens degradation and misery: what Book 11's convert exhorts us to seek is the *inexplicabilis voluptas* ('ineffable pleasure'),[30] that comes from contemplation of the only true *Venus caelestis* in this novel, the goddess Isis. 'There is no ambiguity in the ending of 'Cupid and Psyche', only different perceptions of different readers that reflect their different life-situations and value-systems'.[31] But Penwill's idea, according to which Cupid and Psyche's story is the narrative of the soul's fall from pristine innocence to enslavement to desire, has found scant acceptance from scholars, who stand firm in the orthodox opinion that Psyche's tale anticipates Lucius' tale and represents a Platonist-Isiac myth whose ending prefigures Lucius' salvation in Book 11. Why Apuleius assumed as protector only Isis and not other divinities also linked with mysteries, is perhaps to be found in the exotic fascination of Isiac cult, as well as the authority it enjoyed for its millenarian tradition or its relative compatibility with Platonic positions.

Another useful and explicit indication comes from the *Oneirocritica*, the dream-manual written in Greek by Artemidorus of Daldis, who like Apuleius lived in the second century C.E. He affirms (2, 39) that the Egyptian gods Serapis, Isis, Anubis and Harpocrates [...] appearing during a dream 'signify disturbances, dangers, threats and crises from which salvation will come when one's hopes and expectations have been abandoned'[32] – words that seem to be just written for Apuleius' Lucius.[33] In other words the soul (θυμός), after being stained with the sin of ὕβρις for revealing a mystery which was not to be revealed, must atone through endless humiliations and sufferings, before having the chance to be reunited with god. The religious meaning appears above all through the final intervention of the god Cupid who spontaneously offers himself to aid the repenting sinner. In the same

---

[29] Penwill 1998, 161.
[30] *met.* 11, 24, 5.
[31] Penwill, 1998, 175-176.
[32] Tr. White 1975, 123.
[33] So Fo 2002, 678-679.

manner the whole eleventh book must be explained in a mystagogic key, an addition due beyond any doubt to Apuleius, especially because the young Lucius who, during the whole novel, was defined as Greek, suddenly becomes *Madaurensis*, just like Apuleius, and identifies himself with the author.

The *Metamorphoses* is then a novel of formation, where (as in the *Divina Commedia*) there unfolds the story of the spiritual itinerary of the protagonist who, after falling into sin, passes through the stages of a difficult penance and finally achieves redemption, but only by divine intervention. 'Moreover, Apuleius informed us in advance of the fact that from this novel, where the light is triumphant over the darkness, the leading character would emerge safe, when he gave his name to the protagonist: as a matter of fact Lucius comes from *lux*'.[34]

Apuleius was soon cited (not exactly with favour) by Macrobius in his *Commentarii in Somnium Scipionis*,[35] where he says that the *genus* of fables like those of Petronius and Apuleius *solas aurium delicias profitetur*. Then, as Keulen points out,[36] Macrobius asserts that the plots (*argumenta*) are full of fictitious lovers' affairs (*fictis casibus amatorum referta*). So the author of the *Saturnalia* mentions together Petronius and Apuleius, because the late-antique man of letters regarded fictitious love affairs as representative of the same kind of literature. The *Satyrica* and *Metamorphoses* are sophisticated works and at more than one level; in each of them the author uses his own methods to produce a sort of gap between the writer's protagonists and the everyday life, where they operate.[37] Twenty-five pages later on Keulen wonders: did Apuleius know Petronius? If yes, he imitates him, otherwise the two are joined only by the fact that they adopt independently the same literary genre. If we consider Petronius' and Apuleius' passages together from a different point of view, we find that other elements too operate in a common environment. Both like best low-life settings, such as inns, where they place dramatic and turbulent actions with broken down doors, smashed furniture and shouting people, an ensemble conflicting with the high literary aspirations of the characters.

Jerome in the *Tractatus de psalmo*,[38] after introducing someone who, speaking about magic practices, says *hoc totum lucri causa fecerunt*, through

---

[34] Grilli 2000, 134.
[35] Willis 1994, I 2, 8.
[36] Keulen 2006, 131-167, particularly 131.
[37] Ibidem, 133-134.
[38] Morin 1958, 81, 6, 89.

the Platonic philosopher Porphyrius expresses these words: *homines rusticani et pauperes, quoniam nihil habebant, magicis artibus operati sunt quaedam signa. Non est autem grande facere signa. Nam fecerunt signa in Aegypto magi contra Moysen. Fecit et Apollonius, fecit et Apuleius: et infinita signa fecerunt.* One of the first to testify to the bad influence exerted by Apuleius was Iulius Capitolinus, who in his *Vita Clodii Albini* tells how Septimius Severus reproached him because *neniis quibusdam anilibus occupatus inter Milesias Punicas Apulei sui et ludicra littera consenesceret.*[39] In the fourth century, further to Jerome as cited above, Apuleius is quoted still as a magician, in opposition to the true Christ, by Lactantius,[40] whereas Ausonius, seeking to justify himself with his readers for having composed the obscene *Cento nuptialis*, seems more generous towards the writer from Madauros; in fact, after having mentioned Martial, Plinius and Sulpicia, he quotes Apuleius because he was *in vita philosophus, in epigrammatis amator.*[41]

After this, Augustine, in the *De civitate Dei*, proves himself to have read a good part of Apuleius' works.[42] There is, besides, a central theme common to the Augustinian *Confessiones* and Apuleian *Metamorphoses*: beyond the conventional relation of 'sin' and 'redemption' there is, in fact, the exposure of 'deceit' (*fallacia*) and the search for wrong pleasures:[43] 'both Lucius and

---

[39] *hist. Aug.* 12, 12, in Soverini 1983, 492.

[40] *div. inst.* 5,3,21: *non igitur suo testimonio* (that's 'of Christ') [...] *sed prophetarum testimonio, qui omnia quae fecit ac passus est multo ante cecinerunt, fidem divinitatis accepit, quod neque Apollonio neque Apuleio neque cuipiam magorum potuit aut potest aliquando contingere* (Monat 1973, 44).

[41] Aus. *cent. nupt.* 11, 4, in Pastorino 1971, 670. But the Platonic philosopher is exactly like the magician: in fact the element that allows man to come into contact with the divinity, according to Apuleius, is the magic (cf. what he says in the *Apologia*...'Plus nombreux sont les passages dans lesquels l'initiative revient à l'homme, dans ses sermons et ses prières [...]. Dans les dix premiers livres, ils n'occupent que quelques lignes, à l'adresse de la Fortune [...] dans le dernier, au contraire, c'est le héros du roman, Lucius, qui seul implore longuement une unique déesse égyptienne, Isis». [...] Le recours à la magie a pour conséquence le malheur de ceux sur lesquels elle s'exerce' (Méthy, 1999, 45-46).

[42] The *De mundo* in 4, 2, the *De Platone et eius dogmate* in 8, 12 and the *De deo Socratis* in 8, 14-23 (where he describes very negatively the cult of demons and their intermediary role between gods and men, which Apuleius theorized in the sixth chapter of his work) and, still, in 9, 1-16 and in 10, 9 and 27 (where, comparing Apuleius with Porphyry, he considers the first's mistake more human and tolerable). In 12, 10, on the contrary, he refutes roughly the assertion contained in book 6 of the *De deo Socratis* (according to which men, if taken separately, are mortal, but considered all together are eternal) and finally in 18, 18, where, as we have already mentioned in note 12 above, he quotes the *Golden Ass*.

[43] See the stimulating treatment of Shumate 1988.

Augustine grow increasingly dissatisfied with the pleasure and the successes human society has to offer'.[44] Augustine too speaks of a *pruritus cupiditatis*[45] going back to an ancestral epoch, but again: 'Earlier in the work he had likewise identified the motif for his boyish hook-playing as an itch to gratify his *amor ludendi, studium spectandi, nugatoria et imitandi ludicria*';[46] that corresponds perfectly with the atmosphere which circulates in the first ten books of the *Metamorphoses*, pervaded with the tired search for amusement and *spectacula*. In the two works one can find, then, a substantial crisis of values[47] and a condemnation of *curiositas*, which in Apuleius recurs only in the last book,[48] whereas in the *Confessiones*, which consist of thirteen books, it is found at 10.35.

Fulgentius, in the *Fabula deae Psicae et Cupidinis* (*Mythologiae* 3.6) besides summarising Apuleius, accuses him of spending almost two whole books narrating in detail *tantam falsitatum congeriem*.[49] A very accurate investigation of the presence of Apuleius in Fulgentius has undertaken by G. Hays,[50] who affirms that Fulgentius surely read Apuleius, as shown by the echoes of Cupid and Psyche's fable in the quoted passage of *Myth*. 3, 15, but also in the *Expositio sermonum antiquorum* (116, 21 Helm), where the grammar shows the difference between *pumilior* and *glabrior*, quoting another passage of Psyche's *fabula* (*Met*. 5, 9). There are besides 'programmatic reminiscenses': *Myth*. 3, 15 *aurium sedes* lepido *quolibet* susurro permulceam, which is quite a literal echo of Apul. *Met*. 1, 1, 1 : *omnesque tuas benivolas* lepido susurro permulceam. As already noted by M. Zink:[51] 'Wir können den Stil unseres Autors (*id est* Fulgentius) als Imitation des Appulejus und mehr noch des Tertullian bezeichnen'. Fulgentius (*Myth*. 7, 23 Helm) draws on Apuleian refined terms such as *exantlata* (which recurs four times in *Met*. 6, 4; 7, 6; 11,12 and 11,15).

Another text which probably was influenced by Apuleius' *Metamorphoses* is the anonymous *Historia Apollonii regis Tyri*, usually assigned to the fifth or sixth centuries C.E.[52] Pavloskis, in her preface, writes: 'Like the protagonist of Apuleius' story of conversion, the *Golden Ass*, Apollonius, at

---

[44] ead., 36-37.
[45] *conf*. 2, 8, 16.
[46] *conf*. 1, 19, 30; Shumate 1988, 37-38.
[47] Shumate 1988, 50.
[48] *Met*. 11, 23 (quoted above).
[49] Helm 1970², 68, 22.
[50] Hays 2000.
[51] Zink 1867, 38.
[52] Pavlovskis 1978.

the end of his sufferings, presents the story of his life to the goddess as kind of ritual confession. For this act he is rewarded with complete felicity'.[53] However, Elizabeth Archibald[54] remarks 'I have deliberately restricted this section (= *Sources and Analogues*) to Hellenistic romances because I see so little connection between HA and the Latin 'novelists' Petronius and Apuleius […]' and 'although there is only one verbal echo of Apuleius in c. 8 (not a particularly striking one), Perry argues for a number of parallels and links, particularly in the use of folktale and the way in which independent stories are joined together without adequate motivation; he calls this technique 'contaminatio', and claims that it is much more frequently found in Latin literature than in Greek'.[55] She concludes in a very drastic way: 'HA seems to me entirely lacking in Apuleius' playfulness and in his deliberate ambiguity and challenge to interpretation […] as has been elegantly analysed by the late Jack Winkler'.[56] Garbugino, arguing against Kortekaas' argument that HA is a mere translation of the Greek summary and so replying also to Archibald, writes: 'Eppure l'influenza di Apuleio sulla HA è stata ampiamente documentata da Weyman[57] e da Morelli[58] … e non sembra che le conclusioni dei due studiosi siano impugnabili'.[59] He then quotes a series of *loci parallelli* between the Apuleian *Metamorphoses* and HA, to prove the correctness of the argument.

After the sixth century we have no news about Apuleius till the eleventh century, when the manuscript *F* (Laur. 68.2) was transcribed, and the twelfth century, when he was quoted by John of Salisbury,[60] by Bernardus Silvestris, who based his *Cosmographia* on *De mundo* of Apuleius,[61] and by Geoffrey of Monmouth, who in his *Historia regum Britanniae* mentions again the *De deo Socratis* as an *auctoritas* to testify the possibility of the birth of Merlin the magician by means of the intervention of a demonic *incubus*.[62] Recently

---

[53] *Ead.*, 11.
[54] Archibald 1991, 33.
[55] Perry 1967, 321-324.
[56] Winkler 1985.
[57] Weyman 1893, 380-382.
[58] Morelli 1913, 183-185.
[59] Garbugino 2008.
[60] *policr.* 6, 29: *Haec Apuleius eleganter quidem et splendide; et utinam audiatur* (ed. Webb 1909, vol. II, 86); in chapter 28, in fact, John alluded to some pages of the *De deo Socratis*, where there was the invitation to neglect material goods for searching the wisdom.
[61] Cf. Dronke 1978, 24; cf. above all Bern. *cosm.* 2, 4 and 2, 6 with Apul. *de mund.* 23, 341 and 19, 333, as well as 21, 336.
[62] *hist. reg. Brit.* 6, 18, in Agrati - Magini 1989, 112-113.

Gian Franco Gianotti, in the conclusion of a long and precious paper, observed: 'Come scrittore Apuleio consuma fino in fondo l'esperienza stilistica della 'nuova sofistica' a cui sa aggiungere vertiginosa abilità personale. Il saldo impianto retorico e il sapiente dosaggio di arcaismi e volgarismi, i rapidi passaggi e la costante capacità di controllare le digressioni, la funambolica tensione espressiva, la calibrata miscela tra preziosità formali e sermocinazione quotidiana, gli accorgimenti lessicali di stampo poetico accanto a toni risentiti o paludati o parodici, infine il brillante lavoro di cesello in raffinati pezzi di bravura e il sorridente umorismo fanno del testo apuleiano un *unicum* nella storia della prosa latina'.[63]

Walsh again[64] informs us that, after Bussi's *editio princeps* published at Rome in 1469, in the sixteenth century there followed one after another new printings of all the Apuleian works at Vicenza, Venice, Milan and Florence, to which we must add the editions of the *Golden Ass* only at Bologna and Venice. But already a century before 1469, Petrarch and Boccaccio had a personal copy of the novel. Boccaccio, besides interpreting allegorically the novel of Cupid and Psyche, took as a model two stories of adulterous love from the ninth book to incorporate them into his *Decameron*. The *Golden Ass* gained more renown and diffusion from the year 1518, when, basing himself on Beroaldo's commentary (Bologna 1500), Boiardo published in the year 1517 at Venice his well-known translation, followed thirty years later by the free translation of Agnolo Firenzuola (Venice 1548), where the ninth book is removed. It had many reprints and was one of the most read books in Western Europe. This translation caused a kind of explosion of social satire, which had as main theme the idea of holy stupidity by which Giordano Bruno distinguished himself especially.[65]

In the Spanish novels of the seventeenth century we find Apuleian themes in Ubedas, *La pícara Justina* (1605) and in *La vida del escudero Marcos de Obregón* of the novelist and poet Vicente Espinel (1618). Probably also in Cervantes' *Don Quixote* there is some recall of Apuleius, particularly in the episode where Lucius engages in combat with the wineskins. The Cupid and Psyche myth inspired French writers such as La Fontaine (*Les amours de Psyché et de Cupidon*, 1669) and Corneille, and Italians such as Marino in the *Adone* and Pascoli in *I poemi di Psiche*. In Germany the legend of Lohengrin, so as Wagner offers it to us, sets up a remarkable com-

---

[63] Gianotti 2000, 182.
[64] Walsh 1995, XLIX.
[65] *Lo spaccio della bestia trionfante* (1584), immediately followed in 1585 by *La cabala del cavallo pegaseo*, with the addition of *De l'asino cillenico*.

parison. Nevertheless the most enthusiastic evaluation of Apuleius is in a passage of Gustave Flaubert's *Correspondance* which sounds: 'S'il y a une verité artistique au monde, c'est que ce livre est un chef-d'oeuvre. Il me donne à moi des vertiges et des éblouissements; la nature pour elle-même, le paysage, le côté purement pittoresque des choses sont traités à la moderne et avec un souffle antique et chrétien tout ensemble qui passe au milieu'.[66] Diana Rîncioy[67] notes in the fourth volume of that *Correspondance* (édition Pleîade) that this is one of the 208 letters written to George Sand.

I conclude by considering the extensive use of Apuleius by Boccaccio. In his *Genealogia deorum gentilium* (5.22) Boccaccio develops the story of Clotho, Lachesis and Atropo, the Demogorgon's daughters, who administer human destiny, and at a certain point the Florentine writer quotes the Apuleian *De mundo*:[68] 'Apuleius of Madauros, a philosopher whose authority is not to be despised, writes in the following way about these matters in the book which he calls *Cosmographia* (38): 'But there are three Fates, a number which matches the framework of time, if you relate their power to the image of the same time. For what is already finished on the spindle presents the appearance of time past, and what is being spun on the fingers indicates the extent of the present moment, and what has not yet been drawn off the distaff and submitted to the care of the fingers, this seems to indicate the later elements of a future and following age. This is their condition; and the property of their names fits the case, so that Atropos is the Fate of past time, which not even a god can render undone; Lachesis, the Fate of the future, is named from the end, since god has assigned their end even to things which are to come. Clotho has the care of the present time, so as to urge on actions themselves, and to make sure that there is a diligent concern for all matters.' These are the things that Apuleius says'.

But the first extensive echo by Boccaccio of the ninth book of *Metamorphoses* is the story told by Apuleius at chapters 5-7, which becomes the second tale of the seventh day in the *Decameron*. The Florentine writer adds some particulars, such as the names of two of the three actors (that is the wife, who is called Peronella, and the adulterous lover, whose name is Giannello Scrignario). He tells us that the city where the story takes place is Naples, where Boccaccio lived for a long time in his youth. Otherwise the story is practically the same: a poor man (Boccaccio specifies that he is a

---

[66] 2, 133.
[67] Rîncioy 2002, 55.
[68] Apuleius, *De mundo* 38.

bricklayer, whereas in Apuleius he is a blacksmith) married to an equally poor wife, has a difficult life of poverty. One morning after he had gone out, as habitually *statim latenter inrepit eius hospitium temerarius adulter* (*Met.* 9, 5, 2), but that day the husband 'dove in tutto il dì tornar non soleva, a casa se ne tornò' (*Dec.* 7, 2, 10). *Iamque clausis et obseratis foribus uxoris laudata continentia ianuam pulsat* (*Met.* 9, 5, 3 = *Dec.* 7, 2, 10-11). Then Peronella terrified, but able to improvise defensive action, tells Giannello: 'entra in cotesto doglio che tu vedi costì, e io gli andrò ad aprire' (*Dec.* 7, 2, 13 = *Met.* 9, 5, 4).

Peronella opens the door and reproaches her husband for coming back home idle with his hands in his pockets. The husband replies that, though he has not worked that day, because *forensi negotio officinator noster attentus ferias nobis fecerit* (so in Apuleius *Met.* 9, 6, 1, whereas in Boccaccio the reason of the free day is that 'oggi è la festa di Santo Galeone e non si lavora' 7, 2, 20), he did gain income by selling an old *dolium* for *quinque denariis* (*Met.* 9, 6, 3). Peronella then replies that she (since she strives all day for picking up some money, although she is a woman who all day stays shut in at home) found the chance of selling for seven 'gigliati' the same old *dolium* by then neglected in a corner of the house, half covered with earth and merely taking up useful space. Now the buyer is inside the jar, checking it to see its state.

Happy at his wife's business dealings, more profitable than his own, the poor husband is glad to undress and climb into the *dolium*, to replace Giannello who, being in league with Peronella, immediately comes out of the jar, declaring that, for a definite valuation, it is necessary to scrape away all the dirt accumulated inside. And while the husband, inside the jar, tires himself to clean the different parts pointed out by Peronella, who meanwhile offers Giannello sexual satisfaction: 'Giannello il quale appieno non aveva quella mattina il suo disidero ancor fornito [...] a lei accostatosi [...] in quella guisa che negli ampi campi gli sfrenati cavalli e d'amor caldi le cavalle di Partia assaliscono, ad effetto recò il giovinil disidero'.[69] At the end with *utroque opere perfecto* (the jar cleaned, the lover satisfied), the husband carries the jar to the adulterer's house (*acceptis septem denariis calamitosus faber collo suo gerens dolium coactus est ad hospitium adulteri perferre*).[70] No further remark is needed to understand what Boccaccio did.

The second story of adulterous love, taken from the ninth book of the *Metamorphoses* by Boccaccio, is that of *Met.* 9, 14-31. Boccaccio's version

---

[69] *Dec.* 7, 2, 33-34 = *Met.* 9, 7, 5.
[70] *Met.* 9, 7, 6 = *Dec.* 7, 2, 34-36.

(*Decameron* 5, 10) is much shorter than the original and completely different in character. Whereas the Apuleian tale is particularly dreadful and appalling, full of witches and sorceresses, that of Boccaccio is more light-hearted, because, in his version of the facts, the guilty party is the husband (whose name is Pietro di Vinciolo) who, preferring handsome boys, neglects his wife. Nevertheless Boccaccio's tale is for long stretches very like Apuleius': cf. *Met.* 9, 22, 3: *Nam et opportune maritus foris apud naccam proximum cenitabat* with *Dec.* 5, 10, 26: 'Avvenne che, dovendo una sera andare a cena il marito con un suo amico, [...]'; *Met.* 9, 22, 6 / 23, 1 *puer admodum et adhuc lubrico genarum splendore conspicuus, adhuc adulteros ipse delectans. Hunc [...] mulier cenam iubet paratam adcumbere [...] multo celerius opinione rediens maritus adventat* with *Dec.* 5, 10, 26-27: 'un garzone, che era de' più belli e de' più piacevoli di Perugia [...] Ed essendosi la donna col giovane posti a tavola per cenare, ed ecco Pietro chiamò all'uscio che aperto gli fosse'. And again *Met.* 9, 23, 2-3: *Tunc uxor egregia [...] exsangui formidine trepidantem adulterum alveo ligno, quo frumenta confusa purgari consuerant, temere propter iacenti suppositum abscondit, ingenitaque astuta dissimulatio tanto flagitio, intrepidum mentita vultum, percontatur de marito cur utique contubernalis artissimi deserta cenula praematurus aforet* with *Dec.* 5, 10, 28-29: 'La donna, questo sentendo, si tenne morta, ma [...] essendo una sua loggetta vicina alla camera nella quale cenavamo, sotto una cesta da polli, che v'era il fece ricoverare [...]; e questo fatto, prestamente fece aprire al marito. Al quale entrato in casa ella disse: – Molto tosto l'avete voi trangugiata, questa cena –'.

Further comparison can be made of *Met.* 9, 24, 1-25, 2: *Contubernalis mei fullonis uxor, alioquin servati pudoris ut videbatur femina [...] occulta libidine prorumpit in adulterum quempiam. Cumque furtivo amplexus obiret adsidue, ipso illo denique momento quo nos lauti cenam petebamus, cum eodem illo iuvene miscebatur in venerem. Ergo nostra repente turbata praesentia, subitario ducta consilio, eundem illum subiectum contegit viminea cavea, quae [...] in rectum aggerata cumulum lacinias circumdatas suffusa candido fumo sulpuris inalbabat, eoque iam ut sibi videbatur tutissime celato mensam nobiscum secura participat. Interdum acerrimo gravique odore sulpuris iuvenis inescatus [...] utque est ingenium vivacis metalli, crebras ei starnutationes commovebat. Atque ut primum e regione mulieris pone tergum eius maritus acceperat sonum starnutationis – quod enim putaret ab ea profectum – solito sermone salutem ei fuerat imprecatus et iterato rursum et frequentato saepius, donec rei nimietate commotus quod res erat tandem suspicatur. Et impulsa mensa protenus remotaque cavea producit hominem crebros anhelitus aegre reflantem* [...], with *Dec.* 5, 10, 32-41: 'Pietro allora disse: – Dirolti. Essendo noi già posti a tavola [...] sentimmo presso di noi starnutire, di che noi né la prima volta né la seconda ce ne curammo; ma quegli che starnutito avea, starnutendo ancora la terza volta e la quarta e la quinta e molte altre, tutti ci fece maravigliare; di che Ercolano,[71] che alquanto turbato con la moglie era, per ciò che gran pezza ci avea fatti stare all'uscio senza aprirci, quasi con furia disse: 'Questo che vuol dire? Chi è questi che così starnutisce?'; e levatosi da tavola, andò verso una scala la quale assai vicina v'era, sotto la quale ero un chiuso di tavole [...] da riporvi, chi avesse voluto, alcuna cosa [...]. E parendogli che di quindi venisse il suono dello starnuto, aperse un usciuolo il quale v'era; e come aperto l'ebbe, subitamente n'uscì fuori il maggior puzzo di solfo del mondo [...] E poi che Ercolano aperto ebbe l'usciuolo e sfogato fu alquanto il puzzo, guardando dentro vide colui il quale starnutito avea e ancora starnutiva [...] per le quali cose la nostra cena turbata, io non solamente non la ho trangugiata, anzi non l'ho pure assaggiata, come io dissi'.

And finally we can show some examples which prove once and for all, how much Boccaccio depends on Apuleius: *Met* 9, 26, 1-2: *Haec recensente pistore iam dudum procax et temeraria mulier verbis execrantibus fullonis illius detestabatur uxorem: illam perfidam, illam impudicam, denique universi sexus grande dedecus, quae suo pudore postposito torique genialis calcato foedere larem mariti lupanari maculasset infamia iamque perdita nuptae dignitate prostitutae sibi nomen adsciverit; addebat et talis oportere vivas exuri feminas. Et tamen taciti vulneris et suae sordidae conscientiae commonita, quo maturius stupratorem suum tegminis cruciatu liberaret, identidem suadebat maritum temperius*, with *Dec.* 5, 10, 42-47: 'Udendo la donna queste cose [...] cominciò a dire: – Ecco belle cose! Ecco buona e santa donna che costei dee essere! Ecco fede d'onesta donna, ché mi sarei confessata da lei, sí spiritual mi pareva! [...] Che maladetta sia l'ora che ella nel mondo venne, ed ella altresí che viver si lascia, perfidissima e rea femina che ella dee essere, universal vergogna e vitupero di tutte le donne di questa terra; la quale, gittata via la sua onestà e la fede promessa al suo marito e l'onor di questo mondo, lui, che è così fatto uomo e così onorevole cittadino e che così bene la trattava, per un altro uomo non s'è vergognata di vituperare, e se medesima insieme con lui. Se Dio mi salvi, di così fatte femine non si vorrebbe aver misericordia: elle si vorrebbero occidere, elle si vorrebbon vive vive mettere nel fuoco e farne cenere. Poi, del suo amico

---

[71] The friend at whose house Pietro had gone to supper.

ricordandosi, il quale sotto la cesta assai presso di quivi aveva, cominciò a confortare Pietro che s'andasse al letto, per ciò che tempo n'era'.

In both tales the husbands refuse their wives' invitations and want to have supper. In Apuleius (*Met.* 9, 27, 2) Lucius, changed into an ass, but retaining all his human feelings, takes the opportunity to revenge himself for this woman's ill-treatments. While passing near the chest, where the young lover is hidden, and seeing that his fingertips protrude from it, he deliberately treads on them to crush them, so that the young man, crying out with pain, hurls out of the chest, thus revealing himself. Boccaccio tells the same episode as follows (*Dec.* 5, 10, 48-51): 'Avvenne che, essendo la sera certi lavoratori di Pietro venuti con certe cose dalla villa, e avendo messi gli asini loro senza dar lor bere, in una stalletta la quale allato alla loggetta era, l'un degli asini, che grandissima sete avea, tratto il capo dal capestro, era uscito dalla stalla, e ogni cosa andava fiutando, se forse trovasse dell'acqua; e così andando s'avvenne per me' la cesta sotto la quale era il giovinetto. Il quale avendo, per ciò che carpone gli conveniva stare, alquanto le dita di una mano stese in terra fuor della cesta, tanta fu la sua sventura, o sciagura che vogliam dire, che questo asino ve gli pose su piede, laonde egli, grandissimo dolore sentendo, mise un grande strido. Il quale udendo Pietro si meravigliò e avvidesi ciò esser dentro alla casa; per che, uscito dalla camera e sentendo ancora costui rammaricarsi, non avendogli ancora l'asino levato il piè d'in su le dita, ma premendol tuttavia forte, disse: – Chi è là? – e corso alla cesta, e quella levata, vide il giovinetto, il quale, oltre al dolore avuto delle dita premute dal piè dell'asino, tutto di paura tremava che Pietro alcun male non gli facesse. Il quale essendo da Pietro riconosciuto, sì come colui a cui Pietro per la sua cattività era andato lungamente dietro, essendo da lui domandato – che fai tu qui? –, niente a ciò gli rispose, ma pregollo che per l'amor di Dio non gli dovesse far male'.

But the two stories (as we have already remarked) end in a completely different way. In Apuleius' tale, the miller's wife, when she knew that her husband not only sodomized her young lover, but told everyone that he would apply for a divorce from her, was deeply enraged for being so insulted and found an old witch who murders him with her sorceries. In Boccaccio on the contrary, the trio find an easy way for acting in concert. On the close resemblances between Apuleius and Boccaccio Silvia Mattiacci, in her Introduction to Apuleius' *Met.* Book IX,[72] remarks: 'A noi interessa qui soprattutto la mirabile rielaborazione, nel *Decameron*, delle novelle del IX libro [...] la sezione più amata e imitata del romanzo [...]. Al ritorno del

---

[72] Mattiacci 1996, 22-23.

marito Peronella non mostra la freddezza e la consumata astuzia della moglie del *faber*, ma verbalizza in forma diretta la sua paura e disperazione, pur mostrandosi poi capace di prendere una rapida decisione. Il momento di timore e di esitazione di Peronella rende questa figura umanamente più simpatica e ci mostra l'evoluzione del personaggio che, nel corso della vicenda, si trasforma da inesperta giovinetta in donna abile e attiva, al punto da superare il modello, perché sarà sua l'idea di far ripulire il doglio al marito [...]'. In the image of the last scene 'all'esaltazione dell'intelligenza industriosa e all'emarginazione di ogni giudizio morale, s'accompagna in Boccaccio la sana e giovanile celebrazione dei sensi, che non conosce la crudezza espressiva e la brutale rapidità dell'azione finale dell'amante apuleiano. La scena, infatti, è indirettamente descritta mediante il ricorso a una splendida similitudine di probabile derivazione ovidiana, che allude ad altro codice espressivo, quello della furia d'amore degli animali, e che ci trasporta in un mondo panico, di irrefrenabili istinti naturali'. Even more profound is the reworking of the other tale (= *Dec.* 5, 10): 'Così, mentre Lucio definisce il mugniaio *bonus vir et adprime modestus*, in contrapposizione alla pessima moglie (IX 14), il narratore del *Decameron*, Dioneo, stende subito un'ombra sul marito, accennando nell'introduzione alla sua «disonestà» e aggiungendo poche righe dopo che egli si era sposato «forse più per ingannare altrui e diminuire la generale oppinion di lui avuta da tutti i perugini, che per vaghezza che egli ne avesse» [...] La lussuria della mugnaia è un vizio tra i tanti che possiede, mentre il gagliardo appetito sessuale della moglie di Pietro nasce dal suo corpo giovane e sano e dalla voglia insoddisfatta dal marito: se per Apuleio vittima della situazione è il marito, per il Boccaccio è la moglie'.[73]

Bibliography

Agrati G. – Magini M. L. 1989 (trad., introd. e note a cura di). Goffredo di Monmouth, *Storia dei re di Britannia,* Parma: Guanda.
Archibald E.A. 1991. *Apollonius of Tyre. Medieval and Renaissance Themes and Variations,* Cambridge: Brewer.
Chiarini G. 1983. 'Esogamia e incesto nell'*Historia Apollonii regis Tyri*', *MD* 10-11, 267-292.
Cilento V. 1962 (a cura di). Plutarco, *Diatriba isiaca e Dialoghi delfici,* Firenze: Sansoni.
Dronke P. 1978 (edit. with introd. and notes by). Bernardus Silvestris, *Cosmographia,* Leiden: Brill.

---

[73] *Ibid.*, 24-25.

Ernout A. – Meillet A. 1959. *Dictionnaire étymologique de la langue latine,* Paris: Klinksieck.

Fedeli P. 1988[2]. 'Il romanzo', in G. Cavallo – P. Fedeli – A. Giardina (a cura di), *Lo spazio letterario di Roma antica,* vol. 1, *La produzione del testo,* Roma: Salerno Editrice, 343-373.

Ferrari F. 2001 (ed. con testo greco a fronte a cura di). *Menandro e la Commedia Nuova,* Torino: Einaudi.

Fo A. 2002 (ed., trad. e postfaz. a cura di). Apuleio, *Metamorfosi,* Trento: Frassinelli.

Garbugino G. 2004. *Enigmi della* Historia Apollonii regis Tyri, Bologna: Pàtron.

Garbugino G. 2008. Rev. of G.A.A. Kortekaas, *Commentary of the* Historia Apollonii regis Tyri, *Gnomon* 80, 301-307.

Gianotti G.F. 2000. 'Per una rilettura delle opere di Apuleio', in G. Magnaldi, G.F. Gianotti (a cura di), *Apuleio. Storia del testo e interpretazioni,* Alessandria: Dell'Orso, 141-182.

Grilli A. 2000. 'Titoli e struttura interna del romanzo di Apuleio', *Atene e Roma* 44, 121-134.

Gwyn Griffiths, J. 1970. *Plutarch's De Iside et Osiride,* Cambridge: University of Wales Press.

Helm R. 1970[2] (ed.). *Fabii Planciadis Fulgentii opera,* Stuttgardiae: Teubner.

Keulen W. 2006. 'Il romanzo latino', in L. Graverini, W. Keulen, A. Barchiesi, *Il romanzo antico,* Roma: Carocci, 131-167.

Kock Th. 1888. *Comicorum Atticorum fragmenta,* vol. III, Lipsiae: Teubner.

Laird A. 1990. 'Person, 'Persona' and Representations in Apuleius' *Metamorphoses, MD* 25, 130-163.

Martin R. 1970. 'Le sens de l'expression *Asinus aureus* et la signification du roman apuléien', *REL* 48, 332-354.

Martos J. 2003. Apuleius, *Las Metamorfosis o El asno de oro,* Madrid: Consejo Superior de Investigaciones Científicas.

Mason H. J. 1975. 'Lucius at Corinth', *Phoenix* 25, 160-165.

Mattiacci S. 1996 (a cura di). *Apuleio, le novelle dell'adulterio (Metamorfosi IX),* con testo a fronte, Firenze: Le Lettere.

Méthy N. 1999. 'La communication entre l'homme et la divinité dans les *Metamorphoses* d'Apulée', *LEC* 67, 43-56.

Monat P. 1973 (introd., texte crit. trad. par). Lactance, *Institutions divines,* livre V, tome I, Paris: Cerf.

Morelli C.1913. 'Apuleiana', *SIFC* 20, 183-185.

Moreschini C. 1973. 'Sulla fama di Apuleio nella tarda antichità', in W. van den Boer et alii (a cura di), *Romanitas et Christianitas. Studia I. H. Waszink oblata,* Amsterdam – London: North-Holland Publishing Company, 243-248.

Morin G. 1958 (ed.). Jerome, *Tractatus in psalmos,* Turnhout: Brepols.

Norden E. 1986 (ed. it. a cura di Benedetta Heinemann Campana). *La prosa d'arte antica,* t. I, Roma: Salerno Editrice.

Pastorino A. 1971 (a cura di). Decimo Magno Ausonio, *Opera,* Torino: UTET.

Pavloskis Z. 1978. *The Story of Apollonius King of Tyre,* Lawrence (Kansas): Coronado Press.

Penwill J.L. 1975. 'Slavish pleasures and profitless curiosity: fall and redemption in Apuleius' *Metamorphoses*', *Ramus* 4, 49-82.

Penwill J.L. 1998. 'Reflections on a 'Happy Ending': The Case of Cupid and Psyche', *Ramus* 27, 160-182.

Perry B.E. 1967. *Ancient Romances,* Berkeley – Los Angeles: University of California Press.

Reitzenstein R.A. 1912. *Das Märchen von Amor und Psyche bei Apuleius*, Leipzig – Berlin: Teubner.
Rîncioy D. 2002. *Histoire et mentalité dans l'oeuvre de Gustave Flaubert (Étude sur la 'Correspondance')*, Ploiestii Editura: Universității d'iri Pliești.
Sandy G.N. 1972. 'Knowledge and Curiosity in Apuleius' *Metamorphoses, Latomus* 31, 179-183.
Shumate N.J. 1988. 'The Augustinian pursuit of false values as a conversion motif in Apuleius' *Metamorphoses', Phoenix* 42, 35-60.
Soverini P. 1983 (a cura di), *Scrittori della Storia Augusta*, I, Torino: UTET.
Walde A. – Hoffmann J. B. 1938. *Lateinisches Etymologisches Wörterbuch*, Heidelberg: Carl Winter Universitätsverlag.
Walsh P.G. 1995 (new translation by). Apuleius, *The Golden Ass*, Oxford: Oxford University Press.
Webb C. C. J. 1909 (rec. et proleg., app. crit., comm., ind. instruxit). Iohannis Saresberiensis episcopi Carnotensìs *Policratici sive De nugis curialium et vestigiis philosophorum libri 8*, London: Clarendon Press, 2 vols.
Weyman C. 1893, 'Studien zu Apuleius und seine Nachahmern', *Sitz.-Ber. Königl. Bayr. Akad. der Wissensch. philos.-philol. -hist. Kl.*, 11, 321-382.
White, R.J. 1975, *The Interpretation of Dreams: Oneirocritica by Artemidorus*. Park Ridge, New Jersey: Noyes.
Willis. J. 1994 (repr. of 1970^2). *Ambrosii Theodosii Macrobii Commentarii in Somnium Scipionis*, Lipsiae: Teubner.
Winkler J.J. 1985. *Auctor & Actor: A Narratological Reading of Apuleius' Golden Ass*, Berkeley & London: University of California Press.
Zink M. 1867. *Der Mythologe Fulgentius*, II, Würzburg: A. Stuber's Buchhandlung.

From word to image: notes on the Renaissance reception of Apuleius's *Metamorphoses*

MICHELE RAK
Università di Siena

Introduction

The tale (*fabella*) of Cupid and Psyche, narrated by Apuleius in *The Golden Ass*, entered early modern Europe after being rediscovered in the Middle Ages. Around 1338, Giovanni Boccaccio possessed a copy of Apuleius's work. Since the beginning of Italian humanism, the myth of Cupid and Psyche has been spread and variously interpreted throughout the world, thus becoming a universally recognized symbol of love in the arts. Over the last five centuries, the tale of Cupid and Psyche has been eclectically represented in sculpture, painting, drawing, theatre, music, and dance. Different cultures have often adapted Apuleius's tale to their ideas of love and beauty, resulting in a multifaceted representation of the story in frescoes, paintings, statues, drawings, panels, plays and literary works. In this essay, I would like to focus on the European artistic representation of Cupid and Psyche, traditionally perceived as symbolic icons and often seen as symbolizing philosophical dichotomies such as the body and soul, the different sides of beauty, the consequences of envy – often defined as 'the queen of the court'.

This paper also analyzes how some intellectuals read and interpreted the myth of Eros and Psyche when novels and tales began to circulate among Italian humanists. From humanistic elite circles *The Golden Ass* and the tale of Cupid and Psyche spread in Europe following different routes. Here, I would like to refer specifically to eight literary and visual sources which contain different interpretations of Apuleius's tale. Each of the works analyzed reflects various ways in which love has been conceived in different cultural contexts. In early modern Europe, the myth of Cupid and Psyche circulated through: (i) printed editions (*princeps*, 1469), translations and literary adaptations. These included passages from *Hypnerotomachia Po-*

liphili, 1499, containing 170 engraved images; Matteo Maria Boiardo's translations, Venice, 1517-1519, containing 62 engraved images; Agnolo Firenzuola's translation of the first ten books of Apuleius's work, 1525; (ii) poetic paraphrases written in different metres containing singing sections. These include Galeotto Del Carretto's *Nozze di Psiche e Cupidine*, Alessandro Miniziano, Milan, 1502?, later edited by Augustino di Vimercate, Milan 1520, Io. Antonio da Borgho, Milan, 1545 (iii) Editions of Apuleius's work containing engraved images; (iv) Theatre adaptations including a play performed at Blois Castle for the wedding celebrations of Anne d'Alencon and William Paleologos.[1]

Towards the end of the fifteenth century many intellectuals began to read and interpret Apuleius's work. *The Golden Ass* was mainly read as a pagan and lascivious text whose meanings had to be decoded and manipulated. It narrates the transformation of Lucius into an ass and his encounters with different figures – women, bandits, violent youngsters. Through a series of trials and changes undergone by its characters, *The Golden Ass* reflects upon the difference between sex and love. Stylistically elegant and imaginative, Apuleius's text also deals with magic and astrology. The tale of Cupid and Psyche is a section of *The Golden Ass* which analyzes the ephemeral boundaries between human and animal as well as the idea of transformation experienced by the self when detached from the body. Lucius and Psyche experience sex and body transformations, achieving their goals by overcoming trials and misfortunes – Lucius finally gaining supreme knowledge and Psyche acquiring divine beauty. They share curiosity to the extent of risking their lives. Lucius experiments with magic, Psyche tries desperately to see and kill what cannot be seen or killed.

Towards the end of the fifteenth century humanists in Ferrara read two texts which dated back to the second century. Both texts narrate stories of transformations which were probably inspired by Lucius of Patras' tales (2nd century?). The first text is *Lucius or the Ass* hopefully ascribed to Lucian. It is a short story of changes and sex, translated into vernacular probably by Niccolò Leoniceno. The second is *Metamorphoses* by Apuleius of Madauros (120/125.-170/190.), translated by Boiardo and published in 1518. *Metamorphoses* narrates two stories which both deal with tropes such as mistake and redemption, magic, laughter and eroticism. The first story narrates Lucius's transformation into an ass and then into a human being. The second story narrates the tale of Cupid and Psyche. Some of the printed editions of *Metamorphoses* circulating at the court of Ercole I d'Este con-

---

[1] See Gaidano 1897.

tained engraved images which became models for artists and painters who began representing the story of Cupid and Psyche. It was thus in early modern Ferrara, Rome and Modena that the iconic, allusive and spiritual journey of Psyche began.

In early modern Europe, Cupid and Psyche became a fashionable subject in painting. From decorative and narrative painting to frescoes, from public to domestic spaces, the story of Cupid and Psyche became a popular subject for interior decorations and privately owned objects. Some of the most important representations of Apuleius's tale are: (i) Jacopo Sellaio's *cassone* panel, c.1473, Fitzwilliam Museum, Cambridge; (ii) Ercole de Roberti's, *Sala di Amore e Psiche*, c.1487, Villa di Belriguardo, Voghiera;[2] (iii) Raphael's *Amore e Psiche*, 1518, Farnesina, Rome. Raphael's paintings influenced some works at the Palazzo Te in Mantua frescoed by Giulio Romano who, between 1526 and 1528, also engraved images for Boiardo's edition of *The Golden Ass*. Raphael also influenced Perin del Vaga's paintings on Cupid and Psyche at Castel Sant'Angelo (1545). Raphael probably influenced Niccolò dell'Abate's *Nozze di Psiche*, (1540-1543), *Camerino del Paradiso*, Rocca dei Boiardo, Scandiano; (iv) Francesco Primaticcio's fresco of Cupid and Psyche, 1533-1535, (destroyed in 1757), Chamber of Francesco I, Fontainebleau. Francesco Primaticcio worked with Giulio Romano in Mantua and with Niccolò dell'Abate in Scandiano.

In early modern Europe, sketches and prints narrating the tale of Cupid and Psyche circulated widely, helping spread further Apuleius's tale. The latter also circulated through games and cards on which the story was often represented. Psyche and Patience were part of Matteo Maria Boiardo's *Tarocchi*, a poem on *trionfi* cards, consisting of 78 tercets and 2 sonnets which appeared in Boiardo's unusual deck; possibly for a board game whose suits displayed four human passions: fear, jealousy, hope and love. These were enriched by 22 *trionfi* cards dedicated to mythological, historical, intellectual and biblical figures.[3] Apuleius's work and related images also served as meditative icons on love. To some neo-Platonic humanists Psyche symbolized the ascending journey of the soul from the world of the senses to heaven.

In early modern Europe, the circulation of texts on Cupid encouraged a philosophical analysis of the double aspect of Cupid. On the one hand, Cupid was seen as a gentle and divine being who unveils his body to Psyche's human beauty. His love for Psyche is unique, pure, eternal and celestial. On

---

[2] See degli Arienti 1972.
[3] See Boiardo 1993.

the other, Cupid is perceived as Eros, a dangerous, troubled, disturbing infantile god who strikes indiscriminately. However, he moves the world which would end without him. Eros is so uncontrollable that he appears to be a wild being. Ladies at the court of King Louis XIV saw Eros as a beast; so did Walt Disney in the 20th century.

The wide circulation of *The Golden Ass* was partly due to meditation on the body in Renaissance Italy. The human body, both male and female, and its changes, became a focal point of observation in Renaissance painting, visual arts, medicine, and scientific treatises. The European discovery of new territories and cultures also encouraged the analysis of the idea of metamorphosis. In such a context, Apuleius's engagement with transformation and disguise became a model for early modern European theatre, fairy tales, alchemy, and magic.

The tale of Cupid and Psyche partly repeats the general narrative of *The Golden Ass* by exploring the following themes: (i) contact between a human being and a divine being through Eros and envy; (ii) arrogant desire (*hybris*) and curiosity (*curiositas*) in wishing to see what is forbidden to human beings; (iii) consequent punishment in being taken away from Cupid's palace and being forced to embark on a painful journey on the verge of death; (iv) divine intervention – Cupid saves Psyche, Isis saves Lucius; (v) final apotheosis represented with a wedding celebrated on Mount Olympus. The narrative sequence of Apuleius's tale symbolizes an edifying religious experience of the soul-Psyche, in the shape of a butterfly, from error to salvation.

Over the last few centuries, painters, decorators, graphic artists, and translators have variously represented or interpreted passages from Cupid and Psyche. I would like to suggest that in *The Golden Ass* some terms and passages have a strongly visual impact which has variously inspired other forms of art. Visual representations of Apuleius's work have reflected different perceptions of physical love in history. Nonetheless, visual and literary representations of Cupid and Psyche produced in different times and societies seem commonly to interpret Apuleius's tale as a universal symbol of love and pleasure. The tale of Cupid and Psyche is set within a rich narrative structure describing a variety of settings, actions and dialogues. It is a detailed and flexible text with a strong visual component that has facilitated its reception among different cultures. Over the last few centuries, some passages from the tale of Cupid and Psyche have become artistic icons. Several paintings and prints have variously represented characters, places and episodes from Apuleius's tale such as Zephyr gently raising Psyche, Cupid's palace, nocturnal sexual intercourse, Psyche using a lamp to see her sleeping lover, the role of Juno, Ceres and Venus, and the final episode of Cupid united with Psyche.

The Villa Farnesina

In sixteenth-century art, Raphael's *Loggia di Amore e Psiche* (Villa Farnesina, Rome) became a model.[4] Researchers have been able to establish that Raphael drew from two illustrated literary sources namely Matteo Maria Boiardo's *Asino d'oro* and Niccolò da Correggio's *Psiche*.[5] The Loggia decorated by Raphael served as the hall to the house of Agostino Chigi, a rich Sienese banker. Raphael's celebratory painting represents the gods on Mount Olympus attending Chigi's wedding. His bride, like Psyche, had to overcome difficulties in order to gain status and be accepted in contemporary elitist circles.

Raphael's decorations of Chigi's house entrance loggia consist of 14 frescoed spandrels and two large ceiling pictures which simulate tapestries representing the assembly of the gods and the final nuptial banquet. According to some scholars, a further project aiming at decorating the walls of the loggia with pictures made to look like tapestries and representing Psyche's deeds on earth was never completed. Accordingly, the Loggia would have been divided into three sections: (i) frescoed walls representing the period on earth; (ii) frescoed spandrels representing life in heaven; (iii) ceiling pictures simulating tapestries and representing the final triumph of Psyche and Cupid. Raphael's sketches, some of which bear his signature, were mainly painted by his pupils Raffaellino del Colle, Giovan Francesco Penni, Giulio Romano, and Giovanni da Udine. Scholars have pointed out that Raphael adapted and modified the tale of Cupid and Psyche. Some of the artist's sketches on this subject were printed and regarded both as painting models and as images supporting narrations or representations of Apuleius's tale.

Psyche, loved by Cupid and envied by Venus for her beauty, breaks the rule that prevents mortals from seeing gods. Consequently, Psyche has to

---

[4] The house of the Sienese banker Agostino Chigi became an artistic and architectural model in early fifteenth-century Rome. Chigi's house was commissioned as a venue for business and entertainment. It was designed by Baldassarre Peruzzi (Siena 1481 – Rome 1536) between 1506 and 1509 and located in the vicinity of Porta Settimiana at the feet of the Roman Janiculum Hill. Peruzzi drew from Vitruvius's *De Architectura* to design Chigi's house. In 1590 the villa was bought by Cardinal Alessandro Farnese and renamed as *Farnesina*.

[5] See Da Correggio 1507.

overcome a series of trials in order to marry Cupid on Mount Olympus. Psyche's story is frescoed in ten spandrels situated in the loggia at the villa Farnesina. They represent (i) Venus pointing out Psyche to the young Cupid; (ii) Cupid pointing out Psyche to the three Graces; (iii) Venus, Ceres and Juno; (iv) Venus standing in her chariot drawn by doves; (v) Venus, Jupiter and Mercury; (vi) Psyche's trial; (vii) Psyche's trial; (viii) Cupid and Jupiter; (ix) Cupid pleading his case before Jupiter; (x) Mercury bearing aloft Psyche, to whom immortality has been granted. For the representation of Cupid's trophies artists drew from Niccolò da Correggio's *Psiche* published in 1491.[6] As some sketches seem to suggest, the cycle of frescoes in the loggia may have extended to the lower part of the walls. The Villa Farnesina is an ideal setting for one who wishes to analyze how literature and painting

---

[6] Restorations have modified parts of the Loggia. In 1693, Abbott Felini employed by Duke Ranuccio Farnese, the intellectual Giovan Pietro Bellori and the painter Carlo Maratti worked together on a restoration project of the loggia for which they used lapis and pastel. Other frescoed areas have also been restored (see Shearman, 1964). In the *Sala delle prospettive,* on the second floor of Chigi's villa, the wedding celebration of Agostino Chigi and Francesca Odescalchi took place on 28 August 1519. Pope Leo X attended the wedding banquet. The classically decorated *sala delle Prospettive* was used for banquets, meetings, celebrations and staged performances. Peruzzi's frescoed loggia in the *Sala* is divided by Doric pilasters and overlooks on a landscape. The frieze in the Sala represents stories from Ovid's *Metamorphoses* namely the Flood (*Metamorphoses*, I, 253-312), Deucalion and Pyrrha (*Metamorphoses,* I, 314-414), the Creation and the story of Apollo and Daphne. The northern wall in the *Sala* is decorated with love stories representing Venus and Adonis, Bacchus and Ariadne, Pelops and Oenomaus, Pegasus and Hippocrene, the triumph of Venus). The eastern wall in the Sala deals with the theme of night and day and it represents Selene and Endymion, Aurora, Tithonus and Phosphoros, the Horae and Apollo driving the chariot of the sun across the sky, Apollo among the Hyperboreans, Arion, Pan and Syrinx. The gods frescoed below the frieze are: Mercury, Ceres, Apollo, Venus, Diana, Mars, Neptune, Minerva, Vulcan, Jupiter, Juno and Saturn. Impressive frescoes appear in Chigi's bedroom. Giovanni Antonio Bazzi, also known as *Sodoma* (Vercelli, 1477– Siena, 1549) decorated this room with stories from Alexander's life including the marriage of Alexander and Roxana. The coffering on the ceiling include representations from Ovid's *Metamorphoses*, namely the death of Marsyas, hunting of the Calydonian boar, the judgment of Paris, Apollo and Daphne, the rape of Europa, Mercury, Aglauros and Herse, the judgment of Midas, Diana and Actaeon. Four central stories represent Proserpina's kidnap. Arethusa and Ceres, Jupiter with Mercury and Mars. The representation of mythological themes drawn from Ancient Roman literature seems to suggest that artists decorating Chigi's house read and discussed a core of chosen literary texts in order to select specific stories and characters to be represented in frescoes. For a detailed analysis of the interior decorations of Villa Farnesina see Hermanin 1927, Saxl 1934, Weibel 1957, Shearman 1964, Vertova 1979, La Villa Farnesina 1984, Marek 1984, Lippincott 1990, Noireau 1991, McGrath 1995 and Varoli-Piazza 2002.

work on a common subject. After 1511, other frescoed rooms in the villa were inspired by literary sources. On the ground floor, along the walls in the *Sala del fregio,* there is a Sienese sixteenth [see n.4. above]-century frescoed frieze by Baldassare Peruzzi. To paint his mythologically-inspired frieze, Peruzzi drew both from Boethius's *De Consolatione Philosophiae* and Ovid's *Metamorphoses*. Starting from the marble herm, the frescoes on the eastern wall in the *Sala del fregio* represent the rape of Europa, Jupiter and Danae, Semele, Diana and Actaeon, Midas, Neptune and Amphitrite. The southern wall in the *Sala del fregio* is decorated with sea gods, river gods, the kingdom of Dionysus, Marsia, Meleager, and Orpheus. To paint these subjects, Peruzzi drew from Ovid's *Metamorphoses*. The northern wall and part of the eastern wall depict the labors of Hercules. The frescoes in the *Sala del fregio* symbolize the labors of work and love.

The vault in the *Loggia di Galatea,* frescoed by Baldassarre Peruzzi between 1510 and 1511, is inspired by astrological literature. The vault is divided into three sections and 26 panels. The central octagon in the ceiling panels represents the Chigi coat of arms. The vault depicts the position of planets on the 29th of November 1466, the presumed birth date of the patron, whose detailed horoscope is also represented in the ceiling panels. A series of hexagonal panels represent the planets Mercury, Venus, Mars, Jupiter, Saturn, Apollo, the sun god, and Diana, goddess of the moon. The constellations of the Zodiac are also represented with the symbols and the myths to which they are traditionally associated. These include images narrating the story of Zeus and Leda who were the parents of Castor and Pollux (also known as the Dioscuri). The triangular panels situated above the lunettes depict the position of planets and constellations which include Decans (*paranatellonta*), triangle, Pegasus, Andromeda, Dolphin, Bow, Lyre, Altar, Corona Borealis, Crater, Crow and Snake, Canis Major, Argos, Auriga, Eridanus and Cygnus. Two more constellations represent Perseus and Cynosura (*Ursa Minor*) and Helice (*Ursa Major*: cf. Saxl 1934).

In early modern European art, representations of metamorphoses mainly drew from both Apuleius' *Metamorphoses* (named *The Golden Ass* by Saint Augustine, *De civitate Dei*, XVlll.18) and Ovid's fifteen-book poem *Metamorphoses,* which became the most popular text in the European Renaissance. The stories represented in Sebastiano del Piombo's lunettes in the *Sala di Galatea* (Farnesina) drew from Ovid's *Metamorphoses.* Sebastiano del Piombo was born in Venice in 1485 and died in Rome in 1547. In 1511 he moved from Venice to Rome and became part of Chigi's little court. Del Piombo's lunettes are mythologically-inspired frescoes representing myths of the air: (i) Tereus chasing Philomela and Procne; (ii) Aglauros and Herse; Daedalus and Icarus; (iii) Juno in her chariot drawn by peacocks; (iv) Scylla's cutting of Nisus' lock; (v) the fall of Perdix; (vi) Boreas kidnapping Orithyia, Zephyr and Flora. Peruzzi's mythological frescoes depict transformations into birds which fly away like the soul.

Between 1512 and 1514, Sebastiano del Piombo worked in the Loggia of Chigi's house. Here he frescoed Polyphemus and the nymph Galatea. Between 1511 and 1512, Raphael also completed his first painting in Chigi's house: the Triumph of Galatea. For this mythological subject Raphael drew from Poliziano's *Stanze* (*Stanza* 118), in which the sea-nymph is described in a chariot drawn by dolphins. Galatea is surrounded by Nereids, tritons, sea horses and four small boys with Cupid's bows and arrows. One of the two dolphins drawing Galatea's chariot is biting an octopus. Drawing from Oppian's *Halieutica*, this detail has been interpreted as a symbol of the triumph of good over evil.

Further receptions in art and literature

Between 1527 and 1528, Giulio Romano (1499-1546) frescoed the *Camera di Amore e Psiche* at Palazzo Te in Mantua, a sumptuous building with gardens, fish ponds and a secret apartment decorated with stuccos and frescoes. Once situated on an island, Palazzo Te was commissioned by Federico II Gonzaga. Before moving to Mantua, Romano had worked with Francesco Penni and Raphael on the decoration of Chigi's house loggia. In 1520, Romano inherited Raphael's workshop, some of the artist's sketches and unfinished work. Giulio Romano's decorations of the *Camera di Amore e Psiche* in Mantua drew from Apuleius's tale, employing a different narrative path from Raphael's loggia.[7] To decorate the *Camera di Amore e Psiche*, Giulio Romano used simple materials to achieve an effect of grandiosity. He

---

[7] Invited by Duke Federico II, Giulio Romano moved to Mantua in October 1524. During his period in Rome, Giulio Romano was advised by Baldassarre Castiglione, ambassador to Rome, to send to Mantua some of his projects, sketches and models whilst working on some unfinished work by Raphael. Duke Federico II Gonzaga (1500-1540) appointed Giulio Romano as *vicario,* painter, architect and city planner at the Gonzaga court. Once in Mantua, both Romano and Castiglione went to see a building in the countryside which would become a palace for leisure and entertainment, resembling the *Villa Farnesina*. The Duke required the retention of the old walls and the design of a building for occasional entertainment.

also looked at images circulating in Raphael's and Michelangelo's workshop. Palazzo Te was built for leisurely entertainment and was often used by the Gonzaga family to receive and honour important guests. In 1530, Charles V visited Palazzo Te which was decorated with friezes, stuccos and with some of the finest examples of Renaissance paintings. Francesco da Bologna (also known as *Primaticcio*) worked on the decorations of Palazzo Te too. In 1531, he moved to the court of France where he brought some of his sketches on the subject of Cupid and Psyche.

In 1523, Agnolo Firenzuola, a Tuscan priest (Florence 1493 – Prato 1543), wrote a re-interpreted version of *The Golden Ass*. Firenzuola's work was written in the Tuscan literary language and first published in 1550. Often reprinted, this version of Apuleius's work is a discussion on the body and the disturbing similarities between humans and animals. In Firenzuola's book, Lucius regains his human condition after the apparition of his dead lover.[8]

A story of bodies, birds and donkeys

Readers, translators and artists have often been interested in how the theme of the body is discussed in *The Golden Ass*. Between 1525 and 1532, Vicenzo Tamagni, a pupil of Giulio Romano, frescoed 17 scenes in the *Sala dell'Asino d'oro* at Rocca dei Rossi castle (San Secondo).[9] Tamagni depicted

---

[8] See the following editions of Firenzuola's work: Apuleio, *Dell'asino d'oro, tradotto per Menser Angelo Firenzuola fiorentino*, In Vinegia, appresso Gabriel Giolito de Ferrari 1550 Biblioteca Apostolica Vaticana (BAV segn. R.G.Classici VI.367); Apuleio. *Dell'asino d'oro. Tradotto per M. Angelo Firenzuola fiorentino. Nuovamente da molti errori di voci toscane, mai intese, corretto, e con le figure a' suoi luoghi adornato*, In Vinegia, appresso Gabriel Giolito de' Ferrari, 1565 (BAV segn. Capponi V.458); Apuleio, *Dell'asino d'oro. Tradotto per M. Agnolo Firenzuola fiorentino. Di nuovo ricorretto, e ristampato*. In Firenze, per Filippo Giunti, 1598 (BAV segn. Ferraioli.V.5798). Firenzuola joined a monastic order founded in 1020 by San Giovanni Gualberto in Vallombrosa. The Vallombrosan order was a branch of the Benedictine order whose monastic rules were based on hermitage and abstention from work. Firenzuola was appointed Superior of the order in Rome during the papacy of Leo X and Clemens VII. In 1526, Firenzuola, although still receiving emoluments, was dispensed from his vows due to his lascivious lifestyle.

[9] See Annaratone 1976 which contains some Venetian engraved images resembling the frescoes in San Secondo. Tamagni's seventeen paintings represent: (i) Lucius' journey to Thessaly where he is stays at Milo's house. Milo's wife, Pamphile, is a witch who transforms herself into a bird by rubbing her body with some magic ointment; (ii) Helped by Milo and Pamphile's lascivious maid, Fotis, Lucius rubs his body with the wrong ointment and turns into an ass; (iii) robbers break into Milo's house, and steal Lucius to carry

the journey of Lucius-ass from Milo's house, as told by Apuleius in Book III. Tamagni represented a process of body metamorphosis from animal into human form, drawing partly from some of the engraved images contained in Boiardo's edition of *The Golden Ass*.

Conclusion

This essay is an extract from ongoing research on how European cultures have used the tale of Cupid and Psyche to look at the idea of love. This research analyzes European texts and paintings based on Apuleius's myth from the Middle Ages to contemporary times. In so doing, my approach cannot be framed within the individual histories of literature, art or classics. Some passages narrated by Apuleius have been used in a variety of contexts to symbolize, visualize and reflect on moral values and class behaviour. Moreover, this study aims at reconstructing how different societies have changed the original narrative sequence of Apuleius's tale: Zephyr kidnapping Psyche, Venus's anger, the final wedding celebration on Mount Olympus, are some of the most popular episodes from the legend of Cupid and Psyche which different societies have chosen to represent their love stories.

Cultures use images and texts to communicate their ideas. Language and art produce icons and myths which shape traditions, perceptions and cultural identities. Communities use texts and works of art to hand on their heritage and, in some instances, to enforce it upon other communities. This interdisciplinary study has looked at the ways in which some European societies have represented love through literature and art. It has been demonstrated

---

away their booty; (iv) Lucius is beaten up by the robbers; (v) Lucius is taken to the robbers' cave where he hears the tale of Cupid and Psyche and meets Charite; (vi) Lucius and Charite try to escape from the cave; (vii) Tlepolemus, Charite's lover, helps Lucius and Charite to escape from the cave; (viii) Lucius is tormented by a boy who is later killed by a bear; (ix) the furious boy's mother plans to kill Lucius by sodomizing him with a burnt stick; (x) Lucius is sold to false priests and (xi) risks his life; (xii) Lucius is caught eating some food remains by some slaves; (xiii) the slaves inform their master who takes him into the *triclinium* and tests (xiv) his human taste for food and (xv) sex; (xvi) Lucius performs in the arena; (xvi) desperate, Lucius escapes to the port of Corinth and falls asleep. He dreams of Isis who gives him instructions for his re-transformation through participation in her festival. Following Isis' instructions, Lucius finds the antidote, eats some roses and changes back into human form. He then becomes a priest of Isis. (xvii) Lucius' is a transformation from a disturbing bodily dimension into a religious dimension. For a detailed analysis of *The Golden Ass* in Renaissance art see Scrivano 1993, Rossi 1993, Degl'Innocenti 2000, Acocella 2001.

that in Renaissance Europe a process of rediscovery and interpretation of the idea of love, as discussed in classical sources, began. In this essay, I have focused on the role played by classical sources in representing love and transformations in early modern Italian culture. This study is an aspect of an ongoing project aimed at organizing an exhibition on love in European culture.

Bibliography

Acocella, M. 2001 *L'asino d'oro nel Rinascimento. Dai volgarizzamenti alle raffigurazioni pittoriche*. Ravenna.

Annaratone, C. 1976. *Apuleio: Le metamorfosi o l'asino* d'oro. Milan.

Boiardo, M.M. 1993. *Tarocchi* [ed. S. Foà]. Rome.

Da Correggio, N. 1507. *Opere del Illustre & Excellentissimo Signor Nicolò da Correggio intitolate la Psiche & la Aurora*. Venice.

Degli Arienti, S. 1972. *De Triumphis Religionis, 1496 : Art and life at the court of Ercole I d'Este: the De triumphis religionis of Giovanni Sabadino degli Arienti* [ed.. W. L. Gundersheimer]. Geneva.

Degl'Innocenti, R. 2000. 'La stanza di Apuleio nella Rocca di San Secondo', *Aurea Parma* 89: Fasc.I, Gennaio-Aprile.

Gaidano, C. 1897. 'Una commedia poco nota di Galeotto Del Carretto', *Giornale storico della letteratura italiana* 15: 368–376.

Hermanin, F. 1927. *La Farnesina*, Bergamo.

La Villa Farnesina 1984. *La Villa Farnesina. I luoghi di Raffaello*. Rome.

Lippincott, K. 1990. 'Two Astrological Ceilings Reconsidered: the Sala di Galatea in the Villa Farnesina and the Sala del Mappamondo a Caprarola,' *Journal of the Warburg and Courtauld Institutes* 53: 185-196.

McGrath, Mary Quinlan 1984. 'The astrological Vault of the Villa Farnesina: Agostino Chigi's Rising Sign, *Journal of the Warburg and Courtauld Institutes* 47: 91-105.

McGrath, Mary Quinlan 1995. 'The Villa Farnesina, time-telling conventions and renaissance astrological practice', *Journal of the Warburg and Courtauld Institutes* 58: 29-51.

Marek, Michaela 1984. 'Raffaels Loggia di Psiche in der Farnesina. Überlegungen zu Rekonstruktion und Deutung', *Jahrbuch der Berliner Museen* 26: 257–290.

Noireau, C. 1991. *La Lampe de Psyché*. Paris.

Rossi, S. 1993. *La Rocca di San Secondo*. Parma.

Saxl, F. 1934. *La Fede astrologica di Agostino Chigi*. Rome.

Scrivano, R. 1993. *Il modello e l'esecuzione. Studi rinascimentali e manieristici*. Naples.

Shearman, J. 1964. 'Die Loggia der Psyche in der Villa Farnesina und die Probleme der letzten Phase von Raffaels graphischen Stil', *Jahrbuch der Kunsthistorischen Sammlungen in Wien* 60: 59-100.

Varoli-Piazza, R, 2002. *Raffaello: La Loggia di Amore e Psiche alla Farnesina*. Milan.

Vertova, L. 1979. 'Cupid and Psyche in Renaissance painting before Raphael', *Journal of the Warburg and Courtauld Institutes* 42: 104-121.

Weibel, A.C. 1957. 'The Story of Psyche', *Bulletin of the Wadsworth Atheneum* 1957: 13-16.

Love on a wallpaper: Apuleius in the boudoir

CHRISTIANE REITZ
Rostock

LORENZ WINKLER-HORAČEK
Berlin

1. Introduction

A decorative wallpaper in grisaille which depicts the story of Amor and Psyche is the focus of our research project.[1] This wallpaper consists of a sequence of twelve images. Several copies are preserved, among them one complete set in Rostock and one nearby in the ducal palace in Bad Doberan on the Baltic.[2] The wallpapers were designed by the French painters Merry-Joseph Blondel (1781-1853) and Louis Lafitte (1770-1828). The latter is famous for his decorations of the Château de Malmaison for Empress Joséphine. The Amor and Psyche wallpapers were first printed by the atelier Dufour in Paris from 1815 onward, and were sold (from 1865 in a reprint by the manufacture Defossé) until at least 1924. They were evidently a commercial success.[3]

---

[1] See Reitz/Winkler 2008a for brief information and Winkler/Reitz 2008b for a more detailed treatment in connection with an exhibition (Berlin and Rostock 2009).

[2] The Rostock exemplar is displayed in the Schifffahrtsmuseum in Rostock, formerly Kunst- und Altertumsmuseum. For its history see Reißmann 2003 and 1996. The wallpaper in Bad Doberan was acquired during the erection of the Grandducal palace in the 1820s; documents concerning the negotiations for its purchase have been preserved.

[3] This is evidenced by e.g. the exemplar in the Tapetenmuseum Kassel, a reprint by the manufacturers Defossé and Karth. For the wallpaper's commercial success see Haase 1978, 8f. and O. Nouvel-Kammerer 1990 and Lang, 'Josef Dufour' 1994, 144-149. On the influence of ancient art on 19th cent. interior design see e.g. A. Brunner 2003.

There are several possible interpretative approaches to this interesting combination of ancient subject matter and nineteenth century interior design. We focus firstly on the text and image relationship between the literary version (or versions) and the pictorial design, and secondly on the reception of ancient iconography in the pictures, and on a broader level, on the reception of ancient art and artefacts, including architecture. That later art history plays an important part in the design is evident. From the second half of the 19th century, the wallpapers were industrially produced and disseminated. As such, they can offer broader and more telling insights into the fashions, tastes and conventions current among their buyers than a unique artefact.[4]

2. The context in art history

In ancient art from the fifth century BC, Psyche, the representation of the human soul, is depicted as a young girl with butterfly wings. The wings characterize her as a personification of a floating, shifting condition: the soul descends into Hades and exists there as something floating and dreamlike.[5] But in addition to this more transcendent aspect, the earliest images already show Psyche together with Eros, perhaps alluding to the story of Amor and Psyche. Both aspects, Psyche as a winged personification, and Psyche as princess and Amor's lover, are present in ancient Greek and Roman art. This double aspect is visible in many groups, presenting Amor and Psyche in close embrace. Greek and Roman statuettes, Roman wall painting and (above all) Roman sarcophagi provide well known examples.[6] The frequency of the motif on sarcophagi shows the connexion of the motif with the sepulchral sphere.

Other than in modern art, narrative elements are rare in the ancient pictures. Though the combination of the figures of Eros and Psyche alludes to a narrative context, more concrete hints and details of a sequence of events are lacking. The combination of Love and Soul in their allegorical meaning takes precedence. There are rare exceptions: two late antique sarcophagi of the 3rd and 4th centuries AD probably show the courtship and submission of

---

[4] For a fuller discussion of the influence of Napoleonic ideological imagery, see Winkler/Reitz 2008 and O. Nouvel-Kammerer 2008.
[5] Cf. Homer, *Od.* 11, 220-222. For an overview see Icard-Gianolio 1994.
[6] See Icard-Gionolio 1994, Nr. 120-145.

Ill. 1. Cupid and Psyche. Mosaic from Antioch, 3rd cent. AD. Antakya, Mus. Hatay. Photograph: LIMC VII 2 (1984) 450 Nr. 86a s. v. Psyche.

Psyche;[7] on a mosaic from Antioch Psyche is depicted stealing Amor's weapons;[8] another image shows Psyche while she observes the sleeping Amor,[9] and Psyche's trials are also, if rarely, depicted.[10] Two motifs are present in ancient art which have no place in Apuleius' story: Psyche tormenting Amor,[11] and the other way round, Psyche being tormented by Amor or several Amores.[12] Whether these pictures are part of a story, or allegories for the power of love, is not clear. Again we return to images without a narrative content.

The development of the myth of Amor and Psyche in modern art is a topic that cannot be discussed here. Christel Steinmetz in her dissertation collects the evidence with a focus on the early 19th century. She writes:

---

[7] Icard-Gianolio 1994, Nr. 118-9.
[8] Icard-Gianolio 1994, Nr. 86.
[9] Icard-Gianolio 1994, Nr. 87.
[10] Icard-Gianolio 1994, Nr. 110-3.
[11] Icard-Gianolio 1994, Nr. 114-7.
[12] Icard-Gianolio 1994, Nr. 99-109.

'Amor und Psyche ist ein traditionelles Thema, das ... seit Beginn der Neuzeit in immer neuen Formen und mit unterschiedlichen Schwerpunkten aufgegriffen wurde.'[13] It has to be remembered that there are both whole cycles and works which select single episodes and motifs from the myth. Allegorical interpretations like Giulio Romano's cycle for the Palazzo del Te (1535) and new contextualisations like Raphael's cycle in the Villa Farnesina (1515) offer new possibilities. The symbolic meaning, and the discussion of ancient concepts of death and immortality, influence the shaping of the myth. These are very complex intertextual relationships which include the reception of texts from late antiquity, Boccaccio's treatment of the subject and other pictorial traditions like the Florentine *cassoni*.[14]

In ancient art the topic of Amor and Psyche is present, but it is not the story or the events which predominate in the pictures, rather the transcendent character of the personifications. In this sense the images are, in antiquity, while not a narrative, part of a vigorous and lively religious perception. Since the Renaissance, on the other hand, the pictures are part of a story which is told and interpreted from an inner distance. For this reason in the modern pictures the narrative element is prevalent, whereas it is lacking in ancient art.

3. The literary context

Recent scholarship on Apuleius has concentrated very much on the complex narrative strategies of the novel and on the multi layered interpretative possibilities of the inserted story of Amor and Psyche.[15] Since late antiquity the framing story of the novel and the inserted tales – Lucius' metamorphosis and the overcurious Psyche's trials – have been the subject of allegorical interpretations.[16] Boccacio in his *Genealogia deorum gentilium* (ca. 1350-1367, 5,22) not only alludes to Apuleius' novel, but also draws on Martianus Capella (*Nupt.* 1,7) and Fulgentius (*Myth.* 3,6). Of course, Boccaccio adapts the notions of his predecessors to the theological discourse of his own epoch.

---

[13] Steinmetz 1998, 4. Cf. Leidl 2008; de Jong 1998.
[14] Weiland-Pollerberg 2002. See Michele Rak's preceding chapter in this volume.
[15] Cf. esp. the Groningen commentary by Zimmerman et al. (Zimmerman 2004) with bibliography.
[16] Gaisser 2003.

Of special importance for us is the retelling of the story by Jean de La Fontaine. His prosimetric *Conte, Les amours de Psyché et de Cupidon*, appeared in 1669.[17] The overall structure introduces a group of learned friends who tell the story in the surroundings of the park in Versailles. Multiple editions of La Fontaine's work, of which some were illustrated, were to follow, and book-illustrations by François Gérard especially influenced Dufour's wallpapers. There are, however, substantial differences between the pictures of the printed illustrations and the wallpapers, according to the wishes of Dufour himself. In the print version the protagonists are nude, while they appear fully clothed on the wallpapers. Several attributes and architectural vistas present in the wallpapers do not appear in the print version. The narrative on the wallpapers includes one episode which appears only in La Fontaine, not in Apuleius (Psyche is given shelter by a fisherman). The emphasis placed on individual episodes is different. Thus Psyche's bath is one of the central pictures, after the well known motif of the *Toilette de Vénus*. In Apuleius, the bath as normal part of daily life is only briefly mentioned. But on the whole, the pictorial narrative, in its sequence of events and choice of elements, follows the story as told by Apuleius.

Interpreting the wallpapers involves different approaches. On the one hand, one has to examine the iconographical background. The visual narrative draws on preceding literary versions of the myth, but also on ancient sculpture and motifs which receive a symbolic or allusive significance in their new narrative context. It is especially relevant to investigate which ancient works of art were known at the time when the wallpapers were designed, and which meanings were attributed to them by the artists. But also the narrative strategies of both media must be analysed. The wallpapers featured subtitles for the individual scenes – if those were not cut off for reasons of space – which point the potential viewer to the literary background. A small booklet also seems to have been distributed with the wallpapers.[18] In scholarship, it still remains common practice to regard images as illustrations of texts, or texts as explanations of images, depending on the scholarly perspective. What is needed is an analysis of the capabilities of each medium.

---

[17] Vol. 8, p. 21-234 of the ed. by H. Regnies (1892).

[18] The booklet by one Abel Lanse from 1815 is mentioned by Clouzot 1931, p. 174. It has only recently been made available to me by Philippe de Fabry, Musée du Papier Peint, Rixheim. It is noteworthy that the subtitles are sometimes badly preserved or even lost by cutting down the panels.

4. Analysis

We will proceed as follows. First we give a short overview of the twelve scenes; then we will by way of an example go into two scenes in particular. Lastly, the differences in the appearance of Psyche will be analyzed.

The twelve panels, whose common height is 202 cm (the breadth varies from 100 to 175 cm), show the following scenes: Interrogation of the oracle; Psyche transported by Zephyrus; Psyche's bath in the palace; the visit of her sisters; Psyche trying to wound Cupid; Psyche sitting on the rock; Psyche encountering the fisherman; the delivery of the vase with Stygian water; Proserpina's box – Psyche in the underworld; Psyche opens the box; Psyche reconciled with Venus; the marriage of Cupid and Psyche. The wallpaper panels could be arranged according to the structure of a room. This is evident from the example of their presentation in the oval room of the palace in Bad Doberan.

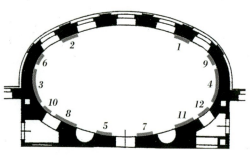

Ill. 2. Arrangement of the wallpapers in the Oval Room, Ducal Palace in Bad Doberan. Photograph: Leaflet 'Großherzogliches Palais Bad Doberan', ed. by Landkreis Bad Doberan.

The interrogation and answer of the oracle.

A small courtyard is enclosed at the back by a wall, into which a niche is set, containing a statue of the god Apollo. Apollo is easily recognizable for the viewer by the iconography which alludes to ancient depictions; the statue

 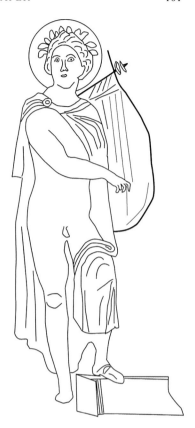

Ill. 3 (left). The oracle (All pictures of the wallpapers from the Oval Room, Ducal palace in Bad Doberan, taken by Edeltraut Altrichter, AVMZ Univ. of Rostock).
Ill. 4 (right). Apollon, Statuette, Clay, 1st cent. BC to 1st cent. AD, Museo Nazionale di Napoli. Drawing by Brigitte Meyer, Univ. of Rostock.

defines the location – the sanctuary of Apollo where the oracle was pronounced. The room itself looks nothing like an ancient sanctuary. Instead it resembles in some ways Roman domestic architecture as it would have been known since the eighteenth century from the excavations in Herculaneum and Pompeii. In the foreground we see three figures. In the light of the sun's rays, we can make out a dignified bearded figure with a long sceptre who with his left hand points at the statue of the god. In the context of ancient iconography, one is reminded of father deities like Jupiter, who here serves as a model for the depiction of Psyche's father. In the shade of the wall stand the two other protagonists of the story. Two female figures, one in the severe dress of a Roman matron, the other in a more sensuous garment, an Aphrodite-like beauty. It is Psyche, who sadly rests her head on her mother's shoulder.

She has just heard the cruel oracle of the god Apollo. The mother underlines the connection between Psyche's grief and the oracle by looking pleadingly at the statue of the god. The shadow which envelops mother and daughter hints at the tragic parting which is to follow. The spectator recognizes the story by the cluster of the single figures – god, father, mother, daughter. Their interpretation and the story itself are articulated through allusion to ancient iconography and symbols. There seems to be a break between image and story. In Apuleius' version it is the father who had to bear the message of the oracle; in La Fontaine's, it is unclear, but both parents are mentioned as present. The bearded figure of the father points to the god as the giver of the oracle. But his position and the iconography characterize him also as a priest. The image can leave this undecided, and use this ambiguity to tell the story even more clearly: the bearded figure presents the oracle in front of mother and daughter. This is the duty of the priest; in Apuleius it is the father's, who undertook the journey to the sanctuary alone. The representation unites the action of father and priest in one image and thus condenses the story.

In the corner, through the open door, Amor is viewing the events within. He is witnessing events, but also stands apart, as part of a different narrative sphere. He takes the position of an uninvolved observer, but simultaneously, the light thrown on him makes it evident that he is the one directing the sequence of events, and pulling the strings.

The recognition

We are looking into a room in which the vanishing point of the walls is situated left of the centre of the image. The open gallery of pilasters in the upper half of the right hand wall opens onto a landscape in the moonshine. The room contains various kinds of equipment, in front of which in the lower centre two figures are visible. Amor and Psyche are placed in the spotlight, to set them off from the detailed background. The winged Amor is lying on a sofa, his head resting on his left arm. The 'gaze' of the sleeping god is directed toward the approaching figure of Psyche. She is shown taking a vigorous step towards the god. Her garment is flowing behind her and exposes her bare legs. Psyche has evidently been running, but now stops and hesitates. In her left hand she is holding a lamp. The right hand is raised in gentle surprise. This is the critical moment when Psyche recognizes Amor. Her inner turmoil is depicted in a subtle, but still explicit way. Her strong movement towards Amor, whether motivated by the desire to kill or to caress, is shown both by the flowing garment and her body posture. The garment is bulging in the other direction to the wind, as we can see from the smoke of the fire in the background. Her hesitation is shown by the position of her arms.

Ill. 5. The recognition.

Apart from this dynamic group, there are plenty of visual codes pointing to the continuation of the story beyond the moment here depicted. The knife as a sign of the planned deed lies on the floor. It has not been dropped by accident, because then it would be in another position: it is carefully arranged. On the right hand side before the sofa we see a helmet, another part of weaponry. The helmet is not part of the story, but it has an important symbolic meaning: Amor is not only the son of Venus, but through her is also connected with Mars. This connection has an allegorical significance – love and war, sympathy and violence are complementary elements, but they belong together. In one sense, war is part of love and the story of Psyche – especially in the continuation after the scene here depicted – is the story of a struggle for love. The Corinthian helmet points to Mars and to the violent aspect of love. The two doves in the upper half of the image, as sacred animals of Venus, stand for love as represented by Venus. The dove over Psyche's head remains still and testifies to Psyche's continuing and constant feelings of love, whereas the dove over Amor's head flies off, pointing to his behaviour at the end of this episode. Further visual codes allude to events to come: a peacock forms part of the wall decoration in the top right hand corner of the image, and as the animal of Juno the bird symbolizes the married state and points to the happy ending of the story. Finally, the candelabrum behind Psyche is remarkable. On the candelabrum hangs a quiver with the arrows of Amor. By such an arrow Psyche was wounded and fell finally and irreversibly in love. But the quiver has more than one meaning. It appears exactly behind Psyche's back, as an elongation of her right thigh and at a right angle to her chest. Psyche and the arrows of Amor are connected, interlinked. The animated figure of Psyche with her gathered skirt and the quiver behind her back recalls a famous ancient statue, the 'Diana of Versailles'. Though one cannot speak of a direct quotation, the dynamic, proactive aspect of Psyche is foregrounded by this allusion to the hunting goddess.

Psyche's appearance

Ill. 6. Diana from Versailles, Roman copy of a Greek original from 350/340 BC, Paris, Louvre, Cast in Berlin. Photograph: Abguss-Sammlung Antiker Plastik Berlin.

It is remarkable that Psyche looks totally different in the different images of the cycle. One might expect that the main figure in a story would in each image be represented in such a way as to be immediately recognisable; this is the usual procedure to make a cycle readable for the viewer. Are the differences due to the clumsiness of the artist? Of course not. In every scene, Psyche's representation is specifically adapted to suit the precise moment depicted, and to her own position within the narrative. Her image alone can tell a story. Recognisability is not the main aim here: the viewer would know who was depicted in this context. The focus is on the interpretation of the role Psyche is playing in each scene. In this context, ancient iconography plays a

Ill. 7: The submission.

crucial part. In several scenes, visual codes deriving from the ancient iconography of the goddess Venus are applied to Psyche. This is as important for the bathing scene as it is for the encounter with her sisters. It is exactly the assimilation of Psyche to Venus which is the starting point and first cause for the whole story. Venus punishes Psyche because she is jealous of her beauty and the resulting reverence shown to her. This is taken up in the visual narrative by the use of the visual code of Venus in connection with Psyche: Venus and Psyche overlap.

Psyche's bodily proportions are especially puzzling. Psyche can be a little girl, when encountering Venus, an alluring beauty, when her com-

Ill. 8: Kneeling personification of a Roman province in front of the emperor. Sestertius of Hadrian. Photograph: Numismatische Bilddatenbank Eichstätt.

petition with Venus is emphasised, and then again a rather corpulent and stout figure. This is evident in the scene where Psyche offers the vase to Venus. The scene takes the form of an ancient *submissio*. Psyche assumes the role of the subjected barbarian woman who offers a gift to her *domina*. She does not look like a girl, but like a strong woman. Female personifications of this type are known from Roman art: they personify conquered countries or provinces. In this context, the image of Psyche in the discovery scene can likewise be explained. Artemis/Diana is not only the huntress, but also the guardian of virginity. The allusion to ancient imagery characterizes Psyche in each situation.

5. Conclusion

On the wallpapers, ancient models are adapted and transformed in varying intensity; sometimes, the allusion is clearly marked, sometimes hardly at all. The different types of reception range from quotation and allusion to topical use of omnipresent antiquarian details and decorations. In a subtle way, the viewer is led to tell his or her own version of the story, and to question, interpret and reinterpret the visual narrative.

Bibliography

Brunner, A. 2003. *Renaissancen: Antikenrezeption in der Angewandten Kunst des 15. bis 19. Jahrhunderts*. Ausstellungskatalog. Hannover: Kestner Museum.
Cavicchioli, S. 2002. *Amore e Psiche*, Milano: Alberto Maioli.
Clouzot, H. 1931. *Psyché et Cupidon, tableaux-tentures en papier peint de la manufacture J. Dufour et Cie.*, Paris: van Oest.

Gaisser, J. H. 2003. 'Allegorizing Apuleius: Fulgentius, Boccaccio, Beroaldo, and the Chain of Receptions', in: *Acta Conventus Neo-Latini Cantabrigiensis*, Tempe/Arizona: Arizona Center for Medieval and Renaissance Studies, 23-41.

Haase, G., 1978. *Bildtapeten*, Leipzig: E. A. Seemann.

Holm, Ch. 2006. *Die Erfindung eines Mythos in Kunst, Wissenschaft und Alltagskultur (1765-1840)*, München: Deutscher Kunstverlag.

Icard-Gianolio, N. 1994. 'Psyche'. *Lexicon Iconographicum Mythologiae Classicae* (*LIMC*) VII, 569-85.

de Jong, J. L. 1998. ''Il Pittore a le volte è puro poeta'. Cupid and Psyche in Italian Renaissance Painting', in: *Aspects of Apuleius' Golden Ass. Vol. II. Cupid and Psyche*, ed. M. Zimmerman, V. Hunink, et al., Groningen: Egbert Forsten, 189-215.

Lang, P. 1994. *Ein Blick auf Amor und Psyche um 1800*. Katalog zur Ausstellung Kunsthaus Zürich 20. Mai-17. Juli, Zürich: Kunsthaus Zürich.

Leidl, C. 2008. 'Räume und Feste der Liebe. Darstellungen von Amor und Psyche bis 1700'. in: Winkler and Reitz 2008, 100-112.

Nouvel-Kammerer, O. 1990. *Papiers peints panoramiques*, Paris: Flammarion.

Nouvel-Kammerer, O. 2008. 'Les ailes du papillon sous l'Empire napoléonien', in Winkler and Reitz 2008, 94-99.

Reißmann, S. 1996. 'Die Psyche-Tapete, eine Kostbarkeit in den Sammlungen des Schifffahrtsmuseums', in: *Unter Wasser – über Wasser. Beiträge zur maritimen Technik- und Kulturgeschichte Mecklenburgs und Vorpommerns, Schriften des Schiffahrtsmuseums der Hansestadt Rostock*, 75-81.

Reißmann, S. 2003. 'Vom Kunst- und Altertumsmuseum zum Schifffahrtsmuseum', in: *Bürgerstolz. 1841-1903-2003 Museum in Rostock*, Peter Danke-Carstensen (ed.), Kleine Schriften des Schifffahrtsmuseums Rostock, Heft 3, Rostock, 21-27 und 48-53.

Reitz, Ch. und Winkler-Horaček, L. 2008. 'Liebe auf Tapeten. Bericht über ein Projekt zur Antikenrezeption', *Gymnasium* 115, 481-483.

Steinmetz, Ch. 1989. *Amor und Psyche. Studien zur Auffassung des Mythos in der bildenden Kunst um 1800*. Diss. Köln 1989.

Weiland-Pollerberg, F. 2002. *Amor und Psyche in der Renaissance. Medienspezifisches Erzählen im Bild*. Petersberg: Michael Imhof.

Winkler-Horaček, L., and Reitz, Ch. 2008. (ed.) *Amor und Psyche. Eine Erzählung in zwölf Bildern.*, Rahden/Westf.: Verlag Marie Leidorf.

Zimmerman, M., et al. 2004. *Apuleius Madaurensis, Metamorphoses, Books IV 28-35, V and VI 1-24*, Groningen: Forsten.

C

The Reception of Petronius' *Satyricon*:

Perennial Patterns

Petronius in West Egg:
The Satyricon and *The Great Gatsby*

NIKOLAI ENDRES
Western Kentucky University

> It is hard to overestimate the benefit which came to Fitzgerald from his having consciously placed himself in the line of the great.
> Lionel Trilling

According to critic Robert Roulston, who has studied the literary influences on F. Scott Fitzgerald's *The Great Gatsby*:

> A catalogue of the authors whose writings have supposedly left traces on *The Great Gatsby* is as full of bizarre incongruities as Nick Carraway's list of guests at Gatsby's parties. Flaubert is there with Stephen Leacock and Dreiser with Edith Wharton. There too are Charles Dickens and Ford Maddox Ford, Joseph Conrad and Anthony Hope, Coleridge and Clarence E. Mulford, Thackeray and Harold Bell Wright, T. S. Eliot and George Eliot, Petronius and Stendhal, Mark Twain and Emily Brontë, Herman Melville and Horatio Alger, Oswald Spengler and Willa Cather, John Keats and the anonymous creator of Diamond Dick, H. G. Wells and his nemesis Henry James, and poor John Lawson Stoddard, who finds himself confused with the racist Theodore Lothrop Stoddard. And not far from the center, as conspicuous as he would have wished, is the sage of Baltimore, H. L. Mencken. (54)

Poor Petronius, the sage of Rome and not quite as conspicuous as he would have wished, has received little attention,[1] which is all the more remarkable

---

[1] The following are all very brief and/or have a focus different from mine: Briggs 1999, "Petronius" and "Ur-*Gatsby*"; Bruccoli 2002, *Documentary* 142-146; Drennan 1989;

considering that Fitzgerald had originally entitled his novel *Trimalchio* or *Trimalchio in West Egg* (see Turnbull 1963, 169); even in the final text, one explicit reference to the *Satyricon* remains: 'It was when curiosity about Gatsby was at its highest that the lights in his house failed to go on one Saturday night – and, as obscurely as it had begun, his career as Trimalchio was over' (*Gatsby* 119).[2] Most critics have focused on Trimalchio's vulgarity and compared it to Gatsby's ostentation or, like Amory Blaine in Fitzgerald's first novel *This Side of Paradise* (1920), have turned to 'the racier sections of ... Petronius' (*Paradise* 106),[3] but a lot more remains to be explained, especially the two *narrators*' desire to be great (everything we know about the great Gatsby, it should be noted, is refracted through Nick's lens.) Both Nick Carraway and Encolpius, sorely disappointed by pedestrian reality, would like to lead a life of fairy tale and romance. Love, sex, or any form of human intercourse thus falls prey to theatricality and inauthenticity, Fitzgerald's famous 'unreality of reality' (*Gatsby* 105). In the patchwork of incongruity, modes of life are denigrated and human values satirized. In both the *Satyricon* and *Gatsby*, the beginning is ashes, the end melodrama. And behind the narrators we find the great authors themselves: The Great Petronius, The Great Fitzgerald.

Let us begin with triviality: poor Nick, poring over boring financial documents, eating little pig sausages and mashed potatoes, sitting in dark restaurants, and dating a girl from, well, New Jersey; falling asleep while listing quotations on stock, he is truly a creature of probity working for Probity Trust. When telling his story, however, he promises to 'unfold the shining secrets that only Midas and Morgan and Maecenas knew' (*Gatsby* 8).[4] He walks down a pastoral Fifth Avenue expecting to see 'a great flock of white sheep turn the corner' (32) and he looks at Gatsby's house 'like Kant at his church steeple' (93). Nick even waxes presidential: 'Americans, while occa-

---

Fraser 1979; Kumamoto 2001; MacKendrick 1950; Rankin 1970, 207-213; West 2000. The promising dissertation by Sheila Hovis Byrd has not (yet) been published.

[2] Fitzgerald read *The Satyricon of Petronius Arbiter: Complete and Unexpurgated Translation by W. C. Firebaugh, in which are Incorporated the Forgeries of Nodot and Marchena, and the Readings Introduced into the Text by De Salas. Illustrations by Norman Lindsay* (New York: Published for Private Circulation Only by Boni and Liveright, 1922. 2 vols.). Latin editions for Petronius used here: Smith for the *cena* section, Müller for the rest; translation used here: Arrowsmith.

[3] This is complemented by an expurgated passage from "Babylon Revisited" (1931), where the narrator witnesses nightlife in Paris as something that "Petronius would have winced at" (Daugherty and West 10).

[4] In the first version, this sentence reads "unfold the shining secrets that only Midas and Morgan and Rothschild knew" (*Trimalchio* 7).

sionally willing to be serfs, have always been obstinate about being peasantry' (93). West Egg is compared to a painting by El Greco:

> a hundred houses, at once conventional and grotesque, crouching under a sullen, overhanging sky and a lustreless moon. In the foreground four solemn men in dress suits are walking along the sidewalk with a stretcher on which lies a drunken woman in a white evening dress. Her hand, which dangles over the side, sparkles cold with jewels. Gravely the men turn in at a house – the wrong house. But no one knows the woman's name, and no one cares. (185)

At the end, we find a passage straight out of *Heart of Darkness*:[5]

> Its vanished trees, the trees that had made way for Gatsby's house, had once pandered in whispers to the last and greatest of all human dreams; for a transitory enchanted moment man must have held his breath in the presence of this continent, compelled into an aesthetic contemplation he neither understood nor desired, face to face for the last time in history with something commensurate to his capacity for wonder. (189)

Wonder of wonders, Nick's narration, unlike his life, is anything but dull.

This glamorization continues with needy Nick's depictions of the great Gatsby. Martin Brody remarks about the funeral scene in John Harbison's opera *Gatsby*: 'Of course, the deceased tenor in question is not Siegfried, not Tannhäuser or Tristan, not even Radames or Rudolfo, but Jay Gatsby – opera's most zealous, if not first, incarnation of an indigenously American breed, the self-made man' (414). An even more striking contrast between the ideal and the real lies in Gatsby's death on a pneumatic mattress. Here is how Nick conjures up the scene (visualize is all he can do since he was absent from the crime):

> There was a faint, barely perceptible movement of the water as the fresh flow from one end urged its way toward the drain at the other. With little ripples that were hardly the shadows of waves, the laden mattress moved

---

[5] There is a circuitous relationship between Petronius, Joseph Conrad, T. S. Eliot, and Fitzgerald. Eliot initially contemplated Kurtz' final exclamation "The horror! The horror!" for the epigraph to *The Waste Land* but then settled on the *Satyricon*. Numerous critics have compared Nick with Conrad's narrator Marlow, but I would give equal prominence to Encolpius.

irregularly down the pool. A small gust of wind that scarcely corrugated the surface was enough to disturb its accidental course with its accidental burden. (*Gatsby* 170)

Nick is alluding to the Germanic funeral pyre, with its most elaborate testimony in Brünnhilde's Trauermarsch in Richard Wagner's *Götterdämmerung*:

> Sturdy branches,
> building his pyre
> now bring to the shore of the Rhine!
> Bright and clear,
> kindle the flame:
> let the hero blaze
> in splendour and radiance on high. (*Ring* 325)

Even though Roulston claims that 'anyone in the 1920s with a taste for apocalyptic visions did not have to reach back to Richard Wagner's *Götterdämmerung*, or out to [Oswald] Spengler's *Decline of the West*' (56), let us stay with Wagner for a moment.[6] *Gatsby*'s valley of ashes (27) may allude to *The Ring*. Wotan (alternatively Odin), the supreme deity, had broken a branch from Yggdrasil, the World Ash Tree whose limbs spread all over the world, forged a spear from it, and carved the runes of treaties on it; at the end, he ordered branches from the tree to be piled around Valhalla in order to set it aflame. Wotan's act entailed a violation of nature, with the tree withering, its Spring of Wisdom at the bottom ceasing to flow, and the Three Norns' cord of destiny losing its home. The rest is ashes. Gatsby's killer arrives like Wotan, an 'ashen, fantastic figure gliding toward him through the amorphous trees' (169). Moreover, presiding over the valley of ashes come the two gigantic eyes, truly godlike. Wotan, to acquire wisdom, had to surrender one of his eyes, but even with only one, he now sees truly like a god. Finally, Siegfried, like Brünnhilde a creature of the otherworld, cannot adjust to the world of politics – Wotan's pacts and pledges, Alberich's gold and curse, Hagen's loyalty and treachery – and dies as soon as he trans-

---

[6] Amory Blaine, a self-professed connoisseur of music, does not explicitly allude to Wagner, but he does mention Wagner's friend and foe Nietzsche (*Paradise* 149); in two later short stories, "Two Wrongs" (1930) and "Emotional Bankruptcy" (1931), however, Fitzgerald refers to *The Ring* specifically, as he does in his Note-Books (*The Crack-Up* 202). Finally, Felix Mendelssohn Bartholdy, whose Wedding March is performed in *Gatsby* (134), influenced Wagner.

gresses from fairy tale into civilization. Gatsby similarly is toppled upon transcending his class and entering into the world of old money, or, as Nick terms it, the Westerners who are 'subtly unadaptable to Eastern life' (184). Both Siegfried and Gatsby, at last, die through betrayal, but typical of the discrepancy, the slain Siegfried is carried to Valhalla by Wotan's favorite valkyrie riding a horse, while Gatsby is ignobly shot by an automobile mechanic.

Back to theatricality, *Gatsby* brims with 'automatic' actions and reactions (for example, 92, 95, 137). Gatsby is 'an elegant young rough-neck, a year or two over thirty, whose elaborate formality of speech just missed being absurd' (53). Gatsby and Daisy's reunion is all staged, with Gatsby frozen 'in a strained counterfeit of perfect ease, even of boredom' (91). Fitzgerald's most famous passage stresses Gatsby's inauthenticity:

> The truth was that Jay Gatsby of West Egg, Long Island, sprang from his Platonic conception of himself. He was a son of God – a phrase which, if it means anything, means just that – and he must be about His Father's business, the service of a vast, vulgar, and meretricious beauty. So he invented just the sort of Jay Gatsby that a seventeen-year-old boy would be likely to invent, and to this conception he was faithful to the end. (104)

The ideal, not the real. Daisy, like Emma Bovary, flourishes at night, in another world, where magic reigns supreme:

> …in the very casualness of Gatsby's party there were romantic possibilities totally absent from her world. What was it up there in the song that seemed to be calling her back inside? What would happen now in the dim, incalculable hours? Perhaps some unbelievable guest would arrive, a person infinitely rare and to be marvelled at, some authentically radiant young girl who with one fresh glance at Gatsby, one moment of magical encounter, would blot out those five years of unwavering devotion. (115)

As a result, Daisy loves not the 'real' Gatsby but the one resembling an 'advertisement' (125). Gatsby similarly elevates Daisy to fairy-tale status, especially her house, where the grass is always greener, the romances always rosier, and the bedrooms always better:

> There was a ripe mystery about it, a hint of bedrooms upstairs more beautiful and cool than other bedrooms, of gay and radiant activities tak-

ing place through its corridors and of romances that were not musty and laid away already in lavender but fresh and breathing and redolent of this year's shining motor-cars and of dances whose flowers were scarcely withered. (155-156)

She even metamorphoses into the holy grail (156). (Wagner again, this time *Parsifal*?).

All this originates in the *Satyricon*, which features a Shakespearean stage (80.9):

> *grex agit in scaena mimum: pater ille vocatur*
> *filius hic, nomen divitis ille tenet.*
> *mox ubi ridendas inclusit pagina partes*
> *vera redit facies, assimulata perit*

> The comic actors strut the stage, bow and grin.
> The cast: old Moneybags, Father and Son.
> The farce ends, the smiles come off, revealing
> the true face below, the bestial, leering one.

Reality, in all its triviality, has worn itself out; therefore, it needs to be spiced up, surpassed, scandalized. There is a Circe, that formidable enemy of Odysseus who threatens his very humanity. Petronius' Circe, though, only goes for trashy slaves, sleazy gladiators, mule drivers, or debauched footmen (126.1–11). Another rogue, Giton (the narrator and protagonist Encolpius' boyfriend), hides, not under a ram, but a bug-infested mattress (which of course makes him sneeze) to escape a two-eyed gouty *senex canus* (97–98). This old lecher earlier cast himself in the role of Zeus abducting the beautiful Trojan shepherd: '*laudo Ganymedem*' (92.3) he says to Giton. Giton is ravished by Ascyltos (the third member of the *ménage-à-trois*) like Lucretia by Tarquin (9.5). Impotent, Encolpius resembles the chaste Socrates ('*non tam intactus Alcibiades in praeceptoris sui lectulo iacuit*,' Giton says; 128.7). Domestic disputes reach the Theban proportions of Polynices and Eteocles' fratricide (80.3). Or why not roll yourself up in a carpet to avoid detection, after all that is how Cleopatra was delivered to Caesar (102.10–11)? Unfortunately, both Nick and Encolpius (and everybody else) fail in their effort to render banality into melodrama. All they can do is regurgitate literary scripts. In his chapter on Encolpius, the 'mythomaniac narrator,' Gian Biagio Conte proposes:

The great literary model provides ready-made a noble and solemn representation, the one dramatized version capable of giving a little meaning to the empty container that is the petty reality of the everyday. Such theatrical treatment is necessary to promote ordinary life in its narrow scope to the level of grandeur. The elevated literary model has been appropriated 'melodramatically' by Encolpius in the sense that he is seeking enhanced significance for his own situation, that is, for his words and gestures. It is as though trivial affairs could acquire grandeur and importance purely by being experienced as theater: as though by giving theatrical voice to experience one could actually make sense of the indifference of reality. [...] For him great literature becomes a universe inhabited by suggestive myths, indeed it becomes the secularized mythology of a culture determined to seek out intense emotions which would otherwise be denied to it by immediate experience. (5–6)

At the end, Nick finds out that like Amory Blaine, he 'had grown up to a thousand books, a thousand lies' (*Paradise* 262).

How about love and sex, (theoretically) two of mankind's most genuine experiences ? Real or ideal? First of all, how did Gatsby get rich? For services rendered to Dan Cody? The great toy boy and boy toy (*puer delicatus*)? Fitzgerald never says anything explicit, but he teases us quite a bit.[7] The strongest evidence for Gatsby's prostitution comes from his model, Trimalchio, and his rise to fame: 'For fourteen years I was my master's pet'; in addition, he served his mistress with equal devotion ('*tamen ad delicias ipsimi annos quattuordecim fui. nec turpe est quod dominus iubet. ego tamen et ipsimae satis faciebam*'; *Sat*. 75.11). Moreover, Fitzgerald's edition of the *Satyricon* contains long explanatory notes on Prostitution (21 pages), Paederastia (13 pages), Legacy Hunting (2 pages), and Greek Love (20 pages), drawing attention to crucial issues in Petronius. If sex is mercenary, how about love? Love is wholly absent from *Gatsby*. We find this out early on in the metaphor of the eggs (symbols of fertility): 'Twenty miles from the city a pair of enormous eggs, identical in contour and separated only by a courtesy bay, jut out into the most domesticated body of salt water in the Western Hemisphere' (*Gatsby* 9). Chikako Kumamoto traces these eggs back to vari-

---

[7] Fitzgerald was no stranger to homosexuality, especially in his friendship with Monsignor Cyril Sigourney Webster Fay; later he was even rumoured to have been sleeping with the macho Ernest Hemingway. Also, let us not forget that Fitzgerald greatly cherished Oscar Wilde and his works, including the homo-erotically charged *The Picture of Dorian Gray*, one of whose aphorisms he used for the epigraph to *Paradise*.

ous egg dishes Trimalchio serves, but I suggest a more revealing source. In Plato's *Symposium*, which the *Satyricon* explicitly parodies (Plato's chalices of wine that give birth to Eros contrasting with Trimalchio's silver piss-pot that relieves his bloated intestines), Aristophanes recounts a fantastic myth. Initially, human beings had four hands and four legs and were terribly strong, but when they aspired to overthrow the gods, Zeus intervened: 'he cut those human beings in two, the way people cut sorb-apples before they dry them or the way they cut eggs with hairs' (*Symp.* 190e). What will eventually turn into Romantic love or the desire and pursuit of the whole, fails not only in Aristophanes, where completion is endlessly deferred, where roundness remains square, where one plus one still equals one, where the glass is always half empty.

'Half' is the key-word here. Nick, for example, is 'half in love' with Jordan Baker (*Gatsby* 187). Gatsby almost marries Daisy, almost elopes with her, almost reunites with her.[8] Daisy loves both Tom Buchanan and Gatsby, that is, half loves each of them. She also has, in one day, half a dozen dates with half a dozen men (158). Fitzgerald's idea of 'emotional bankruptcy' comes in here. His biographer notes: 'He believed that people have a fixed amount of emotional capital; reckless expenditure results in early bankruptcy, leaving the person unable to respond to the events that require true emotion. There is no recoupment after emotional bankruptcy' (Bruccoli, *Grandeur* 289).[9] In the *Satyricon*, Froma Zeitlin similarly calls the erotic relationships 'a 'dance-pattern' which teases us with the possibility of a meaningful pattern but which then is denied' (653). A dance card that is only half full for Encolpius et al. Close encounters, however sublime, usually end pre-orgasmically. Encolpius laments: 'At last I was free to make love to Giton, without restraint, and wrapping the boy in the closest of embraces, I took my fill of a bliss that even happy lovers might envy. We were still at it, however, when Ascyltus came tiptoeing to the door' (*Sat.* 11.1-2). To Circe he complains about his premature ejaculation ('*forsitan animus antecessit corporis moram, forsitan dum omnia concupisco, voluptatem tempore consumpsi*'; 130.5). Climax remains elusive, satisfaction infinitely postponed, bliss forever a wink of an eye away. Halves are never rounded in *Gatsby*,

---

[8] A colleague of mine, Walker Rutledge, made the very suggestive observation that Gatsby may be a virgin. Male virginity compares wonderfully to Petronian impotence.

[9] In the short story "Emotional Bankruptcy," the eighteen-year old Josephine passes a crushing verdict on love: "She was very tired and lay face downward on the couch with that awful, awful realization that all the old things are true. One cannot both spend and have. The love of her life had come by, and looking in her empty basket, she had found not a flower left for him – not one" (*Basil* 287).

where Zeus keeps severing emotional ties: 'They were careless people, Tom and Daisy – they smashed up things and creatures and then retreated back into their money or their vast carelessness, or whatever it was that kept them together, and let other people clean up the mess they had made. . .' (*Gatsby* 187-188). They have achieved Aristophanes' ultimate prediction, humans split in *four* halves, 'sawn apart between the nostrils, like half dice' (*Symp.* 193a).

Halves are both Fitzgerald's and Petronius' favorite conveyor of inauthenticity, addled eggs and monstrous patchworks. Trimalchio, for example, badly garbles his literary dream world: Hannibal capturing Ilium, Cassandra killing her sons, Daedalus shutting Niobe in the Trojan Horse, Diomede and Ganymede having Helen as sister, Electra marrying Achilles, Agamemnon pursuing Diana. Trimalchio's tomb (*Sat.* 71.5–12) owes everything to Gatsby's hybrid house: Norman hôtel de ville (*Gatsby* 9), Gothic library (49), feudal silhouette, Marie Antoinette music rooms, Restoration salons, Scottish architecture or 'Adam study' (96). The most consummate jumble, of course, is the great Gatsby himself, rumored to be a cousin or nephew of Kaiser Wilhelm (37), a killer (48), a spy for Germany during the war (48), an Oxford man (53), a native of the swamps of Louisiana or New York's lower east side (54), a bootlegger and nephew to von Hindenburg and, needless to say, second cousin to the devil (65). While Tom and Daisy are breaking up, the music from Mendelssohn's Wedding March penetrates from below (134-142). Throughout the novel, geographies are ignored, animals misplaced, winners lost: San Francisco situated in the Midwest or Biloxi in Tennessee, tigers pursued in the Parisian Bois de Boulogne, the World Series fixed. The moon is produced from a caterer's basket (47), libraries help people sober up (50), cars are driven without wheels (60), women wear moustaches (64), a female breast is 'swinging loose like a flap' (145), people are helpless without tennis shoes (177).

Petronius' Niceros, who may have given Nick his name (see Drennan 1989), tells the story of a werewolf (*Sat.* 61.6-62), that ultimate shape-shifting, theatrical human beast. No such creature appears in the ruthlessly realistic *Gatsby*, but there is a Mr. Wolfshiem (in whose name itself the letters 'i' and 'e' have been metamorphosed from the more common Wolfsheim), the wearer of the finest human teeth on his sleeves, fixer of the World Series, and creator of Gatsby: 'I raised him up out of nothing, right out of the gutter' (*Gatsby* 179). Trimalchio also rose from an 'attic' (*pergula*) to a 'palace' (*aedes*) or from a 'shack' (*casa*) to a 'shrine' (*templum*) (*Sat.* 74.14 and 77.4), and Tom proudly proclaims: 'I've heard of making a garage out of a stable… but I'm the first man who ever made a stable out of a garage' (*Gatsby* 125). Now, human teeth used for personal beautification make us pause, but Fitzgerald must have read in Petronius that there is no clear difference between beauty and the beast. We are all cannibals, we all eat human flesh with our animal teeth. As Habinnas disturbingly asks, 'if bears eat men, why shouldn't men eat bears?' (*Sat.* 66.6). Then, right after Niceros, Trimalchio tells a story of a Petronian dummy made of straw: no heart, no guts, no nothing (*'non cor habebat, non intestina, non quicquam'*; 63.8). Everybody is a dummy during the day and werewolf at night. Even worse, no one can keep up with what he or she is doing.

Time is running out in the *Satyricon*. After one reminder of death after another, Trimalchio exhorts his guests to pretend that he is dead (78.5). At Gatsby's funeral, conversely, no one shows up, supposedly because no one cared about him. Two words sum it all up: 'Nobody came' (*Gatsby* 182). When Trimalchio is injured, Encolpius has the same worry: 'we dreaded the thought of possibly having to go into mourning for a man who meant nothing to us at all' (*'ne necesse haberent alienum mortuum plorare'*; *Sat.* 54.1). Nick similarly remembers the first party he goes to: 'It made me uneasy, as though the whole evening had been a trick of some sort to exact a contributory emotion from me' (*Gatsby* 22). At the same time, Petronius' characters do not seize the day, they *double* it in their *taedium vitae* (*'de una die duas facere'*; *Sat.* 72.4). William Arrowsmith says it perfectly: 'Like *hybris*, *luxuria* affects a man so that he eventually loses his sense of his specific function, his *virtus* or *aretē*. He surpasses himself, luxuriating into other things and forms' (317). In *Gatsby*, Daisy is 'p-paralyzed with happiness' (13). She has 'been everywhere and seen everything and done everything' (22). Yet there is never enough time: 'an evening was hurried from phase to phase toward its close in a continually disappointed anticipation or else in sheer nervous dread of the moment itself' (17). For Nick, youth is everything: 'Thirty – the promise of a decade of loneliness, a thinning list of single men to know, a thinning brief-case of enthusiasm, thinning hair' (143). When Nick tells Gatsby, who runs down 'like an overwound clock' (97), that one cannot repeat the past, ''Can't repeat the past?' he cried incredulously. 'Why of course you can!''' (116). Like Trimalchio, of course, he has no past as poor James Gatz of North Dakota, so there is nothing to repeat. Tom, who like Trimalchio worships 'Fat Profit, Good Luck, and Large Income' (*'aiebat autem unum Cerdonem, alterum Felicionem, tertium Lucrionem vocari'*; *Sat.* 60.9), dismisses him as Mr. Nobody from Nowhere (*Gatsby* 137). In the end, Nick even talks to the dead Gatsby (172-173), rejecting for the last time the line between life and death.

It has all become a bit confusing – or inauthentic or half true. What is really real? Who is modeled on whom? Who is talking about whom? Yes, Gatsby is as inauthentic as Trimalchio and almost as unsophisticated, but how about Nick? How perceptive is he, after all? Are we supposed to believe him: 'I am one of the few honest people that I have ever known' (64)? And do we not have two Nicks in the story? Attention must be paid, for Fitzgerald follows a crucial Petronian distinction here. Encolpius the *protagonist* is gullible, naive, chaotic, scatter-brained, and falls prey to many illusions; as *narrator*, however, Encolpius is genuinely perceptive. J. P. Sullivan stresses Encolpius' dilemma: 'alternately romantic and cynical, brave and timorous, malevolent and cringing, jealous and rational, sophisticated and naïve' (119). Nick, too, occupies the role of spectator/actor and narrator. When Nick tells Gatsby 'You're worth the whole damn bunch put together' and later adds 'I've always been glad I said that. It was the only compliment I ever gave him, because I disapproved of him from beginning to end' (*Gatsby* 162), Nick is both Nick and Gatsby, both little and great. At the end, Nick says:

> I found myself on Gatsby's side, and alone. From the moment I telephoned news of the catastrophe to West Egg village, every surmise about him, and every practical question, was referred to me. At first I was surprised and confused; then as he lay in his house and didn't move or breathe or speak[,] hour upon hour it grew upon me that I was responsible, because no one else was interested – interested, I mean, with that intense personal interest to which everyone has some vague right at the end. (173)

He then calls Gatsby by the signature 'old sport,' feeling a 'scornful solidarity between Gatsby and me against them all' (173). He has become the actor, drawn into the action as Gatsby's replacement. As we saw all along, Nick wants to be great. *Gatsby* is really his story too, his dull life turned into great fiction.

But where does this leave Fitzgerald? Conte suggests of the author of the *Satyricon*:

> Petronius introduces into the text a character who is like himself in longing for great literature, but who is essentially different because he lacks the critical awareness. The error that makes Encolpius absurd is that of

not seeing the distance – or rather the inaccessibility – of the great literary models. These may seem near, or even easy to imitate, just because they are well known, but any imitation of them can only produce a caricature. (84–85)

Of course, any statement about Petronius must remain fairly speculative, but let us extend it to Fitzgerald. I do not think it is a coincidence that *The Great Gatsby* brims with literary allusions,[10] worlds of heightened reality and sublime abode, great heroes or abject villains, unlike Fitzgerald, the ruined drunk, the frustrated failure, the inadequate (literally) husband. In *Gatsby*'s famous 'inexhaustible variety of life' (40), not surprisingly, Fitzgerald is quoting James Boswell, the small biographer to the great Dr. Johnson. A passage at the end reads like therapy: '[Gatsby] must have looked up at an unfamiliar sky through frightening leaves and shivered as he found what a grotesque thing a rose is and how raw the sunlight was upon the scarcely created grass. A new world, material without being real, where poor ghosts, breathing dreams like air, drifted fortuitously about' (169). Having composed great fiction – a new world, material without being real – Fitzgerald soon saw various ashen figures coming after him. Fitzgerald's biographer paints such a wide-ranging tableau: 'prince charming, the drunken writer, the ruined novelist, the spoiled genius, the personification of the Jazz Age, the sacrificial victim of the Depression' (Bruccoli, *Grandeur* xix). Well, this sounds much like the Petronius of popular culture:[11] the arbiter of elegance, the literary personification of silver Latin, the sacrificial victim of Nero, and (literally) ruined novelist of whose massive work only scraps remain.

Let us finish with another look at the Trimalchio reference in *The Great Gatsby*: 'It was when curiosity about Gatsby was at its highest that the lights in his house failed to go on one Saturday night – and, as obscurely as it had begun, his career as Trimalchio was over' (119). Gatsby is not Trimalchio, only pretending to be like him, making a 'career' or profession or pretence of his Latin model. We would expect nothing less from a novel of inauthenticity. Remember that Petronius' famous portrait by Tacitus ('*nam illi dies per somnum, nox officiis et oblectamentis vitae transigebatur...*'; *Annales*

---

[10] In *This Side of Paradise*, incredibly, about 70 works and around 100 authors are referred to; see Good. On Fitzgerald as a (non)derivative author, see Kuehl.

[11] Tacitus, the Elder Pliny, and Plutarch are our only biographical evidence from the classical period. The bottom line is that we know next to nothing about Petronius. Some recent re-imaginings of Petronius and the *Satyricon* include Eurydice's *Satyricon USA: A Journey Across the New Sexual Frontier*, Ellery David Nest's *The Satyricon: The Morazla Scrolls*, and Jesse Browner's *The Uncertain Hour*.

16.18), depicts Petronius as, not a debauchee, but as a *poseur* of vice ('*vitiorum imitatione*'), whose career as arbiter of elegance was over as obscurely as it had begun.

Bibliography

Arrowsmith, W. 1966. 'Luxury and Death in the Satyricon,' *Arion* 5, 304-331.
Briggs, W. 1999. 'Petronius and Virgil in *The Great Gatsby*,' *IJCT* 6, 226-235.
— 2000. 'The Ur-*Gatsby*,' *IJCT* 6, 577-584.
Brody, M. 2001. ''Haunted by Envisioned Romance': John Harbison's *Gatsby*,' *Musical Quarterly* 85, 413-455.
Browner, J. *The Uncertain Hour: A Novel*. New York: Bloomsbury, 2007.
Bruccoli, M. J., ed. 2002. *F. Scott Fitzgerald's 'The Great Gatsby': A Documentary Volume*, Dictionary of Literary Biography, vol. 219. Detroit: Gale.
— 2002. *Some Sort of Epic Grandeur: The Life of F. Scott Fitzgerald*, second edition, Columbia, SC: University of South Carolina Press.
Byrd, S. H. 1966. *The Inexhaustible Variety of Life: Satire of the Nouveau Riche in Petronius' 'Satyricon', Molière's 'Le bourgeois gentilhomme' and Fitzgerald's 'The Great Gatsby'*, dissertation, Middle Tennessee State University.
Conte, G. B. 1966. *The Hidden Author: An Interpretation of Petronius' Satyricon*, trans. Elaine Fantham, Berkeley: University of California Press.
Daugherty, C. E., and J. L. W. West III. 2002. 'Josephine Baker, Petronius, and the Text of *Babylon Revisited*,' *F. Scott Fitzgerald Review* 1, 3-15.
Drennan, W. R. 1989. ''I Know Old Niceros and He's No Liar': Nick Carraway's Name in *The Great Gatsby*,' *ANQ* n.s. 2, 145-146.
Eurydice. 1999. *Satyricon USA: A Journey Across the New Sexual Frontier*, New York: Scribner.
Fitzgerald, F. S. 1973. *The Basil and Josephine Stories*, ed. J. R. Bryer and J. Kuehl, New York: Scribner.
— 1945. *The Crack-Up*, ed. E. Wilson, New York: New Directions.
— 1992. *The Great Gatsby*, The Authorized Text, New York: Collier.
— 1970. *This Side of Paradise*, New York: Charles Scribner's Sons.
— 2000. *Trimalchio: An Early Version of 'The Great Gatsby'*, ed. J. L. W. West III, Cambridge: Cambridge University Press.
Fraser, K. 1979. 'Another Reading of *The Great Gatsby*,' *English Studies in Canada* 5, 330-343.
Good, D. B. 1976. ''A Romance and a Reading List': The Literary References in *This Side of Paradise*,' *Fitzgerald/Hemingway Annual* 35-64.
Kuehl, J. 1961. 'Scott Fitzgerald's Reading,' *Princeton University Library Chronicle* 22, 58-89.
Kumamoto, C. D. 2001. 'Fitzgerald's *The Great Gatsby*,' *The Explicator* 60, 37-41.
MacKendrick, P. L. 1950. '*The Great Gatsby* and Trimalchio,' *CJ* 45, 307-314.
Müller, K., ed. 1961. *Petronii Arbitri Satyricon cum apparatu critico*, München: Ernst Heimeran.
Nest, E. D. 2004. *The Satyricon: The Morazla Scrolls*, Coral Springs, FL: Llumina Press.
Petronius. 1959. *Satyricon*, trans. William Arrowsmith, New York: New American Library.

Plato. 1989. *Symposium*, trans. A. Nehamas and P. Woodruff, Indianapolis: Hackett.
Rankin, H. D. 1970. 'Notes on the Comparison of Petronius with Three Moderns,' *AAASH* 18, 197-213.
Roulston, R.1984. 'Something Borrowed, Something New: A Discussion of Literary Influences on *The Great Gatsby*,' in *Critical Essays on F. Scott Fitzgerald's 'The Great Gatsby'*, ed. S. Donaldson, Boston: G. K. Hall, 54-66.
The Satyricon of Petronius Arbiter: Complete and Unexpurgated Translation by W. C. Firebaugh, in which are Incorporated the Forgeries of Nodot and Marchena, and the Readings Introduced into the Text by De Salas. Illustrations by Norman Lindsay, New York: Published for Private Circulation Only by Boni and Liveright, 1922, 2 vols.
Smith, M. S., ed. 1982. *Petronii Arbitri Cena Trimalchionis*, Oxford: Clarendon Press.
Sullivan, J. P. 1968. *The Satyricon of Petronius: A Literary Study*, Bloomington: Indiana University Press.
Turnbull, A., ed. 1963. *The Letters of F. Scott Fitzgerald*, New York: Charles Scribner's Sons.
Wagner, R. 1976. *The Ring of the Nibelung*, trans. A. Porter, New York: Norton.
West, J. L. W. III. 2000. 'Almost a Masterpiece,' *Humanites* 21, 14-18.
Zeitlin, F. I. 1971. 'Petronius as Paradox: Anarchy and Artistic Integrity,' *TAPA* 102, 631-684.

'His Career as Trimalchio': Petronian Character and Narrative in Fitzgerald's Great American Novel

NIALL W. SLATER
Emory University

> ...what better right does a man possess
> than to invent his own antecedents?
> *Trimalchio* 117

Both the writing and the titling of F. Scott Fitzgerald's greatest novel were complicated affairs. After drafting the text in the summer of 1924, he sent a complete version to Scribner's in October under the title of *The Great Gatsby*, but only a month later he wrote to his editor, Maxwell Perkins, proposing to call it instead *Trimalchio in West Egg*. The galley proofs that Perkins sent back to Fitzgerald, in the wake of two letters with a number of comments and suggestions, were headed 'Fitzgerald's Trimalchio,' though that is probably the printers' abbreviation of his requested version.[1] In response, Fitzgerald undertook a considerable rearrangement as well as important re-writing of the novel. In this process, the sole explicit reference to Trimalchio survived largely unchanged. Here are both the original and the re-shaped versions:

> It was when curiosity was at the highest about him that his lights failed to go on one Saturday night – and as obscurely as it had begun his career as Trimalchio suddenly ended. *Trimalchio*, ed. West 2000: 88

---

[1] See the full account in West 2000's 'Introduction,' esp. xvii on Fitzgerald's numerous other thoughts for titles. Perkins' letters of Nov. 18 and 20, 1924, are given in Appendix 1. Briggs 2000 argues forcefully that only the full title, Trimalchio in West Egg, is appropriate, although at least four of Fitzgerald's letters that he cites include the suggestion of simply Trimalchio for the title. I cite the text of West 2000 as *Trimalchio* hereafter and the text of *The Great Gatsby* from Bruccoli 1995 as *Gatsby*.

> It was when curiosity about Gatsby was at its highest that his lights in his house failed to go on one Saturday night – and, as obscurely as it had begun, his career as Trimalchio suddenly ended.
>
> *The Great Gatsby*, ed. Bruccoli 1995: 119

Indeed, it could be argued that this Petronian allusion has even gained in prominence in the revision, as originally it closed the fifth paragraph of chapter 7, while in the final text it is the very first sentence of that chapter.

Yet other changes make the equation of the American self-made millionaire with Petronius's Roman freedman even less straightforward than it was in the version that once bore his name. That text, only recently published by James West in the Cambridge edition of Fitzgerald, now allows us to see fuller dimensions of Petronian influence on the novel's original design, which I explore further here. The original text still does not answer the question of how Fitzgerald knew Petronius. The syllabi of the two Latin courses he took at Princeton do not include Petronius (few college courses did in that era), and Fitzgerald portrays himself as an indifferent Latin scholar in a famous letter about the formidable Andrew Fleming West, the classicist who helped drive Woodrow Wilson out of the Princeton presidency and into that of the United States:

> "One time in sophomore year at Princeton, Dean West got up and rolled out the great lines of Horace:
>   Integer vitae, scelerisque purus
>   Non eget Mauris iaculis neque arcu –
> – And I knew in my heart I had missed something by being a poor Latin scholar, like a blessed evening with a lovely girl....[2]

The risqué reputation of Petronius might have been inducement enough for Fitzgerald to read him in Latin on his own – but more likely in English.[3] Fitzgerald was certainly reading Homer in English as well[4] – though a prob-

---

[2] As quoted by MacKendrick 1950. 307.
[3] See Briggs 2000, 582-583 for a succinct and fascinating account of the publication of W. C. Firebaugh's translation of the *Satyricon* in 1922 and the prosecutions of its publisher, Boni and Liveright, for vice, which must have been known to Fitzgerald (a fuller account at Briggs 1999, 226-229).
[4] Briggs notes Fitzgerald's letter to Thomas Boyd, May 1924, in which he promises to 'read nothing but Homer + Homeric literature – and history 54-1200 A.D. until I finish [Gatsby]' [= Bruccoli and Duggan 1980, 141.]. It is intriguing that Fitzgerald chooses Nero's accession date (54) as the beginning point for his reading.

able allusion such as this detail from Daisy's drawing room might even have come third-hand:

> A breeze blew through the room ... and then rippled over the wine-colored rug, making a shadow on it as wind does on the sea. (*Gatsby* 12)[5]

The interest of *Trimalchio in West Egg*, however, lies not in isolated classical or Petronian allusions but in the light it sheds on the theme of time in the novel and the re-structuring of narrative that re-shapes our views of characters therein.

Certain broad parallels are obvious. Like Gaius Pompeius Trimalchio Maecenatianus, Jay Gatsby is a self-made man with a new name and identity he expresses through display of his acquired wealth. At age seventeen the former Jimmy Gatz of North Dakota found a wealthy patron who hired him as crew for his yacht and eventual private secretary – just as Trimalchio progressed from youthful slavery through assiduous attention to his master to become his freedman and heir.[6] When we meet Gatsby, his most obvious attribute is his enormous and lavishly furnished house, where he stages parties. For example, while Trimalchio has three libraries, one Greek, the other Latin (*tres bybliothecas habeo, unam Graecam, alteram Latinam*, 48.4),[7] the narrator Nick Carraway finds Gatsby's library one of his house's most impressive features:

> On a chance we tried an important-looking door, and walked into a high Gothic library, panelled with carved English oak, and probably transported complete from some ruin overseas. (*Gatsby* 49)

---

[5] I suspect a Homeric influence as well on the catalogue of anti-heroes near the beginning of chapter 4: for more than two pages, Nick Carraway lists Gatsby's party guests and their scandalous stories from that long-ago summer (*Gatsby* 65ff.); cf. Briggs 1999, 231, who sees parody of both Greek and Roman epic. There are very few changes between versions, although in *Trimalchio* the Stonewall Jackson Abrams of Georgia are 'still violently impassioned about the Civil War' (53), while *Gatsby* 67 introduces a 'Faustina O'Brien' near the end of the list. Fitzgerald clearly takes great pleasure in these carnivalesque names.

[6] See chapter 6 of *Gatsby* 103ff. Gatsby is actually cheated of his monetary legacy from his patron Dan Cody by the old man's widow (107), but his real inheritance is the education he received in how to reinvent himself.

[7] As MacKendrick 1950, 309 rightly notes, 'The discrepancy is in the manuscripts, and it should stand.'

Another guest discovered in the library admires it enormously – for what might seem a curious reason: the books are real!

> "Absolutely real – have pages and everything. I thought they'd be a nice durable cardboard. Matter of fact, they're absolutely real. Pages and – Here! Lemme show you." ...
>
> "See!" He cried triumphantly. "It's a bona fide piece of printed matter. It fooled me. This fella's a regular Belasco. It's a triumph. What thoroughness! What realism!" (*Gatsby* 50)

As shown by the reference to David Belasco, a theatrical producer famed for the realism of his extravagant sets, the visitor assumes that books in Gatsby's house must just be stage dressing – and only admires the expense of buying real books to create the illusion of a library. When he takes Daisy on a tour of his house, Gatsby describes this room as 'the Merton College Library' (*Gatsby* 96).[8]

Jay Gatsby in the first part of *Trimalchio* creates and presides over a carnivalesque house operating by 'the rules of behavior associated with an amusement park' (34). Music, food, and drink are lavishly omnipresent, including 'salads of harlequin design and pastry pigs'[9] as well as 'cordials so long forgotten that most of his female guests were too young to recognize their names' (33). At Gatsby's request, the orchestra plays Vladimir Epstien's 'Jazz History of the World'[10] to entertain a largely uncomprehending crowd of self-invited parasites. In a paragraph that vanished from the final published version, Nick Carraway describes being rapt by the music, despite its 'weird spinning sounds' and discords, concluding:

> Long after the piece was over, it went on and on in my head – whenever I think of that summer I can hear it yet. (*Trimalchio* 42)

---

[8] Though it may seem pedantic to note it, Gatsby himself presumably did not design the architecture of the library. We hear just a little earlier of a previous failure in self-creation: 'a brewer had built [the house] early in the "period" craze, a decade before' (93) and tried unsuccessfully to bribe his humbler neighbors into thatching the roofs of their houses to set off his grand manor. Gatsby takes the library and incorporates it into his self-portrayal as an 'Oxford man.'

[9] Perhaps reminiscent of the 'pastry piglets' (*porcelli ex coptoplacentis facti*, *Sat.* 40.4) that Trimalchio served with a huge roast boar?

[10] With painfully broad humor Fitzgerald renamed the composer 'Vladimir Tostoff' in *Gatsby* 54-55.

Like Trimalchio, Gatsby is obsessed not only with display but also time. The very first description of Trimalchio in the *Satyricon* (from a servant) tells us that he is:

lautissimus homo ... horologium in triclinio et bucinatorem habet subornatum, ut subinde sciat quantum de vita perdiderit (26.9)

the most elegant of men ... he has a water clock in his dining room and a liveried trumpeter, so he can know right away how much of his life he's lost.

Trimalchio himself later tells his guests that his Greek astrologer has assured him he has thirty years, four months, and two days left to live (76.10, 77.2). There are 87 occurrences of the word 'time' in the text of *Gatsby*. Perhaps the most telling sign of Gatsby's time obsession is revealed only after his death, when his father shows Nick Carraway a battered book in which the young Jimmy Gatz had written a daily schedule for work and self-improvement, divided evenly into quarter hours (*Gatsby* 181-182). Biographical criticism is now seriously unfashionable, but Fitzgerald himself said of his title character in a letter from 1925:

I never at any one time saw him [Gatsby] clear myself – for he started out as one man I knew and then changed into myself...[11]

In this light, Tom Burnam's reading of an essential theme of Fitzgerald's own character is particularly apposite:

Fitzgerald was always haunted by the theory that one's physical and emotional "capital" was a fixed and ordered quantity, to be carefully parceled out along the years of one's life and overdrawn only at one's peril.[12]

If Fitzgerald in some sense wrote himself into Gatsby, there is undoubtedly still more of him in the novel's narrator, Nick Carraway, to whom we now turn directly. The structure of a young and mobile first-person narrator recalling a past in which he was far more observer than participant shows obvious

---

[11] Letter to J. P. Bishop, 9 August 1925, quoted in *The Crack-Up*, p. 271 (taken from Burnam 1963 [1957] 106-107).
[12] Burnam 1963 [1957] 106, approving and summarizing views from Arthur Mizener's biography of Fitzgerald, *The Far Side of Paradise* (Boston 1951).

parallels to Encolpius in the *Satyricon*. Such references as 'whenever I think of that summer' and the often elegiac tone seem to create a wide distance between the past and the narrator's present – although in fact he just 'came back from the East last autumn' (6).[13] On the other hand, unlike Encolpius the scrounging *scholasticus*, the narrator's style here can seem remarkably accomplished for a young trainee in the bond business, even one who describes himself as 'rather literary in college' (*Gatsby* 8).[14] Where Encolpius provides an often satiric but static viewpoint on the Trimalchian spectacle, Nick's changing view of Gatsby over time allows for significant development in both his own and Gatsby's characters as well as a deepened appreciation of the protagonist's self-fashioning.

Most tellingly, Gatsby's 'real' history in *Trimalchio* emerges as a largely coherent autobiography, delivered to Nick; in the later *Gatsby*, essential parts emerge under hostile interrogation by Tom Buchanan. Pivotal to this change is the moment of revelation concerning Gatsby's claim to be 'an Oxford man.' In the original version, this is the beginning of his self-revelation to Nick after the fatal auto accident:

> "You know, old sport, I haven't got anything," he said suddenly. "I thought for awhile I had a lot of things, but the truth is I'm empty, and I guess people feel it. That must be why they keep on making up things about me, so I won't be so empty. I even make up things myself." He looked at me frankly. "I'm not an Oxford man."
>
> "I know it." I was glad that this tremendous detail was cleared up at last.
>
> "I was only there a few months," he continued unexpectedly. "A lot of the officers overseas had a chance to go there after the war."
>
> I wanted to slap him on the back. I had one of those renewals of complete faith in him that I had experienced before. (*Trimalchio* 116-117)

In the final version, the admission is less voluntary, to a hostile questioner and a wider audience – and before the fatal accident:

---

[13] The narrator's present can seem somewhat flexible. Chapter 9 opens 'After two years I remember the rest of that day ...,' suggesting that fateful summer is now at least two years ago.

[14] See Burnam 1963 [1957] 106 on the two narrators and what he calls 'the Fitzgerald theme.'

> "By the way, Mr. Gatsby, I understand you're an Oxford man."
> "Not exactly."
> "Oh, yes, I understand you went to Oxford."
> "Yes – I went there."
> A pause. Then Tom's voice, incredulous and insulting:
> "You must have gone there about the time Biloxi went to New Haven."
> Another pause ... This tremendous detail was to be cleared up at last.
> "I told you I went there," said Gatsby.
> "I heard you, but I'd like to know when."
> "It was in nineteen-nineteen. I only stayed five months. That's why I can't really call myself an Oxford man."
>
> Tom glanced around to see if we mirrored his unbelief. But we were all looking at Gatsby.
> "It was an opportunity they gave to some of the officers after the Armistice," he continued. "We could go to any of the universities in England or France."
> I wanted to get up and slap him on the back. I had one of those renewals of complete faith in him that I'd experienced before.
>
> (*Gatsby* 135-136)

The change both flattens the effect and undermines sympathy for Gatsby. Nick's faith in Gatsby's underlying honesty of character and self-conception is restored, but his is only one perspective in the later novel. And even Nick's faith may not be enduring, since he prefaces the rest of Gatsby's account of himself, which remains in chapter 8 in the final version, following the accident, with this line:

> It was this night that he told me the strange story of his youth with Dan Cody – told it to me because "Jay Gatsby" had broken up like glass against Tom's hard malice ... (*Gatsby* 155)

Vanished too is this original tribute to Gatsby's self-invention:

> ...what better right does a man possess than to invent his own antecedents? Jay Gatsby of West Egg, Long Island, sprang from his platonic conception of himself. He was a son of God – a phrase which, if it means anything at all, means just that. And he must be about his Father's busi-

ness, which was the service of a vast, vulgar, and meretricious beauty. To this he was faithful till the end. (*Trimalchio* 117)

The impetus for these changes in particular we may lay at Maxwell Perkins' feet, for he pressed the point in one of his letters to Fitzgerald:

> ... in giving deliberately Gatsby's biography when he gives it to the narrator you do depart from the method of the narrative in some degree ... I thought you might find ways ... to let the truth come out bit by bit in the course of the actual narrative.[15]

Fitzgerald has only partly followed this advice, with results that neither may have foreseen.

The original narrative structure of *Trimalchio* is more clearly Petronian, more tightly focussed through Nick Carraway's observations of the spectacle of Jay Gatsby. Yet if Nick begins with Encolpian detachment, he soon moves through fascination with the man and his entertainments to a far more sympathetic stance. Fitzgerald's re-ordering and re-structuring of narrative time for the final version adds new focalization which may paradoxically be more Encolpian yet retains a mythic power in which time and place are equally essential. In the last time we hear his voice directly, Gatsby still tells Nick the story of his life through what proves to be his final night, like Trimalchio, dictating the details of the monument to his life. Maxwell Perkins' judgement on the first version is equally valid for the finished product:

> "And all these things, the whole pathetic episode, you have given a place in time and space, for with the help of T. J. Eckleberg and by an occasional glance at the sky, or the sea, or the city, you have imparted a sort of sense of eternity."[16] [17]

---

[15] Letter of 20 November 1924, cited from *Trimalchio* 187-188.
[16] Letter of 20 November 1924, cited from *Trimalchio* 188.
[17] My gratitude is owed to Emory University's late, lamented Institute for Critical International Studies for a grant in support of my participation in ICAN 4, and I am also most grateful to the audience in Lisbon for questions and suggestions that have improved this version.

Bibliography

Briggs, W. 1999. 'Petronius and Virgil in *The Great Gatsby*', *International Journal of the Classical Tradition* 5, 226-235.

Briggs, W. 2000. 'The Ur-*Gatsby*', *International Journal of the Classical Tradition* 6, 577-584.

Bruccoli, M. J. and M. M. Duggan. 1980. *The Correspondence of F. Scott Fitzgerald*. New York.

Burnam, T. 1963 [1957]. 'The Eyes of Dr. Eckleburg: A Re-examination of *The Great Gatsby*', pp. 104-111 in *F. Scott Fitzgerald: A Collection of Critical Essays*, ed. A. Mizener. Englewood Cliffs, NJ. [= *College English* 24 (Oct. 1952) pp. 7-12]

Fitzgerald, F. S. 1991. *The Great Gatsby*, ed. M. J. Bruccoli. New York.

MacKendrick, P. L. 1950. '*The Great Gatsby* and Trimalchio', *Classical Journal* 45, 307-314.

Parr, S. R. 1985. 'The Idea of Order at West Egg', pp. 59-78 in *New Essays on The Great Gatsby*, ed. M. J. Bruccoli. Cambridge.

Raleigh, J. H. 1963 [1957]. 'F. Scott Fitzgerald's *The Great Gatsby*: Legendary Bases and Allegorical Significances', pp. 99-103 in *F. Scott Fitzgerald: A Collection of Critical Essays*, ed. A. Mizener. Englewood Cliffs, NJ. [= *The University of Kansas City Review* 24 (1957) pp. 55-58]

West, J. L. W. 2000. *Trimalchio: An Early Version of The Great Gatsby by F. Scott Fitzgerald*. Cambridge.

Petronius and the Contemporary Novel: Between New Picaresque and Queer Aesthetics

MASSIMO FUSILLO
University of L'Aquila

Petronius' 'splendid evasiveness' (Slater 1990) is the main reason given for his splendid success in contemporary culture. Much of this elusive character comes notably from the text's fragmentary condition, but a careful literary analysis shows the deliberately episodic nature of the *Satyricon*: it is a subversive text that plays with readerly expectations, genre categories, narrative roles, linguistic registers. These features find a profound echo in the novel's manifold transformations at the beginning of the twentieth century, when it became the experimental genre *par excellence*. If Petronius' realism – now a thorny critical category, formerly brilliantly described by Erich Auerbach (1946) in his masterpiece of stylistic criticism – could correspond to novelistic frescoes of the nineteenth century (especially those by Balzac and Zola), his open form vividly corresponds to modernist (and postmodernist) expressive revolutions: especially to Joyce's epic of body and language.

Petronian innovations definitively look towards the modern novel and contemporary experimentation. First of all, his revolutionary transformation of a theme, which is among the specific features of novelistic writing: travel. Compared with the ancient archetype of any fiction of adventure, the *Odyssey*, and with its re-use in the Greek novel, the *Satyricon* shows an impressive absence of teleology: travels are no longer a negative experience, a test to be passed in order to reach the final goal, conjugal reunification (in any case a peculiar kind of negativity, since this series of obstacles comprises the main part of the narrative). As Bakhtin points out, the typical Greek love story is an «extratemporal hiatus between two moments of biographical time» (Bakhtin 1934-5, 90): an effective formula that does not depict, however, the complex variations to be found in each work. On the contrary, in Petronius's novel characters do move from one place to another without following any organic design, frequently just for pleasure's sake. The true propulsive force of narration is encounter (a famous Bakhtinian chronotope), which allows the confrontation with manifold social types and the insertion of a varied encyclopaedic subject-matter. By this route the novel turns out to be a voyage into the labyrinths of language, body and sexuality, in which adventures follow each other in a paratactic, irregular and centrifugal way.

In Petronius the labyrinth is indeed something more than a simple metaphor: it is rather a textual device that characterizes the anarchic course of the narration. At the beginning of our *Satyricon* we are plunged into a complex dialogue between the protagonist, Encolpius, and a professor of rhetoric, Agamemnon, about the decline of oratory and educational systems. This long essayistic insertion is abruptly interrupted by Encolpius, who realizes that his rival Ascyltus has taken flight. He then encounters a mass of students coming back from another declamation, and loses his way in a labyrinth of streets, until an old woman brings him finally to a brothel:

Dum hunc diligentius audio, non notavi mihi Ascylti fugam <...> et dum in hoc dictorum aestu in hortis incedo, ingens scholasticorum turba in porticum venit, ut apparebat, ab extemporali declamatione nescio cuius, qui Agamemnonis suasoriam exceperat. Dum ergo iuvenes sententias rident ordinemque totius dictionis infamant, opportune subduxi me et cursim Ascylton persequi coepi. Sed nec viam diligenter tenebam [quia] nec quod stabulum esse sciebam. Itaque quocumque ieram, eodem revertebar, donec et cursu fatigatus et sudore iam madens accedo aniculam quandam, quae agreste holus vendebat (§ 6).

[I was listening so attentively to this speech that I did not notice the flight of Ascyltos, and while I was pacing the gardens, engulfed in this flood-tide of rhetoric, a large crowd of students came out upon the portico, having, it would seem, just listened to an extemporaneous declamation, of I know not whom, the speaker of which had taken exceptions to the speech of Agamemnon. While therefore, the young men were making fun of the sentiments of this last speaker, and criticizing the arrangement of the whole speech, I seized the opportunity and went after Ascyltos, on the run; but, as I neither held strictly to the road, nor knew where the inn was located, wherever I went, I kept coming back to the same place until, worn out with running, and long since dripping with sweat, I approached a certain little old woman who sold country vegetables] (transl. W. C. Firebaugh).

There is no logic and no teleology in this narrative layout that follows only the free association of encounters. Even the picaresque pattern will be more regular in its alternation of episodes, and in its organization according to a series of obstacles.

As already hinted, a second noteworthy Petronian innovation is its open form: the *Satyricon* frequently follows the course of a conversational novel, full of discussions on art and poetry, quotations, and recitations of entire works of poetry, facilitated by the encounters with characters such as the above mentioned Agamemnon, and especially the poetaster Eumolpus. Finally, a last Petronian feature which looks towards modernity is certainly theatricality: his characters (especially the protagonist and narrator, Encolpius) conceive their adventures in terms of sublime literary models, epic and tragic, and read their experience as a continuous performance.

Petronius's novelty has often been explained and labelled with another elusive category: realism. As a matter of fact, some of the features Ian Watt (1957) considered typical of the English novel as a new, revolutionary genre can be found in the *Satyricon* (and generally in ancient fiction) as well: plots not taken from mythology, stress on everyday life, the pattern of autobiographical memory, and so on. In *An Exemplary History of the Novel* Walter Reed (1981) acknowledged several significant novelistic elements in ancient prose fiction, such as the use of contemporary characters, psychological analyses, reflections on social conditions, and sophisticated awareness of the conventionality of literary tradition. Nevertheless, he denies it the definition of true novel because of its religious idealization, and, in the specific case of Petronius (the only one devoid of any transcendence), because of the aristocratic bias of his parody. On the contrary, in *The True History of the Novel* Margaret Doody (1996) has strongly defended the continuity between ancient and modern novel, totally rejecting the novelty of British novel of the eighteenth century. To find a balance between literary constants and historical variations is always a thorny methodological question, but it is hard to deny now that the classical dichotomy between novel and romance does not portray the complex history of the novel. If we only give a look at the five volumes of the collective work *Il romanzo*, edited by Franco Moretti (2001-3), that dedicates space to ancient fiction as well as to Chinese novels, we have the impression not of a single literary genre, but of a galaxy of similar forms. Personally I do not believe in a direct homology of literary and social structures; I think that the vision defended by Russian formalists (and especially by Tynianov) of two autonomous series, that certainly interact but have a different tempo, is still convincing. If we want to state a link between the novel and historical processes, we might rather speak of parallel and recursive elements. In the ancient world novels emerged in a period of drastic transformations, such as Hellenism, as an underground literature probably addressing a new, larger audience, the global and scattered citizenry of the Greco-Roman Empire. One can find of course similarities in the historical contexts of the periods that are usually considered the birth of the (modern) novel (16th century Spain, 18th century England), but it seems hard to find a direct connexion.

Literary history, like real history, does not follow any teleology, but is mostly ruled by chance and unpredictability. That is the reason why I would like to concentrate now on an example of a desultory continuity between ancient and modern novel, and of a peculiar historical recursivity more generally. In my opinion Petronius's idiosyncratic creation found its true reception first in the 20th century and in the contemporary novel. Actually, canonical picaresque novels seem to have been more influenced by the second Latin archetype, Apuleius' *Golden Ass,* which was translated into Spanish in the early 16th century. If we look especially at the narrative organisation, both follow a quite regular pattern: the potentially infinite series of encounters and adventures are always obstacles to surmount in order to survive and to satisfy primary drives. Indeed, in Apuleius there is a teleological element, the orientation towards the final metamorphosis back into human form, although it is basically obscured by a massive internal focalization on the "I" actor, which provides the single episodes with a great autonomy. From this point of view the Novel of the Ass is a parodic version of the idealized sentimental novel, just as the Spanish picaresque novel is one of pastoral romance. On the other hand, Petronius's adventures are much more irregular, and frequently motivated only by curiosity and aimless pleasure. The *Satyricon* sounds indeed quite anarchic and nomadic; that is the reason why it can be compared, with the necessary caution, to the so called new picaresque novel.

In literary criticism there are two different usages of the term 'picaresque': a restricted one, closely linked to the specific social and historical context of sixteenth century Spain and related areas; and a broader one, sustained, among others, by Claudio Guillén (1987), which identifies a recurrent narrative pattern. Let us read two effective definitions, which synthesize the main features of the picaresque (both quoted and discussed by Rohnert 2001): 'In broad general terms, it (picaresque novel) is usually employed to describe episodic, open-ended narratives in which lower-class protagonists sustain themselves by means of their cleverness and adaptability during an extended journey through space, time, and various predominantly corrupt social milieu' (Bjornson); and: '1) the quasi confession, presented in a first person narrative, of a paradigmatically orphaned protagonist operating on the fringes of society and legality; 2) an action-oriented, hectically episodic plot crowded with sudden peripeties and anagnoreses.' (Klaus Poenicke).

The new picaresque is an interesting example of how the 20th century novel can re-use and transform traditional narrative patterns. The paratactic and associative structure of the canonical antecedents is now aimed at expressing a shattered identity, a cosmic dissatisfaction, a profound nomadism; it is not by chance that the last of these has become a crucial philosophical category, from Deleuze to Rosy Braidotti. That is the reason why scholars prefer to stress the cultural clash using the adjective 'new', or speaking of picaresque echoes. This trend involves works of different areas and periods (from Kafka's *Amerika* to Thomas Mann's *Felix Krull*, from Saul Bellow's *The Adventures of Augie March* to Günther Grass' *Der Blechtrommel*), until postmodern novels and movies, in which the picaresque journey allows the depiction of plural cultural landscapes, especially in the United States, as the recent *Road Book America* by R.A. Sherrill (2000) has brilliantly showed. Moreover, a German dissertation by Werner Reinhart (2001) stressed the American attitude towards picaresque narrative, starting from William Dean Howells, who in 1895 read the *Lazarillo* as a possible model for a future narrative, and reading in these terms Twain, Ellison, Dos Passos; Reinhart focusses especially on the Eighties, considering the flourishing of alternative storytelling a reverse of the Reaganomics mythology (father, family, progress), which opposes to the dominant sense of hierarchy a chaotic destructuration; the main examples of this trend are William Kennedy's *Quinn's Book* (1988), Paul Auster's *Moon Place* (1989), Tom Coraghessan Boyle's *World's End* (1987), John Irving's *The Cider House Rules* (1985) and *A Prayer for Owen Meany* (1989), Kathy Acker's *Quixote* (1986), and finally Thomas Pynchon's *Vineland* (1990).

I will focus on texts coming from different moments of the 20th century, in order to show how productive the new picaresque contemporary novel can be. The first one embodies in my opinion at its utmost the dialectics between literary constants and cultural variations: Céline's *Voyage au bout de la nuit*. In his travels from France to Africa and to the States, the *Voyage*'s autobiographical main character, Bardamu, is driven by a metaphysical disgust and a strongly splenetic disposition, a recurrent literary motif in the last century. The novel shows an incredibly dense thematic system: on the one hand dirt, corruption, degradation, war, obsession, a long negative chain of concepts, visualized by the paratextual metaphor of night; on the other hand a few flashes of positive energy, such as fantasy, dream, music, movies, encounters. Nomadism and lying represent indeed the only solutions, in the Célinian universe, to overcome this strong dichotomy, although in a radically desperate way, as is summarised by the following passage, in which we also find the search for the double as another propulsive force:

> J'en avais trop vu moi de choses pas claires pour être content. J'en savais de trop et j'en savais pas assez. Faut sortir, que je me dis, sortir encore. Peut-être que tu rencontreras Robinson. C'était une idée idiote évidemment mais que je me donnais pour avoir un prétexte à sortir à nouveau, d'autant plus que j'avais beau me retourner encore sur le petit plumard je ne pouvais accrocher le plus petit bout de sommeil. Même à se masturber dans ces cas-là on n'éprouve ni réconfort, ni distraction. Alors c'est le vrai désespoir.
> Ce qui est pire c'est qu'on se demande comment le lendemain on trouvera assez de force pour continuer a faire ce qu'on a fait la veille et depuis déjà tellement trop longtemps, où on trouvera la force pour ces démarches imbéciles, ces mille projets qui n'aboutissent à rien, ces tentatives pour sortir de l'accablante nécessité, tentatives qui toujours avortent, et toutes pour aller se convaincre une fois de plus que le destin est insurmontable, qu'il faut retomber au bas de la muraille, chaque soir, sous l'angoisse de ce lendemain, toujours plus précaire, plus sordide.
> C'est l'âge aussi qui vient peut-être, le traitre, et nous menace du pire. On n'a plus beaucoup de musique en soi pour faire danser la vie, voilà. Toute la jeunesse est allée mourir déjà au bout du monde dans le silence de vérité. Et où aller dehors, je vous le demande, dès qu'on a plus en soi la somme suffisante de délire ? La vérité, c'est une agonie qui n'en finit pas. La vérité de ce monde c'est la mort. Il faut choisir, mourir ou mentir. Je n'ai jamais pu me tuer moi (Céline 1932, 199-200).

[I'd seen too many puzzling things to be easy in my mind. I knew too much and not enough. I'd better go out, I said to myself, I'd better go out again. Maybe I'll meet Robinson. Naturally that was an idiotic idea, but I dreamed it up as an excuse for going out again, because no matter how much I tossed and turned on my narrow bed, I couldn't snatch the tiniest scrap of sleep. Even masturbation, at times like that, provides neither comfort nor entertainment. Then you're really in despair.

The worst part is wondering how you'll find the strength tomorrow to go on doing what you did today and have been doing for much too long, where you'll find the strength for all that stupid running around, those projects that come to nothing, those attempts to escape from crushing necessity, which always founder and serve only to convince you one more time that destiny is implacable, that every night will find you down and out, crushed by the dread of more and more sordid and insecure tomorrows.

And maybe it's treacherous old age coming on, threatening the worst. Not much music left inside us for life to dance to. Our youth has gone to the ends of the earth to die in the silence of the truth. And where, I ask you, can a man escape to, when he hasn't enough madness left inside him? The truth is an endless death agony. The truth is death. You have to choose : death or lies. I've never been able to kill myself] (transl. Ralph Manheim).

Nevertheless, there are many Célinian features that evoke Petronius: the artistic re-use of colloquial language; the absolute prominence of sexuality and physical compulsion as the only true forms of authenticity; a poetics of dirt, degradation and corruption; the exploitation of encounters as the main device to produce narration, and as a way of representing multifarious social typologies; theatricality and performativity as the predominant human reactions to the menace of disease and death. Although we never catch Petronius's *Weltanschauung*, in reading the *Voyage* we feel a strong consonance between distant cultural contexts; a feeling that comes back in Céline's other masterpiece, *Mort à credit*, and in some of his later, more controversial novels (for example, *Le pont de Londres*).

The second example shows a more direct and intertextual relationship. In the second half of the twentieth century Petronius' novel has been rewritten and reinvented by several Italian artists, especially by avant-garde movements (Sanguineti's free translation, Maderna's opera, and even Pasolini's last novel *Petrolio,* and of course Fellini's movie); quite original and idiosyncratic is the register chosen by Alberto Arbasino, member of the avant-guarde group 63, who nevertheless shared a long friendship with Pasolini (an enemy of that group). In his essay *Certi romanzi*, he theorised a new Menippean satire and considered the *Satyricon* as a model for a novel based on continuous digressions and free conversations, namely, on the ironical and cynical observation of contemporary customs. In his masterpiece *Fratelli d'Italia* (1963), Arbasino quotes often the *Satyricon* as a model for the picaresque travels and sexual adventures of a gay couple, interwoven with long discussions and digressions on novels, paintings, music and theatre. In the third, expanded new version of the novel (1993), he adds a futurological and dystopian version of Petronius's novel, presented as a collection of fragments from a lost work, dominated by a cultural entrepreneur, Trimalciozzi, who produces digital programs that enable people to experience strange literary pastiches.

Arbasino's aesthetic attitude leads us to an outstanding category in contemporary Anglo-Saxon culture: camp. First defined by Susan Sontag in 1967, 'camp' predominantly indicates a mixture of irony, theatricality, aestheticism, and juxtaposition of incongruous elements; a playful re-use of consumer culture; a refined contamination of kitsch with cultivated, highbrow elements. It is a mode characteristic of postmodern culture, and in particular of gay communities, which often have strong relationships with a range of icons (see Cleto 1999). Since camp implies a shifting and performative idea of subjectivity, it often uses a picaresque narration: as in Gus Van Sant's *My Own Private Idaho*, a road movie often compared to the *Satyricon* (a comparison supported by the director, who acknowledges however that he read the novel only after the movie was released), and characterized by a campy theatrical artificiality (especially evident in the use of footage for the sexual scenes), and by a profound sense of nomadic dislocation. It is not by chance that Petronian ambivalent resumption of consumer genres (mime, pantomime, sentimental novel), together with his promiscuous vision of homosexuality, and especially with his melodramatic theatricality, has been read by Cecil Wooten (1984) as a first occurrence of a camp sensibility: an embryo archetype.

How can we evaluate the parallelism between Petronius and the new picaresque novel? I am perfectly aware of the criticism that can come from a strictly historicist perspective, that usually denies any metaphorical use of the term picaresque, both in the past and in the future direction. I also know that Petronius's splendid evasiveness can be extremely risky, becoming a container of disparate categories (realism, picaresque, camp). The most serious risk is to frame the novel as an all-embracing concept: this is the case for Bakhtin's theory, which certainly made a fundamental and precious contribution to the history of the novel, especially from the point of view of its genealogy, but tended to hypostasize it as a positive force, just in the same way Lukács did for the epic, forgetting that, for example, in the 19th century the novel was no longer a non-canonical, polyphonic and emerging genre, being on the contrary a more and more hegemonic and official form. My point was just to show how in different cultural contexts, thanks to its open form, the novel can convey a series of narrative and thematic constants – nomadic adventures, autobiographical narration, low and degraded setting, theatricality, anti-idealistic and anti-sentimental attitude, cynical and materialistic ideology, linguistic contamination; and how this recursive mixture can be summarised by the transcultural label of picaresque.

Bibliography

Auerbach, E. 1953. *Mimesis*, Princeton: Princeton University Press (original Bern 1946).
Bakhtin, M. 1981. *The Dialogic Imagination*, Austin: Texas UP, (Russian orig. 1934-5).
Céline, L.F. 1932. *Voyage au bout de la nuit, Paris*: Editions Denoel et Steele.
Cleto, F. (ed.) 1999. *Camp. Queer Aesthetics and the Performing Subject*. Edinburgh: Edinburgh UP.
Doody, M.A. 1996. *The True Story of the Novel*, New Brunswick: Rutgers UP.
Guillén, C. 1987. *The Anatomies of the Roguery. A Comparative Study in the Origins and the Nature of Picaresque Literature*, New York: Garland.
Moretti, F. (ed.), 2001-03. *Il romanzo,* 5 vols., Turin: Einaudi. Engl. part. transl. *The Novel*, Princeton – Oxford: Princeton UP 2006.
Reed, W.L. 1981. *An Exemplary History of the Novel: The Quixotic versus the Picaresque,* Chicago: Chicago UP.
Reinhart, W. 2001. *Pikareske Romane der 80er Jahre. Ronald Reagan und die Renaissance des politischen Erzählens in den USA (Acker, Auster, Boyle, Irving, Kennedy, Pynchon)*, Tübingen: Narr.
Sherill, R.A. 2000. *Road-Book America. Contemporary Culture and the New Picaresque*, Urbana and Chicago: Illinois UP.
Slater, N.W. 1990. *Reading Petronius*, Baltimore and London: Johns Hopkins UP.
Watt, I. 1957. *The Rise of the Novel. Studies in Defoe, Richardson and Fielding,* Berkeley: University of California Press.
Wooten, C. 1984 'Petronius and Camp', *Helios* 11: 133-9.

D

The Reception of the Ancient Novel in Drama

Psyche, Callirhoë and Operatic Heroines Derived from Ancient Novels

JON SOLOMON
University of Illinois at Urbana-Champaign

Opera owes its existence largely to Greek studies in the late Renaissance. At its inception, Girólamo Mei and Vincenzo Galilei revived the study of ancient Greek music theory, Giovanni Bardi rejected Renaissance Flemish polyphony and substituted ancient Greek monody, and Jacopo Peri, Giulio Caccini, and Ottavio Rinuccini adapted the appropriate dramatic format from ancient Greek tragedy. In particular Peri and Rinuccini attempted to recreate the "sweet speech" [*hêdumenos logos*] of Greek tragedy that Aristotle describes in his *Poetics*: Their solution was to appeal to the acoustical distinction made by Aristotle's student, Aristoxenus, between intervallic musical sounds and continuous spoken sounds. The result was the innovative *stile rappresentativo*, or what we generally call "recitative," the most distinctive presentational form of the operatic genre.

The titles of their first *dramme per musica*, *Dafne* (1598) and *Euridice* (1600), and then Monteverdi's successful *L'Orfeo* (1607) and *L'Arianna* (1608) remind us that the poets who created the first opera librettos derived their subject matter from ancient Greek mythology, albeit from versions by such ancient Latin poets as Ovid, Vergil, and Catullus. None of these earliest works derive from the ancient novelists. When the new musical/theatrical genre moved from Florence to Rome, particularly under the guidance of the Barberini family, it began to incorporate stories taken from paleochristian biography, and soon additional titles were developed dependent upon the Italian Renaissance epics of Tasso and Ariosto, a genre equally dependent on Greco-Roman mythology and epic poetry. An additional subject field was added in the 1640s when Monteverdi derived the first historical opera, *L'incoronazione di Poppea* (1642), primarily from Tacitus, Suetonius, and pseudo-Seneca.

One of the axioms of classical reception is that works that do not interest artists, patrons, and audiences at the outset of a revival have a more difficult time interesting them later, so, one of the reasons the ancient novel had relatively little impact on the operatic genre is that the vast majority of operas for the genre's first half century were derived from ancient mythology and history. Interfering with any movement for change was the fact that opera was a relatively conservative artistic genre: operas became so expensive to produce that entrepreneurs, sponsors, and patrons were unlikely to invest their money on unproven material—not unlike film producers; and audiences and critics tend to prefer what they already know. And so for decades the Greco-Roman myths and histories of Greece and Rome provided librettists with their normal fare without interruption.

This changed a bit in that very same year in the very same city. On January 1, 1642, Francesco Cavalli, formerly under the tutelage of Monteverdi but soon to be the most sought-after composer in Europe, produced his version of *Amore innamorato*. That the music has not survived tells us something about its relative lack of success, but the libretto tells the tale of Amor, Psyche, and Venus from Apuleius' *Metamorphoses*. There might be reason to suspect that an opera based on the story of Cupid and Psyche might not provide a bona fide example of an opera derived from an ancient novel because the story had long since taken a path of its own separate from Apuleius' work as a whole.[1] But, Julia Haig Gaisser in her current book, *The Fortunes of Apuleius and the Golden Ass*, illustrates copiously the concatenation of influences and adaptations of the Cupid and Psyche episode in the Renaissance and suggests few incidences in which the author or artist probably did not even know that the story of Cupid and Psyche derived from Apuleius, let alone from an ancient novel.[2]

In addition, there are several reasons for identifying a conscious borrowing. First, I think it is important to observe a continuing phenomenon in the adaptation of ancient myths and narratives, and that is that adaptations from ancient narratives and myths often occur in clusters. The lists in Jane Reid's *Oxford Guide to Classical Mythology in the Arts, 1300-1990s*, frequently illustrate this. For the Psyche story, there were only 75 adaptations from the middle of the fifteenth century until 1640, a rate of one every other year, but

---

[1] I am grateful to the anonymous referee for this suggestion.
[2] Julia Haig Gaisser, *The Fortunes of Apuleius and the Golden Ass: A Study in Transmission and Reception* (Princeton: Princeton University Press, 2008); see also Salvatore Ussia, *Amore inamorato; riscritture poetiche della novella di Amore e Psiche Secoli XV – XVII* (Vercelli: Edizioni Mercurio, 2001), esp. 11-37.

then 23 between Calderón de la Barca's *Psiquis y Cupido* of 1640 and Le Brun's ceiling cycle of 1652, a rate of two per year, including Jacob Jordaens' paintings commissioned by Charles I of England and five commissioned by Queen Christina of Sweden.[3] This is the cluster which produced as well Cavalli's opera.

Second, Ellen Rosand has confirmed that the men responsible for the libretto of Cavalli's *Amore innamorato*—Giovanni Battista Fusconi, Giovanni Francesco Loredano, and Pietro Michele—were not at all casual authors but signatory members of Venice's Accadémia degli Incogniti.[4] The Accademia degli Incogniti included poets, philosophers, and historians who produced prodigious amounts of literature. Loredano, the highly visible patrician founder of the Academy in 1630, penned at least two publications detailing the debates among academy members; Michele was a poet, and it was his *Psiche*, based on a subject provided by Loredano, that gave Fusconi the fodder to prepare the final libretto from which Cavalli could set the opera. It is very unlikely that these three writers were unaware of the pedigree of the story of Psyche.

What is of particular interest about this for the study of early opera is that ancient novels, which for the most part present continuous episodic narratives, allow and even encourage this sort of narrative extraction of a particular episode, while the ancient mythological tradition, from which early opera extracted most of its narrative subject matter, was discontinuously episodic. That is, by and large the mythical stories about Hercules, Perseus, Oedipus, and the like were not told in a connected narrative but transmitted separately in epic, lyric, and tragic poems. Homer tells not of the entire Trojan War but of the episodes of the anger of Achilles and the return of Odysseus. Sophocles tells not of the Labdacid family in a connected narrative but of Antigone, the blinding of Oedipus, and the death of Oedipus in three separate tragedies, the latter being separated from the former by some four decades. In contrast, when Ottavio Rinuccini composed the libretto for the very first opera, *Dafne*, he collected several episodes involving Apollo, mainly the Python and Daphne episodes from Ovid's *Metamorphoses*, and fused them into a single narrative. The same could be said for the operatic version of the Orpheus story set by Monteverdi in 1607 and penned by Ales-

---

[3] On the latter, see Jennifer Montagu, "The Early Ceiling Decorations of Charles Le Brun," *The Burlington Magazine* 105 (1963) 395-408.

[4] Ellen Rosand, *Opera in Seventeenth-Century Venice: The Creation of a Genre* (Berkeley: University of California Press, 1991) 38. n. 11; and "Barbara Strozzi, *virtuosissima cantatrice*: The Composer's Voice," *Journal of the American Musicological Society* 31 (1978) 241-281, esp. 245 with n. 22.

sandro Striggio, for it includes both the *katabasis* episode from Book 10 of Ovid's *Metamorphoses* and the death of Orpheus from Book 11,[5] and then incorporates as well the account from the fourth book of Vergil's *Georgics*.

Reid omits two additional operas that were produced in quick succession Tomaso Breni's *Psiche* (1645) performed in Lucca, and Marco Scacchi's *Le nozze d'Amore e di Psiche*, libretto by Virgilio Puccitelli, performed in Gdansk, Warsaw, and Cracow in 1646. But of the other listed musical works inspired by this reinvigorated interest in the Cupid and Psyche portion of Apuleius' *Metamorphoses* in the middle of the seventeenth century—Lully's 1656 ballet, the Carnival spectacular of 1671, and the Thomas Shadwell/Matthew Locke semi-operatic English work of 1675—only one was an opera per se, Lully's *tragédie en musique* of 1778.[6]

Similarly, operatic adaptations of Heliodorus' novel have been almost non-existent. In his 1953 article in the *Journal of the Warburg and Courtauld Institutes*, Wolfgang Sterchow delineated dozens of borrowings and influences in the literature and painting of the sixteenth and seventeenth centuries.[7] Among these there are only a limited number of stage adaptations, including Alexandre Hardy's series of eight five-act dramatic poems,[8] and only one opera of note: Octave-César Genetay's *L'Éthiopique* (1609), a *tragicomédie*.[9] Racine, who reportedly had memorized the novel, developed a non-extant dramatic adaptation in 1662/1663.[10] Finally in 1695 Henry

---

[5] For the question of which version was original and which performed at the 1607 premier, see F. W. Sternfeld, "The Orpheus Myth and the Libretto of *Orfeo*," in John Whenham, ed., *Claudio Monteverdi: Orfeo* (Cambridge: Cambridge University Press, 1991) 25-27.

[6] Michael Turnbull, "The Metamorphosis of 'Psyche,'" *Music & Letters* 64 (1983) 12-24; and Murray Lefkowitz, "Shadwell and Locke's 'Psyche': The French Connection," *Proceedings of the Royal Musical Association* 106 (1979-1980) 42-55.

[7] Wolfgang Sterchow, "Heliodorus' Aethiopica in Art," *Journal of the Warburg and Courtauld Institutes* 16 (1953) 144-152. Cf. Henry Carrington Lancaster, *The French Tragi-Comedy: Its Origin and Development from 1552 to 1628* (Baltimore: J. H. Furst Company, 1907) 102-116, and 168; and Reid, *Oxford Guide* 2.1019.

[8] Alexandre Hardy, *Les chastes et loyales amours de Théagène et Cariclée, réduites du grec de l'Histoire d'Héliodore en huict poèmes dragmatiques* [sic] *ou théâtres consécutifs* (Paris: J. Quesnel, 1623).

[9] Octave-César Genetay, *L'Ethiopique" Tragicomédie des chastes amours de Théagène et Chariclée* (Rouen: T. Reinsart, 1609).

[10] R. C. Knight, "The Evolution of Racine's 'Poétique,'" *The Modern Language Review* 35 (1940) 21. See also, Gilbert Highet, *The Classical Tradition: Greek and Roman Influences on Western Literature* (New York and Oxford: Oxford University Press, 1957) 648, who also cites the borrowings in Racine's *Phèdre* and *Andromaque* (G. May, "Contribution à l'étude des sources grecques de *Phèdre*," *Modern Languages Quarterly* 8 (1947) 228-234) as well as Shakespeare's *Twelfth Night* [5.1.121-123].

Desmarest composed the score for Joseph-François Douché de Vancy's libretto of *Théagène et Cariclée*, but despite Desmarest's previous successes, the opera failed miserably. In fact, after this failure the French cluster of adaptations comes to a relatively abrupt halt.[11] Nonetheless, it is important to observe, as we did for the librettic adaptation of Apuleius, that Douché de Vancy was experienced in adapting classical literature and writing tragedies. His other *tragedies en musique* include *Céphale et Procris* (1694), *Scylla* (1701), and *Iphigénie en Tauride* (1704).[12]

The reception of *Chariton*'s novel differs from the other ancient novels because of its problematic text, which was not promulgated until Jacques Philippe d'Orville's 1750 *editio princeps*. This eventually inspired an operatic *Calliroe*, which premiered on *February* 11, 1770 at Ludwigsburg for the birthday of Carl Eugen, Duke of Württemberg. In the preface to his libretto, Mattia Verazi cites both Michele Angelo Giacomelli's 1756 Italian translation of Chariton's work and Lopez de Vega's *Giulietta, e Roselo* [*Castelvines y Monteses*]. Both models include a false-death motif, but Verazi preferred Juliet's more humane coma-inducing potion to Callirhoe's being kicked to death.

Calliroe was still another libretto adapted from an ancient novel by a dedicated humanist who was at the forefront of an artistic movement and well aware of the implications inherent in the source material he chose. Indeed, it was Mattia Verazi who followed the lead of Frederick the Great and helped return Greek tragedy to the operatic stage in the 1750s. Verazi's adaptation of *Calliroe* was relatively successful. After the 1770 Sacchini setting performed in Ludwigsburg, Giacomo Rust set it in Padua in 1776, Josef Myslivecek in Naples in 1778 and again in Pisa the following year, Felice Alessandri in Milan in 1778, and Sebastiano Nasolini in Florence in 1792.[13] But the cluster ends there.

One of the requirements for a successful opera is a dynamic protagonistic duo, not simply a couple upon whom fate and/or the gods foist a number of adventures. I would add to that another desideratum at least in the realm

---

[11] E.g. Claude Joseph Dorat's five-act tragedy, *Théagène* (Paris: Imprimerie de Sébastien Jorry, 1766), produced at the Comédie Français in 1762; and Pierre Nicolas Brunet's tragedy-ballet, *Théagène et Charicleé* (1771).

[12] Cuthbert. M. Girdlestone, *La tragédie en musique (1673–1750) considérée comme genre littéraire* (Geneva, 1972).

[13] Oscar George Theodore Sonneck, *Catalog of Opera Librettos Printed Before 1800: Title Catalogue* (Washington, D.C.: Government Printing Office, 1914) I.249-250. For the differences and variations, see Marita P. McClymonds, "Calliroe," *The New Grove Dictionary of Opera*, ed. S. Sadie. Vol. I, 691-692.

of popular culture—a heroine with an exotic name easy to pronounce. Psyche is an excellent example, Callirhoe may qualify, and certainly this is true for Aida.

Auguste Mariette's plot outline for *Aida* parallels that of Heliodorus' novel in several ways. But it is much more likely that Mariette had in mind contemporary politics involving the Khedive of Egypt and Meroe as well as ancient Greek accounts of ancient Egypt and the Rosetta Stone itself as his chief sources of inspiration.

This is a complicated argument which I have made elsewhere, but allow me to summarize. Khedive Isma'il, who commissioned *Aida* to celebrate the inaugural of his Cairo opera house in 1870, was thoroughly involved militarily in Meroe and the slave-trading south of Egypt in the hope of winning Western abolitionist support: this was the source of his interest in Ethiopia. To please Isma'il, Mariette outlined an opera scenario, which, ultimately, was set by Giuseppe Verdi. The name 'Aida' is not found in any ancient, i.e. bronze-age, Egyptian texts or models but closely resembles the feminine Ptolemaic form, '*Aeta*,' of '*Aetos*.' '*Aetos son of Aetos*' is the name of the priest mentioned in just the first few lines of the extant Greek portion of the text of the Rosetta Stone, and he is a priest of Ptah, the chief divinity represented in *Aida*. As a Greco-Egyptian archaeologist and an authority in ancient Egyptian language and scripts, Mariette would have known this quite well, and Mariette himself cites the form '*Aita*' in his correspondence. Moreover, in Diodorus Siculus [1.19] a source which Mariette surely consulted for its Egyptian passages, the name 'Aetus' is equated with the Nile and all of Egypt, which would thereby not only give the name 'Aida' an additional imprimatur of authenticity but also transform her into a historical symbol for the entire Nile region, which Khedive Isma'il was attempting to bring under his control. And as for the Nile, the title of Mariette's original short story was not "Aida" but "La fiancée du Nil."

The adaptations of Longus' *Daphnis and Chloe* have taken a different path. Recognized more for its pastoral atmosphere than its romantic narrative, *Daphnis and Chloe* has not surprisingly found its most familiar home in ballet. Debussy began to develop a balletic version in the 1890s, and then Maurice Ravel's three-part *symphonie chorégraphique* commissioned by Diaghilev, and premiering in Paris' Châtelet theater in 1912, has inspired new choreographies ever since;[14] and two different orchestral suites remain in the orchestral repertoire.[15]

---

[14] Reid, *Oxford Guide*, 1.336-337, lists those by Fokine (1912), Goleizovsky (c. 1922), Littlefied (1936), Wallmann (1938), Massine (1944), Gsovsky (1947), Lifar and Zvereff

The first operatic adaptation does not appear until the middle of the eighteenth century. The libretto for this *Daphnis et Chloé* (1747) was written by Pierre Laujon, who later was elected to the *Académie française*, and set by Joseph Bodin de Boismortier, better known for his operatic setting of another atmospheric novel, *Don Quixote*.[16] Two decades later, Jean-Jacques Rousseau developed a less ambitious musical pastoral, but he never completed the work. It was only after a gap of nearly a century and after the success of his anciently-set *Orphée aux enfers* (1858) that Jacques Offenbach created a one-act operetta version of *Daphnis et Chloé* (1860).[17] Two decades later a mini-cluster developed, first with the Henri Büsser/Charles Raffalli one-act *scenic pastorale*, which premiered in 1897.[18] Two years later saw the Parisian premier of Henri Maréchal's three-act *Daphnis et Chloé*, set to a libretto by the father and son team, Jules and Pierre Barbier.[19] Tchaikovsky's contemporary adaptation seems to be the most innovative of this cluster. Into the second act of *The Queen of Spades* [a.k.a. *Pique Dame*] (1890) he and his librettist (brother Modest) inserted an extended *divertissement*, a pastoral ballet featuring Chloe, Daphnis, and Plutus—Chloe chooses the former over the latter. The composer complicated the adaptation by writing the ballet in the style of Mozart, in part as contrast to the romance of the main plot, and in part as an homage to the eighteenth-century setting of Pushkin's original

---

(1948), Ashton (1951), Skibine (1959), Orlikowsky (1961), Cranko (1962), van Manen (1972), Neumeier (1972), Taras (1975), Tetley (1975), Comelin (1976), and Stowell (1979).

[15] In addition, Amazon.com lists over three hundred recordings for sale. For Alfred Hitchcock's attempt at including a sizable excerpt from Ravel's *Daphnis et Chloé* for *Torn Curtain* (1966), see Jack Sullivan, *Hitchcock's Music* (New Haven and London: Yale University Press, 2007) 287.

[16] *Daphnis et Chloé, pastorale* (Paris: Chez la veuve de Delormel, 1747).

[17] Jacques Offenbach, *Daphnis et Chloé* (Paris: Bertin, 1860). For the success of *Orphée aux enfers*, see Siegfried Kracauer, *Jacques Offenbach and the Paris of His Time* (New York: Zone Books, 2002) 199-213. In between *Orphée* and *Daphnis*, Offenbach composed another operetta based on a historical subject, *Geneviève de Brabant* (1859). For the 1866 Paris revival, see Ute Mittelberg, *Daphnis et Chloé von Jacques Offenbach: Ein Beitrag zur Libretto-Forschung im 19. Jahrhundert* (Köln-Rheinkassel: Verlag Christoph Dohr, 2002) 8-11; for Johann Nestroy's 1861 Vienna production, 122-133.

[18] The libretto which I. Ivanov provided to Yevstigney Fomin for his Russian version of Daphnis and Chloe, which was inserted into his last (posthumously produced) opera, *The Golden Apple* [*Zolotoye yabloko*], has not survived intact.

[19] Jules and Pierre Barbier, *Daphnis et Chloé* (Paris: C. Lévy, 1897). This opera engendered a four-page sheet music version of "C'est Lui Qui Nous A Dit Un Jour" for piano and voice, published by Imprimerie Des Annales in 1899.

1833 novella, although so far as I have been able to determine from English translation Pushkin does not mention the characters from Longus' novel.[20]

Finally, there are the operatic versions of Petronius' *Satyricon*, all of them curiosities. The first was Charles Dibdin's *The Ephesian Matron, or The Widow's Tears* (1769).[21] The Irish-born playwright Isaac Bickerstaff wrote the text for this comic serenata "after the manner of the Italians," that is, a witty short story told in spoken dialogue enhanced by a pastiche of continental music.[22] One of the most interesting and appropriate is Bruno Maderna's last work, *Satyricon* (1973), a pastiche of traditional music and electronic tape intertwined with *commedia dell'arte* motifs and a variable sequence of sixteen scenes—matching effectively the episodic nature of the ancient novel.[23] For the most part the text centers on the *cena Trimalchionis*, though one of the numbers retells the story of "*La matrona di Efeso.*"[24] Itself part of a late-twentieth century mini-cluster, Maderna's opera followed close upon the publication of Edoardo Sanguineti's free translation of Petronius, *The Play of the Satyricon*, and it premiered just three years after the well-publicized 1970 cinematic version of Petronius' novel directed by Federico Fellini.[25]

Out of the tens of thousands of operas composed over the last 410 years, and out of the thousands derived from Greco-Roman mythology and history, this is a very small number of works, some never completed, many of them insignificant, and at least one an utter failure. This is not a condemnation of the ancient novel but does speak to its relative unfamiliarity, its apparent

---

[20] For Tchaikovsky search for "peace and consolation" in the music of Mozart, see John Daverio, "Mozart in the Nineteenth Century," in Simon P. Keefe, ed., *The Cambridge Companion to Mozart* (Cambridge: Cambridge University Press, 2003) 181.

[21] Peter A. Tasch, *The Dramatic Cobbler: The Life and Works of Isaac Bickerstaff* (Lewisburg: Bucknell University Press, 1972) 189.

[22] In this instance the music was composed by Charles Dibdin, primarily because Dibdin produced (and performed in) *The Ephesian Matron* at Ranelagh Gardens, where the law mandated that all texts had to be sung throughout. Some considered it "vulgar." Tasch, *The Dramatic Cobbler*, 190, describes the work's popularity; contra, see Irena Cholij, "The Ephesian Matron, or the Widow's Tears," *Grove Music Online* ed. L. Macy.

[23] For an online version of the libretto, see: http://www.karadar.it/Librettos/maderna_satyricon.html]

[24] Bruno Maderna, *Satyricon* (Paris: Editions Salabert, 1974), specifies that the English translations are by William Arrowsmith [*The Satyricon of Petronius* (Ann Arbor: University of Michigan Press, 1959)].

[25] For Sanguineti, see Tim Whitmarsh, ed., *The Cambridge Companion to the Greek and Roman Novel* (Cambridge: Cambridge University Press, 2008) 332. Ramond Fearn, *Italian Opera Since 1945* (Australia: Harwood Academic Publishers, 1997) 137-146, offers an in-depth analysis of the opera itself.

narrative incompatibility with the operatic format, its relatively obscure protagonists, and the fact that the earliest librettists omitted it from their inchoate operatic repertoire. Despite its high status in the modern era, the dynamics of opera production are much more subject to the rules of popular culture than they are to the patron-artist relationship. And the ancient novel has had only limited presence and even less success across the board in the popular arts, particularly in the non-literary spheres. In opera, which costs more to produce, the ancient novel has had very limited impact.

Bibliography

Daverio, J. 2003. "Mozart in the Nineteenth Century," in Simon P. Keefe, ed., *The Cambridge Companion to Mozart*. Cambridge: Cambridge University Press.

Fearn, R. 1997. *Italian Opera Since 1945*. Australia: Harwood Academic Publishers.

Gaisser, J. H. 2008. *The Fortunes of Apuleius and the Golden Ass: A Study in Transmission and Reception*, Princeton: Princeton University Press.

Genetay, O-C. 1609. *"L'Ethiopique". Tragicomédie des chastes amours de Théagène et Chariclée*. Rouen: T. Reinsart.

Hardy, A. 1623. *Les chastes et loyales amours de Théagène et Cariclée, réduites du grec de l'Histoire d'Héliodore en huict poèmes dragmatiques ou théâtres consécutifs*. Paris: J. Quesnel.

Highet, G. 1957. *The Classical Tradition: Greek and Roman Influences on Western Literature*. Oxford: Oxford University Press.

Knight, R. C. 1940. "The Evolution of Racine's 'Poétique,'" *The Modern Language Review* 35, 21.

Kracauer, S. 2002. *Jacques Offenbach and the Paris of His Time*. New York: Zone Books.

Lancaster, H. C. 1907. *The French Tragi-Comedy: Its Origin and Development from 1552 to 1628*. Baltimore: J. H. Furst Company.

Lefkowitz, M. 1979-1980. "Shadwell and Locke's 'Psyche': The French Connection," *Proceedings of the Royal Musical Association* 106, 42-55.

McClymonds, M. P. 1997. "Calliroe," *The New Grove Dictionary of Opera*, ed. S. Sadie. I,

May, G. 1947. "Contribution à l'étude des sources grecques de *Phèdre*," *Modern Languages Quarterly* 8, 228-234.

Mittelberg, U. 2002. *Daphnis et Chloé von Jacques Offenbach: Ein Beitrag zur Libretto-Forschung im 19. Jahrhundert*. Köln-Rheinkassel: Verlag Christoph Dohr.

Montagu, J. 1963. "The Early Ceiling Decorations of Charles Le Brun," *The Burlington Magazine* 105, 395-408.

Reid, J. D. 1993. *Oxford Guide to Classical Mythology in the Arts, 1300-1990s*. Oxford: Oxford University Press.

Rosand, E. 1978. "Barbara Strozzi, *virtuosissima cantatrice*: The Composer's Voice," *Journal of the American Musicological Society* 31, 241-281.

Rosand, E. 1991. *Opera in Seventeenth-Century Venice: The Creation of a Genre*. Berkeley: University of California Press.

Sonneck, O. G. T. 1914. *Catalog of Opera Librettos Printed Before 1800: Title Catalogue*. Washington, D.C.: Government Printing Office.

Sterchow, W. 1953. "Heliodorus' Aethiopica in Art," *Journal of the Warburg and Courtauld Institutes* 16, 144-152.

Sternfeld, F. W. 1991. "The Orpheus Myth and the Libretto of *Orfeo*," in John Whenham, ed., *Claudio Monteverdi: Orfeo*. Cambridge: Cambridge University Press.

Tasch, P. A. 1972. *The Dramatic Cobbler: The Life and Works of Isaac Bickerstaff*. Lewisburg: Bucknell University Press.

Turnbull, M. 1983. "The Metamorphosis of 'Psyche,'" *Music & Letters* 64, 12-24.

Ussia, S. 2001. *Amore inamorato; riscritture poetiche della novella di Amore e Psiche Secoli XV – XVII*. Vercelli: Edizioni Mercurio.

Whitmarsh, T. 2008. *The Cambridge Companion to the Greek and Roman Novel*. Cambridge: Cambridge University Press.

Le dieu Pan fait pan pan pan de son pied de chèvre: Daphnis and Chloe on the stage at the end of the nineteenth century

SIMONE BETA
Università di Siena

'They were young, educated, and both virgin in that, their wedding night'. This is the incipit of *On Chesil Beach* (2007), by one of the most celebrated contemporary novelists, Ian McEwan. The novel tells the story of a young English couple who get married in 1962 and spend their honeymoon in a hotel on the Dorset coast; it focuses on the embarrassment of the newly-weds Edward and Florence, who both struggle with the problems connected with what is bound to happen – their first embrace, their first night together, the discovery of sex. *Nihil sub sole novi*: still in the twenty-first century the most famous scene of Longus' novel, the shiver provoked by the birth of the wonderful sensation the young shepherds Daphnis and Chloe mutually feel for the first time, can be the starting point of a literary work.

Other forms of artistic production have been inspired by Longus' story, though. This essay deals with one of these forms: music, and in particular the theatrical adaptations of the novel staged in the second half of the nineteenth century. During this period, in fact, the adventures of Daphnis and Chloe drew the attentions of many French composers.

The first musician who wrote an opera on Daphnis and Chloe was Joseph Bodin de Boismortier, who set to music a libretto by Pierre Laujon and composed a pastorale performed at the Parisian Opéra on 28 September 1747. Even the philosopher Jean-Jacques Rousseau (whose interest in music composition is shown by his 'intermezzo' *Le devin du village*, first performed at Fontainebleau in 1752) tried to set Longus' novel to music – but what we have is just a fragmentary work.[1]

---

[1] *Fragment de Daphnis et Chloé, composé du premier acte, de l'esquisse du prologue et de différents morceaux préparés pour le second acte et le divertissement*. Paroles de M ***

The theatrical work that gave rise to the success of the 'Daphnis and Chloe' theme in the second half of the nineteenth century was the vaudeville version by Clairville and Cordier, performed in Paris, at the Théâtre des Vaudevilles, in 1849, and set to music by Jacques Offenbach in 1860.[2] In the following pages I shall try to underline which elements Offenbach and the other composers (together with their librettists) took from the Greek original and how they organized this material in their works.

Offenbach's version deals with the main theme of the novel (the reciprocal discovery of sex) in a way that is both amusing and elegant – and this is quite understandable if one considers the peculiar operatic genre Offenbach devoted himself throughout his long and successful career: the operetta. As in the original, Daphnis and Chloe are the targets of the lust of many other characters. In Longus, Daphnis is loved by the 'young, fair, and buxom' Lycaenium and by the parasite Gnatho; in Offenbach, we have seven Maenads who long for Daphnis' love (Calisto, Xantippe, Locoë, Aricie, Eriphyle, Amalthée and Niobé). As for Chloe, in the novel she is loved by two herdsmen, Dorco and Lampis; in the operetta, her suitor is the god Pan himself.

A large statue of the pastoral god par excellence dominates the rural scene ('une site champêtre dans l'ancienne Grèce') where the action takes place. During the only act of the operetta, the statue repeatedly comes to life, thus letting the god play an important role in the story. In fact, the first, tender love scene between the two young shepherds not only occurs under the eyes of Pan, but is also counterbalanced by the bitter remarks of the jealous god: for instance, when Daphnis tells Chloe that, when he looks at her, he wishes many things but does not know what he really wishes, Pan' s comment is the exclamation of anger 'Petit imbécile' ('Little stupid').

As in the novel, Daphnis is seduced by his temptresses (with the only difference that, in Longus, the goatherd has sex with just one woman – and not with seven), while Chloe succeeds in safeguarding her virginity. But –

(Olivier de Corancez); musique de J.J. Rousseau. Prix 12. A Paris chez Esprit Libraire, au Palais Royal. 1779. In this edition the editors have printed the complete text of the prologue (with the sketches of a couple of musical pieces), the overture and the first act (both complete); what we have of the second act is just a short summary, together with some fragments of the 'divertissement'. Rousseau also wrote *Pygmalion*, a *scène lyrique* in one act composed together with Horace Coignet and performed for the first time at the Hôtel de la Ville of Lyon in the spring of 1770.

[2] The operetta was first performed in Paris, at the Théâtre des Bouffes parisiens, on 27 March 1860. The connections between the *vaudeville* and the novel, the *vaudeville* and the *operette*, the *operette* and the novel have been thoroughly studied by Ute Mittelberg (*Daphnis et Chloé von Jacques Offenbach. Ein Beitrag auf Libretto-Forschung im 19. Jahrhundert*, Beiträge zur Offenbach-Forschung, Bd. 3, Dohr, Köln-Rheinkassel 2002).

and this is the main innovation of the operetta – this double seduction is the turning point of the plot. Since Daphnis' mind is set on Chloe only and he seems not to consider the sexual appeals of the seven Maenads, Calisto has a brilliant idea: if they succeed in making him drink the water of the river Lethe, he will surely forget his fiancée. But, when the boy is about to swallow the magic water, Pan enters the scene, thinks that the servants of Dionysus are trying to make Daphnis drunk and scares them away; they run out with Daphnis, who drops the bottle. Pan picks up the bottle but is soon distracted by the arrival of Chloe, sad because Daphnis is far from her. Pan explains to her why she feels so sad: she is in love! 'But what is love?', Chloe asks. The question is exactly what Pan is looking forward to hearing: on the pretext of explaining to Chloe what love is, the lascivious god starts to seduce her – a very Offenbachian scene: indeed, two years before, in 1858, the musician had composed *Orphée aux Enfers*, with the famous *duo de la mouche*, the duet in which Zeus seduced Eurydice under the shape of a fly.

In the novel, there are three steps to love, according to the lesson taught by the old Philetas: 'kissing', 'hugging', and 'sleeping together naked';[3] according to the teaching of Pan (and to the pruderie of the French theatre), the steps are 'holding the hand' (*serrer la main*), 'grasping the waist' (*prendre la taille*), and 'kissing' (*prendre des baisers*). When Pan kisses Chloe, she draws back at first. But, since her desire to know is too strong, she urges Pan to go on with his lesson.

At this point the old god makes a terrible mistake: in order to take heart, he drinks what he thinks to be inebriating wine (the Maenads' bottle, that is the water of the Lethe) and soon forgets everything. Chloe is very disappointed by the god's incomprehensible reaction. But this feeling does not last too long: Daphnis triumphantly enters the scene crying that, thanks to the Maenads, he now knows that the feeling they felt, the feeling they thought it was a disease, was in reality – *L'amour*, says Chloe.

> 'Ah', says Daphnis. 'Did you already know it?'
> 'Yes', Chloe answers. 'Go on, please!'
> 'When a man and a woman love each other, the young boy must hold the hand of the young girl…'
> 'Yes, I know.'
> 'Did you already know it?'
> 'Yes, go on!'

---

[3] Longus, 2,7,7: 'For there is no medicine for love, neither drink, nor meat, nor any charm, but only kissing and embracing and lying side by side naked'.

When they arrive at the third step (the kiss), the Maenads and Pan (still under the effect of the magic water) enter the scene. Daphnis and Chloe decide to postpone the end of the lesson and the operetta ends with a choral piece in honour of Pan (*Pan, pan, pan, le Dieu Pan fait pan pan pan de son pied de chèvre; pan pan pan, et le Dieu Pan posant sa lèvre sur l'instrument; pan pan pan pan, oui le Dieu Pan pan charme le tympan*).

A quarter of a century after this comic version,[4] a Belgian pupil of Jules Massenet, Fernand Le Borne, composed another *Daphnis et Chloé*, performed in Brussels, at the Societé de Musique, on 10 May 1885 (it is his first theatrical work, dedicated to Charles Gounod).[5] This time we are dealing not with an operetta but with a pastoral drama, according to the definition given by P. Berlier, the author of the libretto.

The structure of this one-act work is very simple: just three characters (Daphnis, Chloe and Dorco), and almost no action. At the beginning of the first scene, we hear the complaint of the herdsman Dorco, who is sad because Chloe ignores him; in the following scenes, Chloe asks herself what is that thing called 'love' and falls asleep. When Daphnis' singing awakens her, she asks him the same question; the young goatherd tells her that 'love is the supreme union' and Chloe urges him to be joined with her through a kiss. Dorco comes back, catches them kissing, and tries to set upon Daphnis, but is driven back by the other shepherds. Daphnis asks Chloe the inevitable question ('Do you want to marry me?'); they go out singing 'let's love each other'; the final, poetic stage-direction is 'little by little the sky opens up; Love envelops Daphnis and Chloe with thousands of sun beams'.[6]

The structure of the 'pastorale en un acte' composed by Henri Busser (a good friend of Debussy) and performed in Paris, at the Théâtre National de l'Opéra-Comique, in December 1897, is as simple as Le Borne's work.[7] Its

---

[4] The operetta was staged again in the same theatre on 15 October 1866 with a few significant differences.

[5] Born in Charleroi in 1862, Le Borne studied at the Paris Conservatory with Massenet first, and then with Saint-Saëns and Franck. After *Daphnis et Chloé* (that was performed in Paris, at the Trianon-Lyrique, on 3 November 1909), Le Borne composed *Hedda* (Milan 1898) and many other operatic works (*Les Gyrondins*, Lyon 1905; *Cléopatre*, Rouen 1914; *Néréa*, Marseille 1926). His masterpieces are the two ballets *L'idole aux yeux verts* (1902) and *Fête bretonne* (1903). He died in Paris in 1929.

[6] 'Peu à peu le ciel s'entrouve; l'Amour enveloppe Daphnis et Chloé de mille clartés'.

[7] Born in Toulouse in 1872, Busser studied at the Paris Conservatory with Ernest Guiraud, who had been Debussy's teacher. In 1893 he won the Prix de Rome with the cantata *Antigone*; *Daphnis et Chloé* was his first stage work to be performed. When Debussy was producing *Pélleas et Mélisande* at the Opéra-comique, Busser was the chorus master. Al-

libretto by Charles Raffalli adds another character: together with the couple of Daphnis and Chloe, we find another one formed by Chromis and Lycaenium. In the first scene Chromis, surrounded by the dancing nymphs, sings the story of Syrinx (the same myth told by Lamon in Longus' novel at the end of the second book). In the following scenes (as in Le Borne's version), Chloe arrives and falls asleep; when Daphnis sees her sleeping, he begs the birds and the wind to keep quiet in order not to awake her. Then, while he bends down to kiss her, she utters his name. But – and here the development of the story differs from Le Borne's – Lycaenium arrives, sees the scene, and asks Daphnis why he avoids her. Daphnis is frank: he finds her pretty, but she scares him because 'her lips exude a dangerous poison'.[8] Lycaenium reminds Daphnis that she knows the secret arts of love and invites the young goatherd to follow her into the forest. As in the novel, Daphnis yields. Chloe wakes up and tells Chromis (who has witnessed the whole scene) the dream she has dreamt: a winged boy, equipped with bow and arrows, with Daphnis' face. Chromis feels sorry for Chloe and for himself. The arrival of the two lovers is the climax of the work: in a quartet which is very similar to the one that ends the third act of Puccini's *La Bohème*, Chromis and Lycaenium argue like Marcello and Musetta, while Daphnis and Chloe, like Rodolfo and Mimì, sing of their eternal love. As they had celebrated the arrival of Apollo's chariot in the first scene, the dancing nymphs sing the rising of Diana's, marking the beginning of the night.

Much more complex is the structure of the *comédie lyrique* composed by Henri Maréchal and performed in Paris, at the Théâtre Lyrique, in November 1899.[9] This time we have a real opera in three acts, whose libretto, written by Jules and Pierre Barbier, follows quite closely (or, at least, less loosely than Le Borne and Busser) the plot of Longus' novel.[10]

The first act begins with the presentation of the two main characters: the nymph Echo tells her sisters the story of Chloe (adopted daughter of Dryas

---

though not always reliable, his autobiography (*De Pelléas aux Indes galantes*, Fayard, Paris 1955) is still an interesting document for the history of the music society of the first half of the XX century. He died in Paris in 1973.

[8] 'Ta lèvre distille un dangereux poison'.

[9] Born in Paris in 1842, Maréchal was a pupil of the composer Victor Massé. In 1870 he won the Prix de Rome with the cantata *Le jugement de Dieu*. He wrote many operas, from *Les amoureux de Cathérine* (1876) to *Ping-Sin* (1918). He died in Paris in 1924.

[10] Together with Michel Carré, Jules Barbier wrote the librettos of other famous French operas such as Gounod's *Faust*, Thomas' *Hamlet*, Offenbach's *Les contes d'Hoffmann*, and many others.

and Myrtale) and Daphnis (adopted son of Lamon).[11] Daphnis and Chloe enter and sit near a spring; while Chloe weaves together some rushes in order to make a cage for cicadas, Daphnis makes a whistle for Chloe. The girl falls asleep in Daphnis' arms. As in the second book of Longus' novel, the old cowherd Philetas arrives and tells them he has met the young god Eros, who was picking flowers from his garden. 'Who is this Eros?', the two shepherds ask. 'The god of love', Philetas answers. 'And what is love?', is the next question. Philetas' reply ('Trees, flowers, waves, all these things are *oeuvres d'amour*') suddenly breaks off at the arrival of Dryas, who tells Daphnis that pirates have landed on Lesbos, entrusts Chloe to Philetas, and goes away with Daphnis. Later, Daphnis returns: the pirates have wounded him and he is bleeding. Echo (who, in this version, plays the role of Lycaenium) comes out of the forest, dresses his wounds and kisses him on the forehead. When Chloe arrives, Daphnis seems to forget what has happened and the act ends with a love duet.

The second act is set (as in Longus' third book) in Dryas' house during a winter afternoon. Philetas asks Chloe's parents if they will marry their daughter to Daphnis; they say they like Daphnis, but he is too poor to be their son-in-law. But when Philetas offers to give them three hundred scudos as part of Daphnis' dowry, they suddenly change their minds and leave their house to go to Philetas' and get the money. During their absence, Daphnis enters the house and is warmly welcomed by Chloe. Her parents too are very kind to him when they come back with Philetas' money: Dryas begs Daphnis to play his syrinx and, when Daphnis finishes, Dryas asks him to choose his reward. The young goatherd asks for Chloe's hand; Dryas and Myrtale agree but tell the couple they have to wait for the permission of their masters. Since it has begun to snow outside, Daphnis is allowed to sleep in the house – but not in Chloe's room, of course. When everybody is asleep, Echo and the nymphs enter the house. They make fun of the two lovers, who are allowed to sleep in the same house but in separate rooms. When Daphnis awakes, he sees Echo. She warns him against Dryas' false promises and invites him outside to learn the truth that lies behind Dryas' words. Daphnis follows Echo and the act ends.

The last act is set in the beautiful gardens of Dionysophanes, the owner of the fields where Daphnis and Chloe live. Winter is finally over; Daphnis is happy because he is going to see Chloe again, but he feels sorry because he has betrayed his fiancée with Echo. Chloe is uneasy as well, because she

---

[11] In the novel, Myrtale is the stepmother of Daphnis; the two librettists lend her name to Chloe's stepmother (whose name was, in the original, Nape).

has heard some rumours about Daphnis' flirtation. But their love is strong enough: when Daphnis asks her to forgive him, she accepts. Before the happy ending, there is still time for a *coup de théâtre* (maybe even three): Dryas and Myrtale arrive, say they have changed their mind and are now determined to give their daughter to Philetas (who has promised them a large sum). But (and this is the second *coup de théâtre*) Philetas reassures the appalled couple: he does not want Chloe as wife, but as a daughter; her parents are not Dryas and Myrtale; Chloe's father is Philetas himself.[12] But (and this is the third *coup de théâtre*) Philetas is not a cowherd, but the god Pan. With this anagnorisis (and with a chorus that celebrates the power of love), the opera finds its conclusion, absolutely in the style of a Menandrean comedy.

Having the same title does not mean telling the same story in the same way. Offenbach's and Maréchal's versions, the longest ones, could not be more different: if the latter can be rightly considered a well-done operatic adaptation of a long and complex novel (whose effectiveness must be doubtless ascribed to the librettists' experience), the first draws out of the ancient story an original cue (the two young shepherds' naiveté) and makes it the turning point of a funny comic opera (the teaching of love and the discovery of sex), modelling both plot and characters according to this brilliant theatrical idea.[13] The much shorter versions by Le Borne and Busser are quite unlike as well: Berlier, Le Borne's librettist, basically focuses attention on the mutual, loving feelings of the couple only, whereas Raffalli, Busser's librettist, chooses to introduce in his abridgement the couple Chromis / Lycaenium in order to counterbalance the couple of the protagonists.

But if one wants to measure the success of a classical subject, serious works are not enough. So, this brief survey would not be complete if I did not mention another *Daphnis et Chloe*, the amusing parody composed by Angelo Casirola and published in 1894, where the three authors of the libretto (Lebrun, Gramet and Larseneur) turn the most famous moment of Longus' novel (Daphnis and Chloe's 'wedding night') into a funny and disrespectful farce.

---

[12] In Longus' novel, Chloe's real father is the old Megacles.
[13] A distinct echo of this story can be read in the amusing plot of *Une education manqué*, a one-act opera composed by Emmanuel Chabrier (1841-1894) and first performed on 1 May 1879 in Paris, at the Cercle de la Presse. It is interesting to note that Chabrier's operatic début, the *opéra-bouffe L'étoile*, had been performed for the first time in 1877 at the Bouffes-Parisiens, Offenbach's theatre.

After having married the young Chloé de Virmoncourt, Daphnis Pachiderme, Duc du Casserole e Seigneur de Videpot, son of the Sénéchal of the Périgord, is sent by his parents to a small country village to celebrate his honeymoon. The reason is made clear right at the beginning of the play: until the day of his marriage, the young husband (who is only nineteen) has been tied to his mother's apron-strings; his wife Chloé (who is even younger: she is just sixteen) is also quite naive as far as sex is concerned, because she has always lived in a nunnery. Since 'they do not know anything about their conjugal duties',[14] the worried Sénéchal begs Pettavent, the mayor of the village, to find a pretty and expert woman willing to teach the young groom how to be the husband of his wife.

Quite obviously (do not forget that we are dealing with a comic parody), although the author of the letter is particularly worried for the groom, the mayor (and above all his slimy secretary Vremulet) are most interested in the bride – it's her whom they would love to train and cultivate. But, since the instructions of the seneschal are straight and clear, they decide to concentrate on Daphnis. After having reflected for a while, their choice falls on two women: Rose Lagâchette (wife of the sergeant of the Royal Police, who works in Paris and is out of the village most of the time) and Françoise Lecornu (wife of the most famous drunkard of the village). They send for the two women and explain their proposal. The women soon understand the mayor's demand: the gentle Rose translates the proposal into 'with kindness and cleverness, acquainting a young count with his marital duties',[15] while the rude Françoise's remark is 'healing a fool from his useless wisdom and changing him into a real expert'.[16] The choice between them is the result of a careful consideration: after having played heads or tails, Rose wins; Françoise does not accept the verdict; and the quarrel between the two women is calmed down with difficulty by the two men.

In the meantime, the young couple arrives. To the usual operatic welcome chorus,[17] Daphnis answers with an aria, asking the mayor to teach him to become a good husband (if he had to choose, he would not try to learn such things, but he is willing to do so for Chloe's sake). The mayor entrusts Chloe to his wife and Daphnis to Rose, who promises to show him off (and, most importantly, to take him into the woods…). Françoise, furious because

---

[14] 'Ils sont dans un état d'ignorance crasse des devoirs conjugaux'.
[15] 'Bien gentiment, avec adresse, mettre un jeune comte au courant'.
[16] 'Le guérissant de sa sagesse, d'un crétin faire un vrai savant'.
[17] 'Amis, pour nous, quelle allégresse de recevoir, en ce pays, Monsieur le Comte et Madame la Comtesse, deux jeunes époux bien assortis…'.

she has lost the interesting reward (a thousand scudos) offered by the seneschal to the 'teacher' of his son, swears she is going to grant everything to whoever will help her get revenge. Monsieur Lagâchette (Rose's husband), who has come back to the village without anybody knowing, hears these words; Françoise tells him everything and suggests that he do for Chloe what Rose is doing for Daphnis. The occasion to do so arises soon: Chloe enters the scene with the secretary Vremulet, who is supposed to bring the young bride to her husband. Vremulet tries to give her a kiss, but Chloe says no – it's not that she refuses a kiss (she doesn't even know what a kiss is), it's that the secretary has bad breath. When Lagâchette threatens the secretary with death, the coward goes away.

The following scene explains why I have indulged in such a long description of a play that so far, apart from the names of the two protagonists, shows so little resemblance to the Greek novel. In chasing away the secretary, the captain of the guards offers Chloe his help if someone else should try to *lutiner* (to woo, to court) her. Chloe, who has never heard that verb before, asks Lagâchette what *lutiner* means. The following duet is a charming piece of irony: Lagâchette says that 'wooing is the advance-guard of love',[18] something that every woman should learn, some day. But such an explanation is not enough for Chloe, who, like her Greek model, asks then what 'love' means (a legitimate question because, as Chloe adds, the subject 'love' has never been touched by the nuns in their lessons). Lagâchette's answer is quite poetic, if you think that, after all, he is a military man: 'Love is an enchanted dream, the sweet trait of the soul from which comes the posterity that the universe owes to women'.[19] After having remarked that, according to the abbess' precepts, babies are born under the cabbages, Chloe asks the soldier to teach her the 'essence of love'. Lagâchette, who had been looking forward to hearing this question, takes her into the same woods where his wife had just taken Daphnis.

When Daphnis comes back, together with Rose, he thanks the mayor for having let him know all the beauties of the village. But the mayor is desperate, because Chloe has disappeared with Lagâchette. When the other couple arrives, the mayor gives orders to put the man under arrest, but Daphnis stops him: quoting the Gospel, he says that he has now understood at his expense what the proverbial saying 'don't do to others what you wouldn't want done to you' means. He then asks for a carriage: they must continue

---

[18] 'Lutiner c'est l'avant-garde de l'amour'.
[19] 'L'amour est un rêve enchanté, le doux trait d'union de l'âme d'où surgit la postérité que l'univers doit à la femme!'.

their honeymoon trip and, most of all, they are both eager to exchange their impressions and take advantage of the lessons they have just received. In the final aria, the Count (and the three authors of the libretto) confess their debt to the source that has inspired the plot: 'The story of Daphnis and Chloe comes from the famous Longus, a Greek author that, in his rotten book, tells this story in details and without circumlocution. In our very prudish century, the translators had to speed up, because otherwise the censor's scissors might have cut everything'.[20]

In the first decades of the Twentieth century Longus' novel enticed other musicians, who planned to compose ballets inspired to the tender story of the two young lovers: if Claude Debussy never wrote the music to the ballet whose subject had been suggested to him by the novelist Pierre Louÿs, between 1909 and 1912 Maurice Ravel did compose a Daphnis et Chloé, his only ballet, for a production by the Russian choreographer Mikhail Fokine, first performed by the Ballets Russes, the celebrated dance company led by Sergej Diaghilev, in Paris, at the Théâtre de Châtelet, on 8 June 1912.[21]

Turning a novel made of words into a ballet made of gestures may seem an absurd decision, a cruel mutilation, a drastic summary. But anyone who has had the chance to attend a performance of Ravel's ballet has surely understood that only the art of dancing can convey the slow birth of Daphnis' and Chloe's love in all its charming nuances. The everlasting success of one of the most celebrated compositions of Maurice Ravel, compared with the oblivion into which the five operatic versions dealt with in this paper have sunken, is clear evidence that, sometimes, music and gestures move the soul more effectively than music and words.

Bibliography

Bodin de Boismortier, J. 1748. *Daphnis et Chloé*, pastorale, représentée par l'Académie royale de musique pour la première fois le jeudi 28 septembre 1747. Paroles de Laujon, Paris: Le Clerc.

---

[20] 'De Daphnis et Chloé, l'histoire / nous vient du célèbre Longus, / auteur grec, qui, dans son grimoire, / la conte, *in naturalibus*! / En notre siècle très pudique, / les traducteurs ont dû gazer / sans quoi, du censeur héroïque, / les ciseaux pouvaient tout couper'.

[21] The roles of the protagonists were played by Vaslav Nijinskij and Tamara Karsavina. Ravel's ballet was also produced in London in 1951 by the English choreographer Frederick Ashton, the leader of the Sadler's Wells Ballet (today Royal Ballet); the dancers were Michael Somes and Margot Fonteyn.

Busser, H. 1897. *Daphnis et Chloé*, pastorale en un acte. Poème de C. Raffalli, Paris: Grus.

Casirola, A. 1894. *Daphnis et Chloé*, opérette en un acte. Paroles de Lebrun, Gramet et Larsoneur, Paris: Bertin.

Le Borne, F. 1885, *Daphnis et Chloé*, drame pastoral. Paroles de P. Berlier, Paris: Manuel.

Maréchal, H. 1895. *Daphnis et Chloé*, comédie lyrique en trois actes de Jules et Pierre Barbier, Paris: Grus.

Mittelberg, U. 2002. *Daphnis et Chloé von Jacques Offenbach. Ein Beitrag zur Libretto-Forschung im 19. Jahrhundert*, Beiträge zur Offenbach-Forschung, Bd. 3, Köln-Rheinkassel: Dohr.

Offenbach, J. 1860. *Daphnis et Chloé*, opérette en un acte. Livret de Clairville et Jules Cordier, Paris: Bertin.

Ravel, M. 1910. *Daphnis et Chloé*, ballet en 3 parties de Michel Fokine; partition pour le piano réduite par l'auteur, Paris: Durand.

Rousseau, J.-J. 1779. *Fragment de Daphnis et Chloé, composé du premier acte, de l'esquisse du prologue et de différents morceaux préparés pour le second acte et le divertissement*, paroles de M *** (Olivier de Corancez), Paris: Esprit Libraire, au Palais Royal.

Widows on the operatic stage:

The 'Ephesian Matron' as a dramatic character in twentieth-century German musical theatre (esp. 1928-1952)

TIZIANA RAGNO
University of Foggia

This paper focuses on some operatic adaptations of the 'Widow of Ephesus' tale, expressly shaped after the Petronian source. A preliminary survey, related to the reception of the novella, shows that all the operatic transpositions of this story (with only a few exceptions)[1] are produced from the 1930s onwards; furthermore, many of these are geographically concentrated in Germany. We will investigate them by adopting a comparative approach, in order to point out the strategies used to 'rewrite' the ancient source (Petr. 111-112).

K. A. Hartmann, Die Witwe von Ephesus, *in* Wachsfigurenkabinett *(1930-)*

Karl Amadeus Hartmann composed *Wachsfigurenkabinett* ('Waxworks') between 1930 and 1932.[2] It is a cycle of five miniature operas,[3] whose genesis can be traced back to Hartmann's experimentation in Weimar musical idioms as well as to his socialist political views during the twenties and thirties. The composer aimed at exploring the form of *Kleinoper* (small opera), a popular 'antidote to the continuing neo-romantic and naturalist music

---

[1] The most famous is Charles Dibdin's *The Ephesian Matron* (1769; libretto by Isaac Bickerstaff). It is also worth mentioning, for example, the opéra comique by Louis Fuzelier (*La Matrone d'Éphèse*, 1714): see Ragno 2009, 381 n. 56 with bibliography.

[2] For the detailed chronology cf. Brehler 2003, 83 n. 6.

[3] The five pieces are: *Die Witwe von Ephesus*; *Chaplin-Ford-Trott*; *Der Mann, der vom Tode auferstand*; *Leben und Sterben des heiligen Teufels*; *Fürwahr...?!*

drama',[4] at that time adopted by German and foreign composers (e.g., Kurt Weill, Ernst Krenek, Paul Hindemith, Darius Milhaud, Bohuslav Martinu); then, Hartmann created musical pastiche by using divergent genres currently in vogue, such as cabaret, *Lehrstück*, jazz cantata or *Zeitoper*. On an ideological level, at least four of these chamber operas reveal the composer's social engagement and, in particular, his purpose of satirising contemporary economic policy or American materialistic lifestyle (the 'Great Crash' had just occurred). The full score of *Wachsfigurenkabinett* was left unfinished except for two short operas:[5] *Leben und Sterben des heiligen Teufels* and *Die Witwe von Ephesus*. This last piece (the first of the cycle) is an adaptation of Petronius' tale: its text (as well as the other libretti) was provided by Erich Bormann, a young opera producer who worked for the Bavarian State Opera as an assistant.[6]

Hartmann's *Die Witwe von Ephesus*[7] is conceived in the form of a *Singspiel*; it is musically and dramatically tripartite (*Ensemble und Duett*; *Marsch*; *Finale*). In the first section a *Bürgermeister* (tenor) and his assistants (a little chorus made up of four *Zylinder* ['cylinders'], two tenors and two basses) pass judgement on an anonymous man (*Er*, tenor) accused of unemployment and eventually decree his condemnation to the gallows. An absurd sentence (people who can't work can't eat, so can't survive and must die!) is solemnly pronounced by the *Zylinder:* according to their name (although it could also allude to the top hat as a middle class status symbol or, more specifically, to diplomatic headgear), they behave just like 'robots' or mechanical 'yes-men' and represent the comic side of drama, by singing in vivacious unison in cabaret style, in six-eight time and major tonalities. In particular, among them, a bass blames poverty in his solo and practises one of the most efficacious means of modernizing the ancient plot by using prophetic tones and hinting at contemporary times ('Man stelle sich vor, in eintausend Jahr, so neunzehnhundertvierzig, die Not wäre groß'). In conformity with the grotesque atmosphere which pervades the whole piece, the condemned 'everyman' starts singing just after dying, while the widow stands

---

[4] McCredie 1982, 255.
[5] Hartmann composed only a (not definitive) piano score of the *Chaplin-Ford-Trott*, *Der Mann, der vom Tode auferstand*, and *Fürwahr...?!* Later full scores of these three operas were produced by W. Hiller, G. Bialas and H. W. Henze for the first performance of *Wachsfigurenkabinett* on 29th May 1988 at Munich (see Kerstan 1988). In the same year the piano reduction of the entire operatic cycle was printed by Schott Music: we depend on this edition for the libretto's excerpts here quoted.
[6] Cf. See 1964, 99; Bormann-Kerstan 1988, 53.
[7] For the musical analysis see Brehler 2003, 86 ff. and McCredie 2004, 33.

on the other half of the scenic space. Then, the female role (*Sie*, again an anonymous character) plays as if reflected against the male character: as in the Petronian story,[8] two scenes are 'paratactically' juxtaposed and at beginning reveal a reciprocal incompatibility, accentuated both by a set of polarities inserted in the text (*Leid* v. *Lust*; *leben* v. *sterben* [pain v. joy, life v. death]) and by the same melodic line assigned to the two characters on the stage. But, after thirty-seven beats, this opposition seems to turn into a perfect unity, announced in advance by a musical unison and, soon after the sung parts, by a full sympathy clearly expressed in the declaimed dialogue. In fact the prisoner and the young widow, after summarizing their absurd condition (*Er* would like to live, but he has died because he could not survive because of unemployment; *Sie* would like to die, so she laments because she has survived her husband), suddenly fall in love with each other. Their 'erotic idyll' is as unexpected as it is absolute and only scarcely troubled by a soldier: the guard enters to verify the hanged man's presence, thus performing the same function as in the ancient story, but he takes no active part in the drama; in fact he is only evoked by a march rhythm and remains completely voiceless, except for the last speech pronounced in front of the substituted corpse ('WÄCHTER: Erledigt'). In the meantime, in agreement with the usual exchange of roles as provided in the original literary source, the husband has been sacrificed and exchanged for the equally dead prisoner; similarly both the condemned man and the Ephesian Matron have done a convenient 'swap' (*Er* has given her a partner and *Sie* has given him the most important gift, life): so, their strong 'community of interests' is finally realized in the love-duet, expressly quoted in a metatheatrical allusion.[9]

If compared with the Petronian version, Bormann clearly produced a 'travesty' which consists, in this instance, chiefly of a modernization of the plot by anachronisms: therefore, this new hypertext (like all 'travesties') is characterized by a simple relationship of 'transformation'[10] with or without burlesque purpose. It is also worth mentioning that Bormann realizes, in terms of intersemiotic translation,[11] the combination of different systems of signs. So, by using an expressive medium such as music, foreign to the original hypotext, Bormann on the one hand provides a text that follows the frame of the ancient storyline, and on the other hand exploits the original

---

[8] For this effect, achieved in the Petronian text by means of 'cum inversum' (Petr. 111,5), see, e.g., Pecere 1975, 63 and Vannini 2010, 242.

[9] 'SIE und ER: [...] Jetzt schnell ein Liebesduett und dann ins Bett!'.

[10] Cf. Genette 1997, 8 ff., 29 ff. (about 'transformation' in comparison with 'imitation'), 63 ff. (about 'travesty' with or without the practice of anachronism).

[11] On intersemiotic translation see, e.g., Dusi 2000.

fabula as a 'pre-text' and manipulates it, by turning its meaning into up-to-date references. In order to attain such a result, the librettist deprives the characters of any specific identity and makes them explicitly anonymous (*Er*, *Sie*): therefore, the text, only after being reduced to its 'degree zero', is submitted to a process of overall 're-semantization'. This operation, consisting of a form of abstraction from the previous text, prevents the occurrence of a dull 'masquerade' and allows new meanings to bestow a symbolic perspective on the ancient material.

Bormann uses 'quantitative transformations'[12] in order to reduce the ancient episode. Firstly, the Petronian novella, almost unmodified on the level of 'narrative time', is instead drastically cut on the level of 'story time': this restriction, although not unexpected in a theatrical re-writing (on the stage the narrative time must be equivalent to the story time), leads to other types of 'transformation' relating also to the 'quality' of the original source. Bormann rewrites some parts of the tale by 'concision':[13] for example, he summarizes the mourning sequence (Petr. 111,2 ff.) and afterwards he recalls it ironically while the widow exhumes her husband's corpse;[14] then, the librettist puts into practice a form of 'excision'[15] by removing completely the back-story about the *pudicitia* of the *matrona* being admired by women from the neighbouring towns (Petr. 111,1) and the 'seduction scenario' originally furnished by the persuasive soldier (Petr. 111,8 ff.). These operations of 'quantitative reduction' lead to effects of 'compression' on the qualitative level of the plot: Bormann, indeed, compresses the transition from the mourning to the erotic scene into a very short time[16] in order to strengthen the grotesque element and improbability inherent in the ancient source. Therefore the love which arises spontaneously between the widow and her partner makes unnecessary the function of the *ancilla*, who in the original story (following a convention of mime, comedy and elegy) acts as a 'procuress' in the love-affair between her mistress and the soldier.[17] Then, this fe-

---

[12] Genette 1997, 272 ff.
[13] Genette 1997, 280 ff.
[14] 'SIE: Hier in dieser Erde ruht mein Herr Gemahl. [...] Sein allzu früher Tod bereitet mir nun Qual'.
[15] Genette 1997, 273 ff.
[16] 'ER: Aber es gibt doch noch andere Männer. SIE: Daran hatte ich noch nicht gedacht in meiner Trauer. ER: Ich zum Beispiel wäre gern bereit die Stelle Ihres Gatten einzunehmen. SIE: O du schöner Mann, komm herab und werde mein Gemahl'.
[17] Cf., e.g., Morenilla Talens 1994. In particular, about the Petronian *ancilla* and the comic *anus ebria* type (Petr. 111,10), see already Burman 1743, I, 668: cf. Ragno 2009, 346 ff. with other bibliographical references. It is also worth mentioning, 'per incidens', that the servant does not take part in the plot in many other adaptations of this tale: it is enough to

male stock-character is abolished in Hartmann's opera. Moreover, here two roles, previously kept separate (the male lover, played by the soldier, and the condemned man), coincide by means of an unusual operation of 'reductio ad unum': thus this contraction of the cast supplies the plot with a bipolar and more simple structure, focused chiefly on the two protagonists, the widow and the prisoner. Bormann proceeds by synthesis also in other circumstances: for instance, the same character (the widow) both offers the husband's corpse as a replacement and, before doing it, steals the condemned man's body, whereas, in the original version, relatives remove the crucified man from the cross in order to bury him[18] and the *matrona* replaces the stolen corpse. The capacity, ascribed to the widow, of rendering life not to a near-suicide (such as the 'soldier-lover' in the ancient story) but even to a dead man stands for the aptitude for regeneration generally assigned to the *matrona*:[19] hence in Hartmann's opera the exchange of one man for man shows clearly not only the *ingenium* of the widow (Petr. 112,8), but also her extraordinary power to manage life and death for the purpose of recreating the former by means of a descent to the latter.

In Hartmann's *Witwe von Ephesus* two themes are recognizable at first sight, that of adultery (already belonging to the original Milesian tale and a common subject in the *Zeitoper* tradition of the 1920s and 1930s)[20] and that of antimilitarism, expressed in music (especially in the second section of the

---

consider, for example, Aesop. 299 Hausrath and Vita Aesopi 129 GW (cf. Ragno 2009, 136 ff. n. 6 with bibliography and Vannini 2010, 23 ff.) as well as the vast majority of the Medieval versions from the Italian (see, e.g., Galimberti Biffino 2003) and French areas (see, e.g., Pearcy 2007, 11 ff.).

[18] The variant consisting of hanging instead of crucifixion is common owing to the influence of La Fontaine's famous *conte* (see on this, e.g., Martin 2003). However it is permissible to suppose that, in this instance, Bormann's text was meant to allude to the final scene of *Die Dreigroschenoper*: this successful Brechtian drama (transposition into *Zeitoper* form of a 'ballad opera' of John Gay) had been set into music by Kurt Weill and performed from 1928 onwards. Also, the death sentence for poverty seems to contain a Brechtian echo (this motif appears in *Aufstieg und Fall der Stadt Mahagonny*, set to music again by Weill and performed for the first time in 1930 at Leipzig). I am grateful to Prof. Heinrich Kuch for his suggestions in support of this hypothesis concerning the Brechtian presence in Hartmann's opera.

[19] It is worth mentioning that in the recent past some scholars have distinguished in the tale of the Widow of Ephesus the ancient 'folkloric complex' (including the generation of new life), by applying Bakhtinian theories to the Petronian story (e.g., Fedeli 1986, esp. 33 and McGlathery 1998).

[20] Cf., e.g., Paul Hindemith's *Hin und zurück* (1927) and *Neues vom Tage* (1929): Max See quotes the former among the dramatic-musical patterns of *Wachsfigurenkabinett* (cf. See 1964, 101).

opera, the march) and in the text. In particular, Bormann amplifies the role of a character that gains significance despite its lack of relevance in the original version: in fact the *imperator provinciae* (Petr. 111,5), presented in the Petronian story merely as having an official duty, becomes an important person (the *Bürgermeister*, Mayor, the protagonist of the first scene) given a voice and 'multiplied' into the *Zylinder*, acting as 'body doubles' (in a lower degree) of the Mayor. This very instance of amplification[21] links with a drastic 'transmotivation'[22] of the action: indeed, the prisoner is condemned not for the generic crime of thievery (Petr. 111,5 *imperator provinciae latrones iussit crucibus affigi*) but, more specifically, for his unemployment (a modern 'crime', here illustrated according to its full judicial articulation). The ridiculous authoritarianism of the Strong State is also symbolized by a modest walk-on part (the dumb *Wächter*), into whom Bormann converts a Petronian composite character (the soldier), formerly based on comic-elegiac patterns (especially the topic of *militia amoris*)[23] and on a parodic reception of the Virgilian hypotext: the soldier and the widow act obviously as parallels for the 'eloquent' Aeneas and the 'unchaste' Dido.[24]

Moreover it is also meaningful that the antimilitarism constituted a common motif in the operatic German productions of the same period.[25] In other words, it is possible to say that, in spite of its ancient subject, this first of Hartmann's *kleine Opern* follows contemporary operatic tendencies in elaborating not only the motif of conjugal infidelity but also the satire against war by means of evident references to present-day events. At the same time such a way of combining on the one hand amusing entertainment and on the other hand social engagement matches well the 'serious farce' of the *Satyrica*, available more and more to be revised and rewritten for the German operatic stage before and after the tragedy of the Third Reich.

---

[21] Genette 1997, 316 ff.
[22] Genette 1997, 393 ff.
[23] See on this issue Cicu 1986, 265 and McGlathery 1998, 322 ff.
[24] The Virgilian quotations (Verg. *A*. 4,34 and 4,38), almost unadulterated, are in Petr. 111,12 and 112,2 (see, recently, Heuzé 2003 and Vannini 2010, 252, 256). On Dido's 'lasciviousness' see, e.g., Macr. 5,17,5.
[25] *Wachsfigurenkabinett* was influenced, for example, by E. Krenek, *Das Schwergewicht, oder Die Ehre der Nation* (cf. See 1964, 101) belonging to a triptych inspired by antifascist beliefs and performed in 1928 (cf. Bormann-Kerstan 1988, 52).

K. A. Hartmann and a new (failed) Die Witwe von Ephesus (1949)

During his years of maturity Hartmann reconsidered his early works (especially those composed before 1933) and rewrote some of them.[26] Though *Wachsfigurenkabinett* was not selected, it is relevant that Hartmann attempted to update just *Die Witwe von Ephesus*. This operation was urged in 1949 by the young composer Hans Werner Henze,[27] interested as resident composer at Deutsches Theater in Konstanz[28] in realizing a *Ballettabend* in the autumn of that year. In particular, Henze's suggestions concerned not only the musical form (that of pantomime), but even the performance-time (not more than 20 minutes) and the mode of representation[29] (e.g., unadulterated mimetic gesture without dialogue, of course out of bounds to pantomime, or a narrating voice).[30] This request, at the beginning all but approved,[31] was rejected. So Henze's entreaties, however earnest,[32] were never responded to: nevertheless, whereas for his part Hartmann finally gave up the purpose of revising *Die Witwe von Ephesus* on 16th November 1949,[33] Henze's teacher, Wolfgang Fortner, was hardly less disappointing than his colleague when he realized another musical adaptation of the Petronian tale some years later.

W. Fortner, Die Witwe von Ephesus (1952)

Fortner composed a pantomime (*Die Witwe von Ephesus*, performed for the first time in Berlin on 17th September 1952)[34] but he did not at all reject the narrative form: in fact in this work the gestures of mute characters are illustrated by an external narrator (*Sprecher*), who (according to the *Moritat* [street-ballad] style)[35] is required to give a clear explanation of the action. The author of the text is Grete Weil, known also for her collaborations with

---

[26] See Brehler 2003, 19 ff.
[27] On the relationship betweeen Hartmann and Henze see Henze 1999, 110 ff.
[28] Henze 1999, 80 ff.
[29] Cf. Genette 1997, 334 ff.
[30] The text of the whole letter is reported by Wagner 1980, 188-189.
[31] Hartmann's letter in reply was written on 25th September 1949 (cf. Brehler 2003, 21).
[32] Cf. Wagner 1980, 189 for another letter dated on 19th October 1949.
[33] Cf. Brehler 2003, 21.
[34] About this performance see Koegler 1960, 74 ff. The libretto's excerpts, here quoted, are from full score published in 1952 by Schott Music (I am grateful to editor for allowing me to see the score).
[35] Cf. Koegler 1960, 74.

Henze: hence, we have enough reason to suppose that Fortner's pupil himself could have played a part in this pantomime's genesis (it was exactly at this period when Weil and her husband travelled to Italy with Henze).[36]

The twelve sections of the pantomime *Die Witwe von Ephesus* do not show significant differences in comparison with the Petronian version (named almost explicitly in the subtitle: 'Pantomime nach einer antiken Novelle'). Notwithstanding the need to reduce the story, Weil does not apply any form of 'amputation' (the only case of 'concision' concerns the backstory, before the husband's death), but she provides mere slight variations on the ancient version. In particular, her treatment of the subject consists of the following strategies: modified disposition of some scenes (e.g., acquaintances and local authorities try to dissuade the widow from suicide after [and not before] the entrance of the soldier, while the praise of the *matrona*'s fidelity[37] is sarcastically postponed to the stage of her quasi-bestial consumption of food); amplification of some episodes (the widow's heroic purpose to spend all days and nights in the tomb is emphasized by suggesting a decree banning this; the theft of the corpse is finally effected after two failed attempts); compression of the most scabrous events, also achieved by means of (vain!) reticence, as well as the brevity of the stage direction about the sexual intercourse.[38] This self-restraint in the text is however neutralized by the fact that, according to a paratextual indication ('Beischlaf' is the title of the eighth part), an entire section is devoted to the sexual intercourse's mimic representation, in spite of the fact that it is just briefly referred to in the recited text.

Moreover it is apparently unparalleled that Weil's text contains frequent references to sleep, here ascribed to the *ancilla*. Indeed this element is justified not only by some dramatic demands (in order to keep the *ancilla* on the stage, even in the most intimate circumstances), but also perhaps by the author's purpose to quote indirectly an illustrious adaptation of the same Petronian tale, with little connection to Fortner's pantomime except for the occasion of a performance of both pieces. The use of sleep as a tool of deception inside the tomb had already been used, perhaps for the first time on the

---

[36] Cf. Henze 1999, 96 ff.
[37] 'SPRECHER [gesungen]: Solche treue Gattenliebe, wie bei dieser Frau im Grabe, sei sehr selten […]. Und das Seltne soll man kennen lernen […] wenn man jung ist, ah ah'.
[38] 'Der Soldat schläft bei der Frau ein'. Also the reference to the widow's first *cenula* is concise ('SPRECHER: […] schließlich läßt sich auch die Frau bereden, ein halbes Hühnchen zu verspeisen').

stage,[39] by Gotthold Ephraim Lessing, author of *Die Matrone von Ephesus*. It was composed after September 1767 when Lessing wrote, in a section of his *Hamburgische Dramaturgie* (36. Stück), a composite judgement about the feasibility of transposing the Widow of Ephesus subject from the narrative form to the dramatic one. In particular, Lessing considered it intolerable to stage the Petronian tale without modification and with the inevitable result of depriving it of its own symbolic valence as provided in the ancient version.

Without recapitulating in full either this matter,[40] or the fact that Lessing failed in his attempt to follow his own suggestions in writing a play on this theme (as the fragmentary status of *Die Matrone von Ephesus* certifies),[41] it is useful remembering that Lessing's fragmentary play was staged on 17th September 1952 in Berlin, on the same night as the first night of Fortner's pantomime. So, perhaps in order to create a mutual opposition, that pantomime, which contains a combination of narration and gesture, was juxtaposed with the fully dramatic experiment, by means of which Lessing might have effected a suitable and definitive translation of the Petronian tale to the stage.

Moreover, this confrontation between Lessing's production and Fortner's ballet did not escape a reviewer (H. Koegler),[42] still mindful of the Berlin performance a few years later: in particular, it was clear that the two adaptations of the ancient story were completely different because, on the one hand, Lessing had tried to attenuate every possible bad impression produced by the unfaithful widow (his purpose had been to capture audience sympathy illusionistically by means of his play) whereas, on the other hand, Fortner kept an atmosphere of horror in his 'narrative pantomime', especially in the last scene.[43] So, this *Moritat*, as well as Hartmann's *Zeitoper*, pointed to a manner of musical-dramatic development of the ancient tale: the same reviewer credited Fortner's *Die Witwe von Ephesus* (although it was a not very successful production)[44] for attaining an aesthetic legitimacy based not on identification between audience and actors (established, for instance,

---

[39] In spite of the thesis about the Lessingian source of this variant (cf. Ragno 2009, 395 n. 102 with bibliography), it should not be excluded that Lessing was inspired by Phaed. *app.* 13 Müller 13-14 *dominae tunc adsistebat suae / dormitum eunti* (see, on this detail, Müller 1980, 120 n. 51 and Massaro 1981, 228 n. 30 for a possible emendation of *eunti* to *euntem*).

[40] Cf., for this question, Ragno 2009, 367 ff. (with bibliography).

[41] Ragno 2009, 389 ff. (with bibliography) for Lessing's fragmentary drama.

[42] Cf. Koegler 1960, 74.

[43] Cf. Koegler 1960, 75.

[44] In a work, devoted to Fortner's *Opernkompositionen* (Weber 1995), this pantomime is not even quoted.

by Lessing's *Mitleid* dramatic theory), but on emotional distance from the subject of his ballet. Fortner achieved this result above all by employing a strongly 'stylized' dramatic form (dumb show) supported by mere narration and a 'diaphanous' musical score.[45] Therefore, Fortner and Weil successfully transposed the Petronian tale, achieving this neither by strong adulteration of the source (contrary to Hartmann and Bormann, who had realized a musical-dramatic adaptation by updating the ancient subject and mixing it up with social and political meanings), nor by escaping the original narrative mode of the story, but by showing (as if at a distance) the horror effects produced by depicting on stage the unfaithful widow.

E. d'Albert, Die Witwe von Ephesus *(1928);* R. Wagner-Régeny, Die Witwe von Ephesus *(1950)*

Twentieth-century German operatic history reveals at least two other cases of musical-theatrical transposition of the Widow of Ephesus theme before 1952: left unpublished, the libretti are still in typescript and will be the object of a forthcoming investigation. They were composed by Karl Michael von Levetzow[46] and Caspar Neher.[47] The only point worth mentioning here is that the former text, dated 1928, is the result of a strategy of amplifying the ancient tale (the piece consists of three acts) and giving it a securely happy ending, again by means of unimagined alterations to the original plot. In Levetzow's work the *ancilla* takes in marriage the *vir*, just resurrected from apparent death, while the 'widow' becomes the 'wife' of a new suitor. The librettist clearly exploited a famous version of the Widow of Ephesus tale (according to which the husband unexpectedly returns to life), contained in a Chinese novella[48] and well-known also for being been rewritten by Voltaire.[49] Furthermore, whereas in this text the most impressive modification

---

[45] Cf. Koegler 1960, 76.

[46] The text (*Die Witwe von Ephesus*) was set to music by Eugen d'Albert, but it was never performed. On this opera see Cornaro 1950, 124 ff. and Pangels 1981, 401 ff.

[47] Cf. Wittig 2005 about this fragmentary libretto (*Die Witwe von Ephesus*), now in the Akademie der Künste at Berlin. The score, left unfinished, was produced by Rudolf Wagner-Régeny.

[48] On this Chinese novella see, e.g., Hansen 2002, 270 ff.

[49] The reference is to the second section (*Le nez*) of *Zadig ou la destinée* (1747), which contains the story of Azora, 'widow' until the return to the life of her husband Zadig.

lies in the different frame-tale (the 'Dinner of Trimalchio':[50] Trimalchio is the husband; the widow [his wife] is Phryne, substitute for Fortunata), the happy ending is equally remarkable, since here the author applies the greatest adjustment to the 'Chinese' plot, which originally contained a final punishment for the *matrona*'s infidelity. The act of punishment, ultimately escaped by Levetzow's *Witwe*, occurs, instead, at the end of Neher's piece, composed in 1950, when Germany was exhausted by the war and the Nazi recent past. As in Hartmann's transposition, the ancient tale was rewritten by Neher in the light of antimilitarist beliefs, but in this instance, contrary to the *Zeitoper* produced in 1930s, neither laughter nor an incredible resurrection form could disperse the atmosphere of death, which remains from the first scene (*Trauerzug*) to the last. Hence, despite its substantial conformity to the Petronian version, the dramatic action presents a gloomy 'day-after' by means of an inventive 'proleptic continuation'[51] which prolongs the story of the widow beyond the substitution of her husband's corpse and seals the deadly fate of both the Ephesian Matron and her beloved soldier. In the twenty-third section, in front of the dying soldier, the *ancilla* reports the last horrible moments of the widow: she has been violently killed, just like (we add) many people who, slain by the Nazi regime, would like to have opted for life, as the ancient *matrona*. Moreover, in Neher's text, the murderers of the Widow of Ephesus, urged on by their savagery and contempt, had dared to 'kill' also the thousand-year reputation of one of the most famous female Petronian characters: thus, in their words, a renowned antonomasia (*die Witwe von Ephesus*) and its ironic implications had finally given way to an uncouth value judgement, expressed by means of an obscene and hateful insult (*die Hure von Ephesus*, 'the whore of Ephesus').[52]

Bibliography

Bormann, E. – Kerstan, M. 1988. 'Karl Amadeus Hartmann, München und die Oper. Ein Gespräch', in: H. W. Henze (ed.), *Neues Musiktheater. Almanach zur I. Münchener Biennale*. Munich, 50-56.

---

[50] Cf. Müller 1980, 111 ff. about the relationship, in the *Satyrica*, between the *Cena Trimalchionis* and the Petronian novella.
[51] On continuations see Genette 1997, 206 ff.
[52] 'ANCILLA: Geht dort nicht die trauernde Witwe von Ephesus, / deren Trauer wir alle so rühmten? / Dort geht die Hure von Ephesus […]'.

Brehler, C. L. 2003. *Karl Amadeus Hartmann. Untersuchungen zum Frühwerk der Jahre 1927 bis 1933*. Adliswil/Zürich.
Burman, P. 1743. *Titi Petronii Arbitri Satiricon quae supersunt curante Petro Burmanno*, editio altera, I-II. Amsterdam.
Cicu, L. 1986. 'La matrona di Efeso di Petronio', *SIFC* 79: 249-271.
Cornaro, B. 1950. *Karl Michael Freiherr von Levetzow*. Diss. Wien.
Dusi, N. 2000. 'Introduzione. Per una ridefinizione della traduzione intersemiotica', *VS* 85/86/87: 3-54.
Fedeli, P. 1986. 'La matrona di Efeso. Strutture narrative e tecnica dell'inversione', *MCSN* 4: 9-35.
Galimberti Biffino, G. 2003. '*La Matrone d'Éphèse*: quelques exemples de sa fortune littéraire en Italie', *CEA* 39: 101-111.
Genette, G. 1997. *Palinsesti*. It. trans. Turin.
Hansen, W. F. 2002. *Ariadne's Thread. A guide to international tales found in classical literature*. Ithaca (N.Y.).
Henze, H. W. 1999. *Bohemian Fifths*. Princeton.
Heuzé, P. 2003. 'Sur un *color* virgilien du récit d'Eumolpe', *CEA* 39: 53-58.
Kerstan, M. 1988. 'Wachsfigurenkabinett', *NZ* 149: 16-21.
Koegler, H. 1960. 'Ballette, Ballettaufführungen', in: H. Lindlar (ed.), *Wolfgang Fortner*. Rodenkirchen/Rhein, 67-76.
Martin, R. 2003. 'De Phèdre à Pétrone et de Pétrone à La Fontaine: quelques variations sur un thème', *CEA* 40: 33-45.
Massaro, M. 1981. 'La redazione fedriana della «Matrona di Efeso»', *MCSN* 3: 217-237.
McCredie, A. D. 1982. 'Karl Amadeus Hartmann's aspirant Kunstideologie and its transmission through the Music Theatre', in: J. Schläder and R. Quandt (eds.), *Festschrift Heinz Becker*. Laaber, 249-267.
McCredie, A. D. 2004. *Karl Amadeus Hartmann. Sein Leben und Werk*. Wilhelmshaven.
McGlathery, D. B. 1998. 'Petronius' Tale of the Widow of Ephesus and Bakhtin's Material Bodily Lower Stratum', *Arethusa* 31: 313-336.
Morenilla Talens, C. 1994. 'De lenae in comoedia figura', *Helmantica* 45: 81-106.
Müller, C. W. 1980. 'Die Witwe von Ephesus. Petrons Novelle und die Milesiaka des Aristeides', *Antike und Abendland* 26: 103-121.
Pangels, C. 1981. *Eugen d'Albert*. Zürich/Freiburg.
Pearcy, R. J. 2007. *Logic and Humour in the Fabliaux*. Cambridge-Rochester.
Pecere, O. 1975. *Petronio: la novella della matrona di Efeso*. Padova.
Ragno, T. 2009. *Il teatro nel racconto. Studi sulla* fabula *scenica della matrona di Efeso. Con un' introduzione di G. Cipriani*. Bari.
See, M. 1964. 'Erinnerungen an Karl Amadeus Hartmann', *NZ* 125: 99-102.
Vannini, G. 2010. *Petronii Arbitri* Satyricon *100-115. Edizione critica e commento*. Berlin-New York.
Wagner, R. 1980. (ed.), *Karl Amadeus Hartmann und die Musica Viva. Essays. Bisher unveröffentlichte Briefe an Hartmann. Katalog*. Munich-Mainz.
Weber, B. 1995. *Wolfgang Fortner und seine Opernkompositionen*. Mainz.
Wittig, P. 2005. 'Wir haben keine Leiche!', in: P. Csobádi et al. (eds.), *Das Fragment im (Musik-) Theater*. Salzburg, 379-391.

Apuleius On the Radio:
Louis MacNeice's BBC Dramatisations[1]

STEPHEN HARRISON
Corpus Christi College, University of Oxford

1: Introduction – MacNeice and the BBC

Louis MacNeice (1907-1963) was a major Anglo-Irish poet who was also an expert in classical literature.[2] Born in Belfast, he studied classics at Oxford and was a lecturer in classics at the Universities of Birmingham (1930-36) and London (Bedford College, 1936-9), before turning to work for the BBC (below); in 1936 he published an admired verse version of Aeschylus' *Agamemnon* for performance on the London stage (with music by Benjamin Britten), and his celebrated long poem *Autumn Journal* (1939) contains much reflection on classical topics.[3] At Birmingham he was a friend of the classical scholar E.R. Dodds, who later edited MacNeice's *Collected Poems* (1966).

MacNeice was one of the most prolific authors of radio plays of his time. He worked for the BBC 1941-1963, writing more than 100 scripts for radio, some based on classical themes; the majority of these scripts remain unpublished in the BBC archives.[4] Initially, he was recruited by the BBC during the Second World War to write morale-boosting material which had some propaganda colour: his *The March of the 10,000* was an adaptation of Xeno-

---

[1] This piece could not have been written without the help of my former Oxford colleague Dr Amanda Wrigley, who alerted me to the existence of MacNeice's Apuleian plays. I am most grateful to her for this, and for her practical help in obtaining copies. In what follows I will cite MacNeice's scripts in their BBC format by numbered item.

[2] For his life see Stallworthy 1995.

[3] For MacNeice and the classics see e.g. Peacock 1992, McDonald 1998, Arkins 2000.

[4] Some selections from these plays have been published in MacNeice 1947, 1969 and 1992. For MacNeice at the BBC see Coulton 1980, for his radio plays in general see Holme 1981 and for his radio plays on classical subjects see Wrigley 2007 and 2009.

phon's *Anabasis* which had clear links with the British retreat from Dunkirk in 1940 and was broadcast as Germany invaded Greece in 1941. Amongst the series of MacNeice's wartime classical radio plays are two based on Apuleius' *Metamorphoses*, 'The Golden Ass' and 'Cupid and Psyche', both originally produced late in 1944, when the end of the war was in sight.[5] Both are unpublished, and it is the aim of this paper to provide a first critical assessment of these two works for radio as literary adaptations of Apuleius by a considerable English poet and set them in a contemporary context.[6]

2: 'The Golden Ass', written and produced by Louis MacNeice
First broadcast on BBC Home Service, 3/11/1944;
revived for BBC Third Programme 1951/2
(31/12/1951, 2/1/1952, 25/1/1952).
60 minutes.

This piece is a version of Apuleius' eleven-book *Metamorphoses* or *Golden Ass* in a single radio-play; the length of the broadcast meant a radical abbreviation of the plot in MacNeice's script, and the result is an epitome which is not unlike the pseudo-Lucianic *Onos* (which is certainly a summary of a longer Greek ass-tale). All the embedded tales are removed apart from a reference to Cupid and Psyche (see below), and many episodes are left out (e.g. the stories featuring Pythias in Book 1 and Byrrhaena in Book 2).[7] The announcer's introduction (item 3 in the script) says 'Here follows a dramatisation by Louis MacNeice of the Latin novel written by Lucius Apuleius in the second century AD. Much of the dirt and daintiness has had to be sacrificed but the central theme remains – and remains topical: the man who becomes an ass'. This suggests some current relevance of the plot of Apuleius' novel in a wartime context where Nazism and its followers, now at last being defeated, could be described as asinine. In particular, MacNeice (as a classical scholar with some knowledge of German)[8] might well have known the

---

[5] 'The Golden Ass' was revived at New Year 1951-2, 'Cupid and Psyche' at New Year 1966, perhaps with some notion of entertainment for the pantomime season.
[6] Only Barry Baldwin amongst novel scholars has (briefly) noted the existence of these plays and (more fully) of MacNeice's 1948 adaptation of Petronius' *Cena Trimalchionis* ('Trimalchio's Feast') – see Baldwin 2008.
[7] MacNeice 1992 (originally published 1944) gives an interesting account of the various constraints of the radio play form and the need for simple and effective construction.
[8] In 1951 he published a version of Goethe's *Faust*, also originally broadcast as a series of radio plays.

famous 1935 article of the anti-Nazi Hamburg classicist Bruno Snell on the noise made by the ass in Apuleius' novel,[9] which concluded with the thought that Greek asses could only say 'no' (*ou*), while German asses could only say 'yes' (*ja*); Snell later explained that this was a satirical reference to a Nazi functionary in Hamburg urging the German people to say 'yes' to Nazi power,[10] and this anti-Nazi reference seems to have been known at the time in academic circles.[11]

Apart from its required radical abbreviation of its original, 'The Golden Ass' contains some interesting further modifications. For example, Photis, the slave-girl lover whose carelessness leads to Lucius' transformation into an ass, is given a speech of regret for the harm she has done Lucius, something not found in Apuleius. This makes her more sympathetic, gives her a role after she disappears in the original and (in terms of the drama's practicalities) results in a good speech for an actress, for which the play otherwise offers few opportunities (item 157).

> 'O rising sun, forgive me, during whose absence this night past has seen me fall from grace and my master Milo robbed and my lover Lucius turned to an ass and driven away by hulking thieves. Never was such a night. But you, o rising sun, you shine as gaily as ever – on rippling streams, on waking birds, unshuttering windows, opening roses. May one rose open for *him*, so that he regain his human shape and escape from the murdering thieves and perhaps – but no, he will never come back to me'.

Likewise, the treatment of the novel's central embedded story of 'Cupid and Pyche' is clearly determined by the existence of MacNeice's separate play on this subject which was to be broadcast a week later (see on 'Cupid and Psyche' below), and which echoes some lines from this part of 'The Golden Ass' (see items 2-4 in 'Cupid and Psyche'). The very beginning and end of the lengthy tale are narrated with a teasing gap in between:

> 195. HAG. ... Now : once upon a time there was a certain king and he had three daughters passing fair.
> 196. MUSIC no.8 : FADE UP FAIRY MUSIC BEHIND

---

[9] Snell 1935.
[10] Snell 1966, 200-1.
[11] Skutsch 1992, 400.

> 197. HAG. Now the elder two were beauties but people had seen their like before. But the youngest, my girl, she was a different story. Her beauty was such that people couldn't believe it; they thought she must be a goddess. And that's what began the trouble.
> 198. MUSIC no.8 : FAIRY MUSIC OUT
> 199. HAG. Ah, that was a feast, that was. Talk about weddings ! The Hours adorned the house with roses, the Graces pelted each other with balm, the Muses all nine of 'em sang in chorus and Pan he played on his pipes.
> 200. CHARITE. And Cupid and Psyche, mother ?
> 201. HAG. Them ? *They lived happy ever after.*
> 202. ROBBER CAPTAIN. Happy ever after ? More than either of you'll be.

This arch gesture must have been somewhat mystifying for the original audience, especially since the 'Cupid and Psyche' episode is likely to be the part of Apuleius' novel which was most familiar to them. The use of fairytale formulae ('once upon a time', 'happy ever after') and of 'fairy music'[12] suggest that MacNeice is fully aware of the reception of Apuleius' tale as a Grimm-style fairy story, an interpretation which still has advocates today.[13] The Robber Captain's words to the narrating Hag and listening Charite are nicely ironic for a reader of Apuleius, who knows that both will end up dead before long.

The Hag who tells the story of 'Cupid and Psyche' is like Photis given a larger part than her counterpart in the original (though she is still not individualised by being given a name). Once again we find an added speech for an actress to show her skills, an exit speech of black comic character, covering her last appearance in suicide (moved by MacNeice to a later point in the plot than in the original, to after the defeat of the robbers):

> 289. HAG. O Fire ! Murder ! Rape ! Robbery ! Masters, wake up, wake up ! …. Oh, they must all be dead. Captain, Captain – Ach, he's dead too.
> And where's that girl ? Gone.
> And that stinking ass ? Gone too.

---

[12] On the use of music in radio plays to create an atmosphere see MacNeice 1992 (originally published in MacNeice 1944).

[13] E.g. Anderson 2000, 61-71.

> Our noble band is scuppered, our captives gone, the fire dying. And here, at my feet, look – here's an end of rope. I will make it the end of all things : where's that ring in the roof ? Ah yes, I've made a slip-knot before. Now, if I can get up on this brass-bound chest – so : what could be better ? One, two – hey ! What's that there in the jug ? Just a moment, ye Fates – just one last mouthful of wine.
> GULPS NOISILY
> Good. Now where was I ? Ah yes, up on the chest, the noose around my neck, to shut my eyes and jump. One ! … Two ! …. Three ! ….
> O-o-o-o-h !

This addition of characterising speeches is something of a concession to the conventions of radio drama, and is a fine feature of MacNeice's version. Like the Hag and Photis, the corrupt priest Philebus too is given lines not in the original:

> 410. PHILEBUS. Ass, come with me : you're in holy orders now. From this day forth you'll march through the streets in procession – in a surpliced band with pipe and cymbal, and yourself caparisoned with purple and bearing the sacred image. Ah, it's a great life, ass, a great and holy calling – and apart from that, there's money in it. [a few lines omitted] …Wine and milk, cheese and meat, and there's other pickings too. I remember a young girl once who – What are you pricking up your ears for ? Ah, come on, you'll learn it all soon enough.

Though MacNeice, working within the decorous environment of the BBC, edits out the allusions to homosexuality and bestiality in the corresponding scenes in the original (*Met.* 8.26), it is fitting that Philebus was played by the famously louche poet/actor Dylan Thomas, a friend of MacNeice, in the 1951 production.[14]

In the famous scene where Lucius-ass prays to Isis and she appears to him (*Met.* 11.2 and 11.5-6), MacNeice uses verse to render the originals (*Met.* 11.2 and 11.5-6):

---

[14] As recorded on the script in the BBC Written Archives. The scripts preserved in the Archives are both from the revived productions, of 1951 (produced by MacNeice himself) and 1966 (produced by Christopher Holme).

644. LUCIUS.
Queen of Heaven, whatever thy name,
Whether Ceres giver of corn,
Or Venus yoker of man and woman,
Or Diana lightener of childbirth,
Or Proserpina wardress of ghosts,
Thou whose light illumines the world,
Whose fires foster the seeds,
Though who art Thou in every shape and
by every name art Thou,
End my misery, raise my fallen fortune,
Give me release and peace,
Peel off these abhorrent hoofs and hide
And make me once more Lucius.

Met.11.2
Regina caeli, — sive tu Ceres alma frugum parens
originalis... seu tu caelestis Venus... seu Phoebi
soror, quae partu fetarum medelis lenientibus
recreato populos
tantos educasti ... seu nocturnis ululatibus horren-
da Proserpina triformi facie larvales impetus
comprimens ... ista luce feminea conlustrans
cuncta moenia et udis
ignibus nutriens laeta semina ...fas est invocare:
tu meis iam nunc extremis aerumnis subsiste,
tu fortunam collapsam adfirma,
tu saevis exanclatis casibus pausam pacemque
tribue; ...Depelle quadripedis diram faciem ...
redde me meo Lucio.

652. ISIS
Lucius, this is I. In answer to your prayers,
I the mother of all things, mistress of all the elements, source and nurse of epochs,
Godhead supreme, queen of the dead, highest in heaven,
Who govern the lofty lights of the sky, the life-giving winds of the sea and the sad silence of Hell:
The whole world worships me under divers names
But my truer name is Isis.
I come to heal your sorrow, the day of your rescue dawns.
This day shall my priest walk in procession, his right hand holding a timbrel,
And next to the timbrel, over his wrist – mark well my words – a garland of roses.

Met. 11.5-6
En adsum tuis commota, Luci, precibus,
rerum naturae parens, elementorum omnium domina,
saeculorum progenies initialis, summa numinum,
regina manium, prima caelitum...
quae caeli luminosa culmina, maris salubria flamina,
inferum deplorata silentia nutibus meis dispenso:
cuius numen unicum multiformi specie, ritu vario,
nomine multiiugo totus veneratus orbis ... Aegyptii
caerimoniis me propriis percolentes appellant
vero nomine reginam Isidem. Adsum tuos miserata
casus, adsum favens et propitia. ... iam tibi providen-
tia mea inlucescit dies salutaris. [6] Nam meo
monitu
sacerdos in ipso procinctu pompae roseam
manu dextera sistro cohaerentem gestabit coronam.

In using verse MacNeice astutely picks up the strongly poetic and elevated colour of Apuleius' prose in both these speeches, which has been noted by Apuleian scholars;[15] for variation's sake, he chooses two different verse-forms (with shorter and longer lines) for the Apuleian prose periods. He also picks up the traditional language of prayer employed by Apuleius here, with the repeated *seu* echoed in the repeated 'or' and the repeated to echoed in the repeated 'Thou'. In this last word he clearly turns to the archaic pronouns of traditional Anglican liturgy in the *Book of Common Prayer* to evoke a religious texture for a modern radio audience, perhaps even echoing the Lord's Prayer in his similar opening line ('Queen of Heaven, whatever thy name' ~ 'Our father, which art in heaven, hallowed be thy name').

In Isis' reply to Lucius, MacNiece neatly replicates with assonance and alliteration some of the splendid euphony of the original: 'source and nurse', 'the lofty lights of the sky', 'the sad silence of Hell'. Such aural effects especially befit the medium of radio, where as MacNeice himself emphasised, the sound of the spoken word is naturally crucial.[16]

MacNeice's most interesting modification of the original is his version of the ending. Where Apuleius' novel ends with Lucius a faithful follower of Osiris/Isis in Rome (*Met.* 11.30), MacNeice's version ends with a metafictional allusion to the writing of the novel itself:

> 671. LUCIUS….From this day on I intend to eschew all frivolities. Except maybe …except…
> 672. PRIEST. Except *what* ?
> 673. LUCIUS. Except just one. Writing.
> 674. PRIEST. Writing, young man ! You mean books ?
> 675. LUCIUS. Not books, High Priest, just a book. And I'll call it – you'd never guess – I'll call it The Golden Ass !

This self-referential ending nicely recalls several metafictional allusions in Apuleius' novel to its own writing. Most notoriously, this includes the reference to the narrator as *Madaurensem,* 'man from Madauros' at *Met.* 11.27, apparently ascribing the birthplace of the novel's real author to its fictional narrator; the aged crone narrator of the tale of Cupid and Psyche (MacNeice's 'Hag') refers to herself at 4.32 as *huius Milesiae conditorem*, 'the author of this Milesian tale' and implies that she is a Latin speaker, another example of the real Apuleius appearing behind a fictional speaker; and

---

[15] Cf. e.g. Harrison 2005.
[16] MacNeice 1992, 394-6 (first published in MacNeice 1944).

most fully Lucius receives a prophecy at 2.12 which claims *historiam magnam et incredundam fabulam et libros me futurum*, which can only be a reference to the *Metamorphoses* itself.[17]

3: 'Cupid and Psyche', written and produced by Louis MacNeice
First broadcast on BBC Home Service, 7/11/1944;
revived for BBC Third Programme 11/2/1947
and again 28/12/1966.
75 minutes.

This version of 'Cupid and Psyche', the famous central two-book embedded tale of the *Metamorphoses* (some 17% of the whole in length), had a 25% longer broadcast time than that allocated to the adaptation of the whole of the rest of the work in the 'The Golden Ass', originally broadcast less than a week earlier. Consequently, this is a much fuller version of its original than the 'The Golden Ass': very little is wholly omitted, though much is abbreviated. As we saw in the brief allusion to the Cupid and Psyche story in 'The Golden Ass', there is some emphasis on the fairy-tale aspect of the story and its amusing features, fitting with some of MacNeice's other radio work[18] and contrasting with the more rumbustious 'The Golden Ass'. The announcer's introduction (item 1) says : 'The author, Apuleius, by inserting it into his great picaresque fantasy, The Golden Ass, made it a story within a story. Out of the harsh came forth beauty'. The play begins by pretty much repeating the hag's introduction to the non-narrated story in 'The Golden Ass' (items 2-4), a back-reference to the previous week's play, which might be picked up by an alert listener. The play contains no evident references to its wartime circumstances, and topicality seems to be limited to an allusion to Walt Disney: Psyche's line 'Oh mirror, mirror, why can't you tell me I'm ugly?' (item 21) may well allude to the famous line of the evil Queen in Disney's *Snow White and the Seven Dwarves* (1938) 'Mirror, mirror on the wall / Who is the fairest of them all ?'; MacNeice mentions Disney in his writing elsewhere[19] and it would be hard not to know in 1940's Britain that this famous film contained that line. This casting of Psyche as a kind of Snow White figure, overcoming tribulations to achieve a successful marriage, is

---

[17] For these metafictional allusions see the convenient discussion and further bibliography in Harrison 2000, 231-2).
[18] E.g. 'The Heartless Giant' of 1946 and 'The Two Wicked Sisters' of 1948.
[19] MacNeice 1992, 396 (first published in MacNeice 1944).

thus a cultural updating for the listener as well as a reference to the literary genre of fairy tale (the lines occur in a similar form in *Schneewittchen* by the brothers Grimm, 1812).[20] 'Cupid and Psyche' contains some interesting modifications of the original. The Latin verse oracle in elegiac couplets which precipitates Psyche's exposure on the rock is rendered in neat rhyming lines:

53. ORACLE.	*Met.* 4.33
Unhappy king , who ask your daughter's doom, Know ; Psyche's bridal bed must be her tomb.	*Montis in excelsi scopulo, rex siste puellam ornatam mundo funerei thalami.*
These are your orders: dress the maid in black,	*Nec speres generum mortali stirpe creatum, sed saevum atque ferum vipereumque malum,*
Expose her on the mountain – look not back,	*quod pinnis volitans super aethera cuncta fatigat flammaque et ferro singula debilitat,*
For her appointed bridegroom is not even A man, but a dread monster darkening heaven;	*quod tremit ipse Iovis quo numina terrificantur, fluminaque horrescunt et Stygiae tenebrae.*
None other must your tender daughter wed – Tomorrow married and tomorrow dead !	

Here MacNeice removes some of the clues that the oracle in fact refers to Cupid rather than to a 'real' monster: the Latin refers to his flying through the skies and attacking with fire and iron, and being feared by Jupiter – all characteristics which give the reader a broad hint as to the 'monster''s true identity. Here some of the narratological subtlety of the Apuleian original is removed; this may be partly explained by the difference of media, since a reader can turn back to an ironic anticipation of this kind while a radio listener cannot.

The medium of radio has some added advantages, however. The availability of incidental music leads to several effectively humorous moments in the play, for example the argument between Psyche's parents as she goes to her apparent death :

> 61. MOTHER. If my daughter must go to her death, it ought to be done properly. You've remembered about the musicians ?
> 62. FATHER. No, I'm afraid ! –
> 63. MOTHER. You must be losing your memory. I *will* have music for Psyche's wedding.

---

[20] 'Spieglein, Spieglein an der Wand, / wer ist die Schönste im ganzen Land?'.

64. FATHER. Psyche's funeral.
65. MOTHER. Well, don't let's dispute about words. The ascent of that mountain must be conducted to music. It will help Psyche too.
66. MUSIC FUNERAL MARCH.

Or Jupiter's complaint about his royal trumpeters:

530. CUPID. I am going to speak to Jupiter.
531. MUSIC. JUPITER FANFARE
532. JUPITER. Trumpeters, cease !
533. MUSIC. FANFARE BREAKS OFF.
534. JUPITER. This prelude is not really necessary every time I have visitors. Let him or her come in.

The use of music can also create its own narrative effects. In MacNeice's version Mercury is presented in the act of making two proclamations, both similarly accompanied by trumpets (items 380, seeking Psyche the escaped slave, and 540, summoning the gods to assembly), where there is only one reported at length in the original (the first, *Met.* 6.8; the second is only summarised, *Met.* 6.23).[21]

The magical atmosphere of Cupid's palace is invoked both by the use of music and by Psyche's use of verse to describe it :

87. MUSIC. ENCHANTMENT MUSIC AND BEHIND.
88. PSYCHE. Citron, ivory, silver, gold,
    One room, two rooms, three rooms, four rooms,
    Chests of treasure without a lock,
    Door after door without a keeper,
    Bright mosaics that no one treads,
    Carven chairs where no one sits –
    And listen, listen :
89. MUSIC. UP MUSIC AND QUICKLY BEHIND AGAIN.
90. PSYCHE. Music rising from floors and creeping
    Out of the dazzling walls and dropping
    From coffered ceilings and broidered arras –
    Music without musicians !

---

[21] MacNeice seems to like to insert this kind of mirror-scene even without music: compare the two extended auctions of the ass in 'The Golden Ass', items 354-409 and 490-544, again replacing one in the original.

Verse and music similarly combine to mark the solemn ascent of Psyche from the Underworld:

517. MUSIC. BRING IN ASCENSION MUSIC BEHIND.
518. PSYCHE. Upwards, upwards, upwards, upwards,
      Out of the poppied dark of Death,
      Up to the green of trees and grass,
      Away from the souls that squeak like bats,
      Up to the life of birds and men,
      Climbing, climbing, climbing, climbing
      Up to the chorus of stars at night,
      Up to the clangour of sun by day:
      Daylight, daylight, daylight, daylight,
      Light !

MacNeice inserts several comic scenes to lighten the mood, for example one in which Cupid almost gives his identity away to Psyche like a husband returning from a business trip :

293. CUPID. …Come, let us kiss and sleep: I am so tired, I have had such a long flight.
294. PSYCHE. Flight ?
295. CUPID. Ride – such a long ride. Come, kiss me. Goodnight, Psyche.

Here and elsewhere the play is coy about sex – Psyche does not evidently have intercourse with Cupid, and certainly does not become pregnant. The BBC's standards of decorum are observed. A similar comic tone is struck in the scene where the mythical Cerberus of the original (silently appeased by drugged food, *Met.* 6.20) is replaced by a lively porter (recalling that of *Macbeth* Act 2 Scene 3) with the manner of a comic policeman (not unlike Aeacus in Aristophanes *Frogs,* 464-78) :

504. PORTER. Here, here, here, young lady, where do you think you're going ?
505. PSYCHE. I want to see Proserpina.
506. PORTER. You do, do you ? What for ?
507. PSYCHE. I have a favour to ask, I –

508. PORTER. A favour, eh ? The Queen of Death don't deal so much in favours. And take it from me : she ain't in a very good mood.

4 : Conclusion – MacNeice's reception of Apuleius

In an article in the *Radio Times* in 1945, written in response to audience feedback on his Apuleian radio plays, MacNeice suggested that it was inevitable that Apuleius' novel (which he had admired since schooldays) provided some content shocking for a modern audience.[22] A year later, MacNeice enlarged on these comments in an introduction to a reprint of Adlington's 1566 translation of Apuleius (the first in English and very likely used by Shakespeare).[23] It is enthusiastic in praise of Apuleius (v) : 'It is hard to find a writer who combines such dissimilar qualities – elegance and earthiness, euphuism and realism, sophistication and love of folk-lore, Platonism and belief in witchcraft, mysticism and salty irony'. He picks out Apuleius' robust sense of humour (comparing him with Petronius and Catullus), the sensuousness of his style, and his strong characters (vii) : 'His Venus, like Homer's goddesses, is a jealous and touchy woman, and Psyche ... remains an almost too human girl, an amplified version of the Third Sister of folk story, a charming but naïve Cinderella'. He regards Apuleius as a sincere believer in both high religion and low magic (vii): 'He had then a foot in both worlds, as was natural in an age when rival mystery religions were fighting for man's allegiance while traditional paganism and the rationalistic philosophies were alike out of the running'. Here MacNeice seems to be influenced by the views on the second century CE of his friend and erstwhile colleague E.R. Dodds, later author of *Pagan and Christian in an Age of Anxiety*, 1966, an interesting case of scholarly work colouring literary reception. This view about Apuleius' mixture of mysticism/religion and magic/humour is borne out by the two radio plays, although humour and entertainment are naturally more emphasised there than in the essay.

In conclusion, we find in these two radio plays versions of Apuleius's *Metamorphoses* which are full of interest, both in terms of their adaptation of this Latin novel for the specialised modern environment of radio and in terms of their intrinsic literary form and texture. They contain a number of

---

[22] For the article see MacNeice 1945, for MacNeice's early taste for Apuleius Baldwin 2008.

[23] MacNeice 1946 (reprinted in MacNeice 1987, 127-32); for full accounts of Adlington's version see Carver 2007, 298-326, Gaisser 2008, 288-95.

poetic passages as yet unrecorded in MacNeice's published output,[24] and deserve publication in their own right. In fact, these radio plays fully conform to the historic mission of the BBC to provide 'information, education and entertainment',[25] since they are educative and even informative in providing versions of a literary classic for a modern environment and entertaining in retaining Apuleius' emphasis on humour and amusement in a medium of modern mass consumption.

Bibliography

Anderson, G., 2000. *Fairytale in the Ancient World*. London: Routledge.
Arkins, B., 2000. 'Athens no longer dies: Greek and Roman themes in MacNeice, *Classics Ireland* 7, 1-15.
Baldwin, B., 2008. 'Eee, bah gum, Petronius, Lad', *Petronian Society Newsletter* 38, 22-23.
Carver, R.H.F., 2007. *The Protean Ass*. Oxford: OUP.
Coulton, B., 1980. *Louis MacNeice in the BBC*. London: Faber and Faber.
Devine, K. and Peacock, A.J., 1998 (eds.). *Louis MacNeice and his Influence*. Gerrard's Cross: Colin Smythe.
Gaisser, J.H., 2008. *The Fortunes of Apuleius and the Golden Ass*. Princeton: Princeton UP.
Harrison, S.J., 2000. *Apuleius: A Latin Sophist*. Oxford, OUP.
Harrison, S.J., 2005. 'The Poetics of Fiction : poetic influence on the language of Apuleius' *Metamorphoses*' in T. Reinhardt, J.N. Adams and M. Lapidge (eds.), *The Language of Latin Prose*. Oxford: OUP, 273-86.
Holme, C., 1981. 'The Radio Drama of Louis MacNeice' in J. Drakakis (ed.), *British Radio Drama*. Cambridge: CUP, 37-71.
MacNeice, L., 1944. *Christopher Columbus : A Radio Play*. London: Faber and Faber.
MacNeice, L., 1945. 'The *Golden Ass* or *Metamorphoses* of Apuleius', *Radio Times* 2.2.1945: 8.
MacNeice, L., 1947. *The Dark Tower and Other Radio Scripts*. London: Faber and Faber.
MacNeice, L., 1969. *Persons from Porlock and Other Plays For Radio* [ed. W.H.Auden]. London: Faber and Faber.
MacNeice, L., 1946. 'Introduction', pp. v-ix in *The Golden Ass of Apuleius*. London: John Lehmann.
MacNeice, L., 1966. *Collected Poems* [ed. E.R. Dodds]. London: Faber and Faber.
MacNeice, L., 2007. *Collected Poems* [ed. P. McDonald]. London: Faber and Faber.
MacNeice, L., 1992. *Selected Plays of Louis MacNeice* [ed. A. Heuser and P. McDonald]. Oxford: OUP.
MacNeice, L., 1987. *Selected Literary Criticism of Louis MacNeice* [ed. A. Heuser]. Oxford: OUP.

---

[24] Such incidental verses in plays (and complete verse plays) are understandably excluded from Peter McDonald's recent excellent *Collected Poems*: MacNeice 2007, xxix-xxx.
[25] A formula found several times in the 2006 renewal of the BBC's Royal Charter, available at http://www.bbc.co.uk/bbctrust/assets/files/pdf/about/how_we_govern/charter.pdf (accessed 18.9.2009).

McDonald. P., 1998. ' 'With eyes turned down on the past': MacNeice's Classicism' in Devine and Peacock, 34-52.

Peacock, A.J., 1992. 'Louis MacNeice: Transmitting Horace', *Revista Alicantina de Estudios Ingleses* 5, 119-30.

Skutsch, O. 1992. 'Recollection of Scholars I Have Known', *Harvard Studies in Classical Philology* 94, 387-408.

Snell, B., 1935. 'Das I-Ah des goldenes Esel', *Hermes* 70, 355-356.

Snell, B., 1966. *Gesammelte Schriften*. Göttingen: Vandenhoeck & Ruprecht.

Stallworthy, J., 1995. *Louis MacNeice*. London: Faber.

Wrigley, A., 2007. 'Stages of Imagination: Greek plays on BBC Radio' in C. Stray (ed.), *Remaking the Classics, Literature, Genre and Media in Britain, 1800-2000*. London: Duckworth, 57-73.

Wrigley, A., 2009.'Louis MacNeice's Radio Classics : 'All so unimaginably different'?', in D. Lowe and K. Shahabudin (eds.), *Classics for All: Reworking Antiquity in Mass Culture*. Cambridge: Cambridge Scholars' Publishing, 39-63.

Abstracts

Hugh J. Mason
Charikleia at the Mauritshuis

Bloemaert's painting, of *Theagenes and Chariclea,* commissioned for Amalia, the wife of Prince Frederik Hendrik of Orange (1584-1647), portrays a scene from the *Aithiopika* of Heliodoros, 4.4. It is a "history" painting, the equivalent in art of an historical *exemplum* in rhetoric, illustrating a human quality of interest to the artist or his patron. History paintings came into fashion in the 16th century, just when the ancient novels were becoming known in Western Europe, and the *Aithiopika* became a popular source for history paintings. I argue that the topic of the painting was suggested to the Prince by his secretary, Constantijn Huygens (1596-1687); that the painting commemorates the Prince's marriage to Amalia; and that the Prince or his secretary saw in the *Aithiopika*'s account of a royal marriage achieved despite incredible difficulties, a comparison to the unusual circumstances of their wedding.

Faustina C.W. Doufikar-Aerts
Susanna and her Sisters. The Virtuous Lady Motif in Sacred Tradition and its Representation in Art, Secular Writing and Popular Narrative

The Biblical Story of Susanna and the Elders has always appealed to the imagination of audiences. It became a favorite subject of iconography from early Christianity, a.o. in medieval illuminated Bibles and later it became a popular theme in the representations of painters like Rembrandt, Tintoretto, and Van Orley.

In the past century research and criticism, predominantly from the field of theology, literature and gender studies, concentrated on the origin and relationship of the Susanna story in the Septuagint and Theodotion.

So far, little attention has been paid to other testimonies of 'Susanna' in a non-biblical context, as preserved in the traditions of the Samaritans,

Shi'ite and Sunnite Muslims, Copts and Ethiopian Jews, which were handed down in Arabic and Ge'ez. This paper focuses on these particular traditions. Investigation of the novelistic character of the Susanna story reveals that the conditions, such as the dramatic turns and an appealing plot are essential for the heroine's survival, literally as well as literarily.

GERALD SANDY
Apuleius, Beroaldo and the Development of the (Early) Modern Classical Commentary

To rephrase the well known statement of the grammarian Terentianus Maurus, *Pro captu commentatoris habent sua fata libelli*. Apuleius' *Golden Ass* became widely known in western Europe through the medium of Beroaldo's commentary (1500). He did not, however, "almost single-handedly establish the rules for writing commentaries," as his colleague Codro Urceo at the University of Bologna claimed. As Beroaldo himself recognised, he was working within a well established mediaeval tradition. Beroaldo was not even the first humanist of his generation to produce a commentary on a classical Latin author, as Beroaldo himself acknowledges. To what, then, can we attribute the success of Beroaldo's commentary on the *Golden Ass*? One of his remarkable achievements was to produce publications that simultaneously met the demands of scholars (*docti*), the educated public (*studiosi*) and students (*scholastici*), so much so that the younger Henri Éstienne pays tribute to Beroaldo (and Calderini) as the teacher of his generation. As the teacher of his age Beroaldo had a wealth of erudition and insight to offer to his hundreds of students each day in 1500, and we today would be well advised to take some of his lessons to heart.

FERRUCCIO BERTINI
The *Golden Ass* and its *Nachleben* in the Middle Ages and in the Renaissance

After a brief reference to the Homeric Ulysses in Dante, this paper defines the meaning of the word *curiositas* using these words of Plutarch's *De curiositate*: "Curiosity, that is the longing for knowing other people's troubles, is a malady of the mind, a disease which seems to be lacking in neither envy nor malice." The offence of the young protagonist of Apuleius'

Metamorphoses is *curiositas*, in particular for magic. The paper ends with a discussion of Boccaccio's adaptations from the ninth book of *Metamorphoses*.

MICHELE RAK
From word to image:
notes on the Renaissance reception of Apuleius's *Metamorphoses*

The tale of Cupid and Psyche from Apuleius' *Golden Ass* entered Renaissance Europe about 1338. Since the beginning of Italian humanism the myth has been interpreted as a universal symbol of love. In European artistic representation it is perceived as a symbolic icon and as portraying philosophical dichotomies such as the body and soul, the different types of beauty, the consequences of envy, and 'the queen of the court'. In early modern Europe the myth circulated through printed editions, translations, literary adaptations, and paintings – from *Hypnerotomachia Poliphili* to M.M. Boiardo and Agnolo Firenzuola, from Jacopo Sellaio to Raphael and the *Palazzo Te* in Mantua frescoed by Giulio Romano.

BEATRICE BAKHOUCHE
Martianus Capella's *De nuptiis Philologiae et Mercurii*
or the Subversion of the Latin Novel

In the *Weddings of Philologia and Mercury* by Martianus Capella, the use of the novel is the pretext for a work which focuses on the academic disciplines. The novel is subverted and used as an attractive package for a common handbook. I intend to study all transgressions committed by the author: the frontiers are blurred between humanity and divinity, between microcosm and macrocosm, within the framework of a very cryptic construction. The result is polyphony within a work which intends to reflect an entirety. I will try to show that the novel aims at reflecting a whole – be it cosmic, academic or literary.

Christiane Reitz & Lorenz Winkler-Horaček
Love on a wallpaper: Apuleius in the boudoir

A French scenic wallpaper, first produced in 1815, and a commercial success up to the first half of the 20th cent., depicts the story of Cupid and Psyche. It consists of a sequence of 12 images. Both the literary background, esp. Apuleius, and Jean de La Fontaine's *Conte en prose* (1669), and the iconographical background are of importance for the interpretation: The visual narrative draws on preceding literary versions of the myth, but also on ancient sculpture and motifs which receive a symbolic or allusive significance in their new narrative context. The wallpapers provide an interesting example to analyse the different narrative strategies of both media, text and image.

Massimo Fusillo
Petronius and the Contemporary Novel:
Between New Picaresque and Queer Aesthetics

The paper aims at defining Petronius' contemporary reception, and especially its profound consonance with the manifold transformations of the twentieth-century experimental novel. The analysis involves two significant trends: the so-called 'new picaresque' (especially Céline), which recalls the non-teleological organisation of the *Satyrica*; and the postmodern aesthetics of the camp (especially Arbasino), which concerns the ironic re-use of a popular, consumerist literature.

Nikolai Endres
Petronius in West Egg:
The Satyricon and *The Great Gatsby*

F. Scott Fitzgerald's *The Great Gatsby* was originally entitled *Trimalchio* or *Trimalchio in West Egg*; even in the final text one explicit reference to the *Satyricon* remains: 'It was when curiosity about Gatsby was at its highest that the lights in his house failed to go on one Saturday night – and, as obscurely as it had begun, his career as Trimalchio was over.' Most critics have focused on Trimalchio's vulgarity and Jay Gatsby's ostentation, while I am more interested in the two narrators, Nick Carraway and Encolpius, and *their* desire for great theatricality. Petronius' Niceros, who may have given Nick his name, tells the story of a werewolf, that ultimate shape-shifting, theatrical human beast, which reappears in Fitzgerald's Mr. Wolfshiem, the wearer of finest human teeth on his sleeves, fixer of the World Series, and creator of Gatsby. But who is ultimately great in the *Satyricon* and in *Gatsby*? I end by applying Gian Biagio Conte's thesis about Petronius (*The Hidden Author*) to Fitzgerald, the self-confessed failure in his private life who aspired to giddy heights in his noble fiction: The Great Fitzgerald.

NIALL W. SLATER
'His Career as Trimalchio': Petronian Character and Narrative in Fitzgerald's Great American Novel

In revising the novel he once called *Trimalchio in West Egg* into *The Great Gatsby*, F. Scott Fitzgerald significantly transformed both his portrayal of Gatsby as profligate host and the novel's narrative structure, showing in the process a significant Petronian influence on time and character in the novel. Although what the Encolpius-like narrator Nick Carraway labels Gatsby's "career as Trimalchio" remains, Carraway's perspective changes and grows with his deepened appreciation of Gatsby's self-fashioning. Fitzgerald's re-ordering and re-structuring of narrative time from *Trimalchio* to *Gatsby* shows a more clearly Petronian chronotope at work in the former yet still powerful beneath the surface of the latter.

JON SOLOMON
Psyche, Callirhoë and Operatic Heroines Derived from Ancient Novels

Though opera owes its existence largely to Greek studies in the late Renaissance and several thousand operas are derived from Greco-Roman myth and history, very few operas derive from ancient novels. The works described here include Francesco Cavalli's version of *Amore inamorato*, written by Giovanni Fusconi, Giovanni Lordano, and Pietro Michele; Henry Desmarest's score for Joseph-François Douché de Vancy's libretto of *Théagène et Cariclée*; Mattia Verazi's adaptation of *Calliroe* set by Sacchini, Rust, Myslivecek, Alessandri, and Nasolini; Verdi's *Aida*; Pierre Laujon's *Daphnis et Chloé* set by Joseph Bodin de Boismortier; and Charles Dibdin's *The Ephesian Matron, or The Widow's Tears*.

Simone Beta
Le dieu Pan fait pan pan pan de son pied de chèvre:
Daphnis and Chloe on the stage at the end of the nineteenth century

In 1860 Offenbach composed a comic operetta based on Longus' novel. In 1885 F. Le Borne composed a 'drame pastoral' performed in Brussels; in 1897 and 1899 Paris hosted the 'pastorale en un acte' by H. Busser and the 'comédie lyrique en trois actes' by C. Maréchal. In 1894 A. Casirola set into music a parody where the turning point of the novel – Daphnis and Chloe's discovery of sex – becomes a funny farce. Through the analysis of these librettos, the paper throws new light upon the appeal of this Greek novel at the end of the nineteenth century.

Tiziana Ragno
Widows on the operatic stage:
The 'Ephesian Matron' as a dramatic character
in twentieth-century German musical theatre (esp. 1928-1952)

This paper focuses on some operatic adaptations of the 'Widow of Ephesus' tale, expressly shaped after the Petronian source. A preliminary survey, related to the reception of the novella, shows that all the operatic transpositions of this story (with only a few exceptions) are produced from the 1930s onwards; furthermore, many of these are geographically concentrated in Germany. We will investigate them by adopting a comparative approach, in order to point out the strategies used to 'rewrite' the ancient source (Petr. 111-112).

Stephen Harrison
Apuleius On the Radio: Louis MacNeice's BBC Dramatisations

This paper looks at two unpublished radio plays by the poet Louis Macneice derived from Apuleius' *Metamorphoses* – *The Golden Ass* and *Cupid and Psyche*, first broadcast in 1944, of which the scripts are preserved in the BBC archives. It considers the different treatments of Apuleius in the two pieces, owed at least partly to their different scale, and the strategies of selection and modification applied by Macneice to Apuleius, as well as the plays' use of the resources of broadcasting (such as sound effects) to enhance the narrative. It also sets these pieces against the broader background of Macneice's use of classical texts in his poetry and in his work for radio.

Contributors

BEATRICE BAKHOUCHE is University Professor (Latin Language and Literature) at the Université Paul Valéry (Montpellier III). She is author of a major edition of Chalcidius' commentary on the *Timaeus* of Plato (Paris, 2011), on which her research centres. This unique and rich work occupies a crucial but little-known place in the transmission of Platonism until the Renaissance. She has published numerous articles on science (astronomy, optics, medicine), phylosophy and neo-platonism (Macrobius and Martianus Capella's *De nuptiis Philologiae et Mercurii*).

FERRUCCIO BERTINI is a specialist in medieval Latin and classical Latin literature, who has taught at the University of Sassari (Facoltà di Magistero, 1969-1978) and the University of Genoa (Professor in Facoltà di Lettere e Filosofia, 1978-2003; Dean, 1990-6, director of Dipartimento di Archeologia, Filologia Classica e loro tradizioni 1997-2003). Since 1991 he has been editor of the classical journal *Maia*.

SIMONE BETA is Associate Professor of Classical Philology at the University of Siena.His research centers on Greek and Roman drama, sympotic poetry, and the reception of classical antiquity. He has published the book *Il linguaggio nelle commedie di Aristofane. Parola positiva e parola negativa nella commedia antica* (Rome 2004), an anthology of Greek sympotic epigrams (*Vino e poesia. Centocinquanta epigrammi greci sul vino*, Milan 2006), and the essay "The Metamorphosis of a Greek Comedy and its Protagonist: Some Musical Versions of Aristophanes' Lysistrata" (P. Brown & S. Ograjensek, edd., *Ancient Drama in Music for the Modern Stage*, Oxford 2010, 240-57).

NIKOLAI ENDRES received his Ph.D. in Comparative Literature from the University of North Carolina-Chapel Hill in 2000. As an associate professor at Western Kentucky University, he teaches Great Books, British literature, classics, mythology, and gay and lesbian studies. He has published on Plato, Petronius, Gustave Flaubert, Oscar Wilde, E. M. Forster, F. Scott Fitzgerald,

Mary Renault, Gore Vidal, Patricia Nell Warren, and others. His next project is a "queer" reading of the myth and music of Richard Wagner. He is also working on a book-length study of Platonic love as a homoerotic code in the modern gay novel.

STEPHEN HARRISON is Professor of Latin Literature in the University of Oxford, and Fellow and Tutor in Classics at Corpus Christi College. He has worked and written extensively on the Roman novel of Apuleius and its reception, has worked on the team producing the Groningen Commentaries on Apuleius, and is a member of the editorial board of *Ancient Narrative*. He is author of the monograph *Apuleius : A Latin Sophist* (2000), co-author of the translations *Apuleius : The Rhetorical Works* (2001) and of the Groningen commentary on Apuleius' Cupid and Psyche (2004), editor of *Oxford Readings in the Roman Novel* (1999), co-editor of *Space in the Ancient Novel* (2005) and *The Greek and The Roman Novels: Parallel Readings* (2007), and recently edited *Living Classics: Greece and Rome In Contemporary Poetry in English* (OUP, 2009).

HUGH MASON retired on 31 Dec 2011 from the University of Toronto, where he has taught in the Classics department since 1968. He has attended all the meetings of ICAN since Bangor. His research on Novels has focused mainly on Apuleius and Longus; it is the author of *Daphnis and Chloe* who introduced him to his other area of specialisation, the history and culture of the island of Lesbos from the Bronze Age to the present. The present paper is a direct result of the 2000 conference in Groningen, which gave him an opportunity to visit the Mauritshuis along with other art galleries in the Netherlands.

FAUSTINA DOUFIKAR-AERTS studied Arabic, Turkish and Persian languages and cultures at the universities of Leiden and Utrecht. She took her doctoral degree at Leiden University with the dissertation *Alexander Magnus Arabicus. A Survey of the Alexander Tradition through Seven Centuries: from Pseudo-Callisthenes to Sūrī*. She is specialized in the oriental Alexander tradition and the transmission of literary and religious motifs from antiquity into Islamic cultures. She has been researcher in Leiden and Cambridge and substitute professor of Islamic Studies at Mainz university. Currently she is associate professor at the Center of Islamic Theology at the VU (Free University) of Amsterdam and project leader of the multidisciplinary research program *Beyond the European Myth. In Search of the Afro-Asiatic Alexan-*

der Cycle and the Transnational Migration of Ideas and Concepts of Identity.

MASSIMO FUSILLO is Professor of Literary Criticism and Comparative Literature at the University of L'Aquila; and Coordinator of the PhD Program in Literary Genres. His main Fields of Interest are Ancient Narrative, Modern Reception of Classical Literatures, Thematic Criticism, Cinema and Literature; he published *Il romanzo greco: polifonia ed eros* (Venice 1989; Paris 1991); *La Grecia secondo Pasolini: Mito e cinema* (Florence 1996); *L'altro e lo stesso. Teoria e storia del doppio* (Florence 1998); and *Il dio ibrido. Dioniso e le Baccanti nel Novecento* (Bologna 2006).

MICHELE RAK has taught at the universities of Siena (full professor), Napoli, Palermo, and LUISS-Roma. He is a cultural historian who has written widely on traditions, identities, popular culture, the relationship between written texts and images and baroque culture, and a media expert who studies media culture, cultural management and the book market.

TIZIANA RAGNO is Assistant Professor of Latin Literature at the Faculty of Letters, University of Foggia. Her main area of research deals with Petronius' *Satyrica* and its reception especially in the theatre of XXth century. She is also interested in the *Fortleben* of Latin authors and themes, especially in the history of art and music. Tiziana Ragno's first monograph *Il teatro nel racconto. Studi sulla* fabula *scenica della matrona di Efeso* was published in 2009.

CHRISTIANE REITZ is Professor for Classical Philology (Latin) at the Heinrich Schliemann-Institute for Classical Studies at Rostock University (Germany). Her main fields of research are ancient epic, technical literature and reception studies.

GERALD SANDY is Professor Emeritus of Classics at the University of British Columbia. He has published books, book chapters and articles on a range of subjects that include the ancient Greek and Roman novels, their reception, Catullus, Virgil, Guillaume Budé, French Hellenism, Filippo Beroaldo and humanist commentaries.

NIALL W. SLATER is the Samuel Candler Dobbs Professor of Latin and Greek at Emory University. His research interests focus on the ancient theatre and its production conditions, the later reception of classical drama, and prose fiction. His books include *Spectator Politics: Metatheatre and Performance in Aristophanes* (Penn 2002); *Reading Petronius* (JHUP, 1990); and *Plautus in Performance: The Theatre of the Mind* (Princeton, 1985; 2nd, revised edition 2000), as well as translations of Middle Comedy for *The Birth of Comedy* (ed. J. R. Rusten, JHUP, 2011).

JON SOLOMON, Robert D. Novak Professor of Western Civilization and Culture, and Professor of the Classics at the University of Illinois at Urbana-Champaign, works on the classical tradition in opera and cinema, ancient Greek mythology and music, as well as ancient Roman cuisine and The Three Stooges. His publications include *Ptolemy's Harmonics* (Brill), *The Ancient World in the Cinema*^{2} (Yale), and (co-authored) *Up the University*. He recently published volume I of the I Tatti translation and edition of Boccaccio's *Genealogy of the Pagan Gods*. He is presently working on a book on *Ben-Hur*.

LORENZ WINKLER-HORACEK Studium der Klassischen Archäologie, Alten Geschichte und Islamwissenschaften in Heidelberg und Berlin. Promotion in Heidelberg 1991 mit einer Arbeit über "Salus. Vom Staatskult zu politischen Idee" (Heidelberg 1995). HHabilitation in Rostock 2004 über "Monster in der griechischen Kunst" (im Druck). 1993-2007 Assistent und wissenschaftlicher Mitarbeiter für Klassische Archäologie an der Universität Rostock. Seit 2007 Kurator der Abguss-Sammlung Antiker Plastik der Freien Universität Berlin.

Indices

Index locorum

Apuleius
   Apology 56.2, 39
   Met. 4.33, 189
      6.8.7, 56
      8.2.2, 49
      9.33.5, 54
      11.2, 185
      11.5-6, 185
      11.21.2, 65
      11.27, 187
Artemidorus
   2.39, 69
Augustinus
   conf. 2.8.16, 72
Ausonius
   cent.nupt. 11.4, 71
Boccaccio
   Gen.deor.gentil. 5.22, 98
Dante
   Inf. 24.94-99, 61
        26.112-120, 62
Fitzgerald
   Gatsby 49, 127
      104, 115
      105, 112
      119, 122, 126
      135-136, 131
      137, 120
      170, 113
      173, 121
      185, 113
      187, 118
   Trimalchio 116-117, 130
      42, 128
      88, 125
Fulgentius
   Myth. 3.6, 98
Heliodorus
   4.4.1-2, 4
   9.4-5, 9
Longus
   2.7.7, 159
Martianus Capella
   1.2, 38
   1.7, 98
   1.22, 39
   1.36, 35
   2.100, 37
   7.727, 35
   9.998, 35
Petronius
   6, 136
   60.9, 120
   80.9, 116
   111.5, 171
Plato
   Symp. 190E, 118
Plutarchus
   de curios. 515D, 62
   de Is. et Osir. 362F., 64

General Index

Accursius, 54
Albertus Magnus, 54
allegory, 96, 98, 103
allusion
   metafictional –, 187
Amyot, J., 9

antimilitarism, 179
    20th cent. German musical theatre, 174
Apuleius
    17th cent. reception, 74
    and Fulgentius, 72
    and Petronius, 70
Apuleius' *Golden Ass*
    early modern reception, 74
    significant title, 64
Arabian Nights, 20, 26
Arbasino, A.
    Fratelli d'Italia, 141
Archibald, E., 73
Arrowsmith, W., 120
Artemidorus, 69
Auerbach, E., 135
Augustinus, 71
Ausonius, 71
Bakhtin, M.M., 135, 142
Berlier, P., 160
Beroaldo, Filippo, 74
    interpretation Apul. *Met.*, 57
    on commentator's task, 48
Bloemaert, Abraham, 3
Blondel, Merry-Joseph, 95
Boccaccio, 74, 83, 98
Bodin de Boismortier
    Daphnis et Chloé, 153, 157
Boiardo, M.M., 74, 84, 87
Book of Common Prayer, 187
Bormann, E., 170
Brody, M., 113
Bruccoli, M.J., 122
Bruno Maderna
    Satyricon, 154
Bruno, Giordano, 74
Burnam, T., 129
Busser, Henri
    Daphnis et Chloé, 160
'Calliroe'
    opera (1770), 151
camp, 142
Casirola, Angelo
    Daphnis et Chloé, 163
Cavalli, Francesco
    Amore innamorato, 148

Céline, L.F., 139
    and Petronius, 141
Charikleia
    ~ Amalia van Solms, 17
Chigi, Agostino, 87
Chinese novella, 178
chronotope, 136
Conrad, Joseph
    Heart of Darkness, 113
Conte, G.B., 116, 121
Correggio, N. da
    Psiche, 87
Cupid and Psyche
    in 17th cent. music, 150
curiositas, 86
    Apuleius and Mart. Capella, 39
    cupiditas sciendi, 61
d'Urfée, H., 12
Daniel
    'Book of the Child – ', 24
Dante, 62
Daphnis and Chloe
    ballets, 152
David of Antioch
    'story of Sūsan', 21
Diphilus, 63
Dodds, E.R., 192
Doody, M.A., 137
Douché de Vancy, J.-F., 151
Drennan, W.R., 119
Dubois, Ambroise, 7
Dufour
    wallpapers by –, 95
Dylan Thomas, 185
ekphrasis, 7
Encolpius
    and Nick Carraway, 112, 129
    protagonist vs. narrator, 121
enkyklios paideia, 43
Ercole I d'Este, 84
fabula, 37
fairy tale, 189
Ferrari, F., 63
Firebaugh, W.C., 136
Firenzuola, A., 74, 91
Flaubert. G., 75
Fortner, W.
    Die Witwe von Ephesus, 175

Fulgentius, 72
Gaisser, J.H., 148
Garbugino, G., 73
Gaster, M., 25
genre
    generic mixture, 36
Gérard, François, 99
Gianotti, G.F., 74
Gijsen, Marnix
    Het Boek van Joachim van Babylon, 19
Grilli, A., 64, 66
Grimm Brothers
    Schneewittchen, 189
Guillén, C., 138
Hadīth al-Jumjuma ma'a al-Malik
    'The Story of the Skull and the King', 24, 29
Harbison, J.
    opera *Gatsby*, 113
Hardy, Alexandre, 150
Hartmann, K.A.
    Die Witwe von Ephesus, 170
    Wachsfigurenkabinett, 169
Hays, G., 72
Heliodorus
    Aeth. in paintings, 7
    and Dutch Calvinism, 10
    and Mariette's *Aida*, 152
    in 17th cent. France, 150
Henze, Hans Werner, 175
Hieronymus, 70
Historia Apollonii regis Tyri, 72
Honthorst, G. van, 7, 15
Horions, Hans, 8
Huygens, Constantijn, 11, 15
hybris, 86
iconography
    Cupid and Psyche, 83
    Psyche in ancient –, 105
    Susanna motif, 29
intersemiotic translation, 171
intertextuality, 36
    allusion, 104
    A. Amasino ~ Petronius, 141
    Boccaccio ~ Apuleius, 75
    contaminatio, 73
    Fitzgerald ~ Wagner, 114

intertextuality (*cont.*)
    metafictional allusion, 187
    proleptic continuation, 179
    text ~ illustration, 99
    transformation, 171
    travesty, 171
Keulen, W.H., 70
Kleinoper, 169
Knüpfer, Nicholas, 8
Konstan, D., 10
Kumamoto, C.D., 117
La Fontaine, Jean de
    Psyché et Cupidon, 99
labyrinth, 136
Lactantius, 71
Lafitte, Louis, 95
laughter and education
    Mart. Capella, 38
Le Borne, Fernand
    musical drama *D&C*, 160
Leoniceno, N., 84
Lessing, G.E.
    Die Matrone von Ephesus, 177
Levetzow, K.M. von
    Die Witwe von Ephesus, 178
literary history, 138
Longus
    in opera, 153
Lucius
    and Apuleius, 36
    and Faust, 65
    and Odysseus, 65
MacNeice, L., 181
Macrobius, 70
Maerlant, Jacob van
    Rijmbijbel, 19
Mander, K. van, 6
Maréchal, Henri
    Daphnis et Chloé, 161
Mariette, Auguste
    Aida, 152
Martianus Capella
    'authorial intermezzos', 40
Martin, R., 64
Mattiacci, S., 79
McEwan, Ian
    On Chesil Beach, 157
Menippean satire, 141

metaphor, 117, 140
Milesian tale, 37
Monteverdi, 147
   Orfeo, 149
Moretti, F., 137
Moritat
   'street-ballad', 175
motif
   'clever child' –, 28
   late-night work, 43
   Psyche tormented by Amor, 97
   Psyche tormenting Amor, 97
   Scheintod, 151
   Toilette de Vénus, 99
myth
   Adonis, 28
   in early opera, 149
narrative
   actorial, 138
   actorial ~ auctorial, 121, 129
   homodiegetic –, 43
Neher, C.
   Die Witwe von Ephesus, 179
Nick Carraway
   and Encolpius, 112
Nuchelmans, G., 44
Odysseus
   cupiditas sciendi, 61
Offenbach, Jacques
   Daphnis et Chloé, 153, 158
opera librettos
   Greco-Roman sources, 147
painting
   and literature, 88
   Cupid & Psyche in –, 85
   'history' painting, 6
   '*portrait historié*', 13
   Susanna tradition, 29
parody, 138
Pavloskis, Z., 72
Pennacchietti, F., 24
Penwill, J.L., 66, 68
Perkins, M., 132
Perry, B.E., 66
personification, 106
   Satura, 41
Peruzzi, B., 89
Petrarca, 74

Petronius
   encounters in *Sat.*, 136
   in opera, 154
   open form of *Sat.*, 137
   theatricality, 137
picaresque
   new –, 139
picaresque novels, 138
Piombo, S. del, 89
Porphyrius, 71
ps. Lucianus
   The Ass, 84
Psyche
   as Venus, 105
   in ancient art, 96
   ~ Snow White, 188
Qisas al-Anbiyā'
   ('Lives of the Prophets'), 27
Raphael, 98
   Loggia di Amore e Psiche, 87
Ravel, Maurice
   Daphnis et Chloé, 166
realism, 135, 137
Reed, W.L., 137
Reid, J., 148
Reinhart, W., 139
Reitzenstein, R., 64
Renaissance
   Greek studies in –, 147
Rîncioy, D., 75
Romano, Giulio, 98
   Camera di Amore e Psiche, 90
Rosand, E., 149
Rosetta Stone, 152
Roulston, R., 111
Rousseau, Jean-Jacques, 157
Russian formalists, 137
Sandy, G., 65
satire, 170, 174, 183
satura, 35
Septuagint
   Book of Daniel, 20
Slater, N.W., 135
Snell, Bruno, 183
Sontag, Susan, 142
sphragis, 57
Steinmetz, Ch., 97
Sterchow, W., 150

Sullivan, J.P., 121
tales
    embedded –, 37
Tamagni, V.
    Sala dell' Asino d'oro, 91
Tchaikovsky
    Pique Dame, 153
themes
    adultery, 173
    antimilitarism, 173
    travel, 135
time
    in Petron. and Fitzgerald, 120, 129
Titian, 7
travesty, 171
Trimalchio
    and Gatsby, 122, 127
Vcrazi, Mattia, 151
Verdi, G.
    Aida, 152
Veronese, 7
Villa Farnesina, 87, 98
Wagner, R.
    Götterdämmerung, 114
Walsh, P.G., 67
Walt Disney, 86, 188
Weil, Grete, 175
West, J.L.W., 126
Willis, J.A., 36
Wolf, E., 37
Wooten, C., 142
Zeitlin, F.I., 118
Zink, M., 72

13W12828